LAST WORD

A LIFE WORKING WITH MANAGERS

Ivor Kenny

Published by
OAK TREE PRESS
19 Rutland Street, Cork, Ireland
www.oaktreepress.com

© 2006 Ivor Kenny

A catalogue record of this book is
available from the British Library.

ISBN: 1904887139
ISBN-13: 9781904887133

Printed in Ireland by ColourBooks.

LAST WORD

Also by Ivor Kenny

Industrial Democracy

The Atlantic Management Study

Government and Enterprise in Ireland

In Good Company

Out on Their Own

Boardroom Practice

Talking to Ourselves

The Death of Shibboleths

Freedom and Order

Leaders

Can You Manage?

Achievers

For Maureen and the family

CONTENTS

ACKNOWLEDGEMENTS

This is my 13th book – *absit omen*. For this one, more than any other, I have seen clearly how much I owe to friends.

First to a good friend who wishes to remain unsung. His generous sponsorship made the book possible.

Second to three friends, Tom Cox, Don Thornhill and Joe Gilmartin, who unerringly put their finger on mistakes, ranging from ropey English to insensitive references to individuals, to dated arguments suspended in mid-air. When they pointed things out, I saw immediately where I was wrong.

To Gillian Acton, my friend and colleague in UCD for 18 years, an unerring and encouraging editor who never reaches the end of her tether, despite provocation.

This is the fifth book that Brian O'Kane of Oak Tree Press has published with me. He is always supportive. When I feel I've written irrelevant rubbish, he reassures me that it's not quite that bad.

If men could learn from history, what lessons it might teach us! But passion and party blind our eyes, and the light which experience gives is a lantern on the stern, which shines only on the waves behind us!

                             - Samuel Taylor Coleridge, 1772-1834

We do not know very much of the future
Except that from generation to generation
The same things happen again and again.
Men learn little from others' experience.

                             - T.S. Eliot, 1880-1965

               (Thomas in *Murder in the Cathedral*, 1935)

1

INTRODUCTION: JUST LIKE YESTERDAY

For almost half a century (46 years to be precise), I have been working with managers. A long time, yet those first days in the Irish Management Institute are as fresh as yesterday. The Institute occupied a pleasant red-brick terraced house in Leeson Park in Dublin 4, a suburb that did not have then the cachet it has now. There was a staff of 10 and a budget of £25,000. The Institute now occupies an award-winning building on green acres in Sandyford with 60 staff, half the number it had in earlier days. The Institute's singular achievement has been to survive and remain relevant, despite vicissitudes and predators.

The changes in the Irish business scene over the half-century are well-documented. Tiger cubs would not recognise the Ireland in which I started work. I might as well tell them I went to school in my bare feet bringing a sod of turf.

There has, however, been one constant. The fundamental changes in the environment for enterprise have all come from government.

Organised business – unlike organised labour – has always lacked firepower. Businessmen, unlike farmers, are not going to block the bridge at Athlone or stop the trains like organised labour. This is a universal phenomenon. The difference for Ireland is that we are an intimate community with easy access – "I had a word with the Taoiseach". So do many other interests to whom the Taoiseach – any Taoiseach – will pay more attention. Government's role is now to avoid crises, not by invoking authority, but by compromise with, and appeasement of, other governing institutions, particularly the powerful public sector unions, representing the employees of State monopolies, while the "employer" representatives fight rearguard actions. This startlingly undemocratic ritual has now broadened from simple wages into social policies.

In 1981, when I suggested we might have too much government, Deputy Barry Desmond of the Labour Party said in the Dáil: "We have an example recently of the Director General of the Irish Management Institute launching a tirade – that is what I would call it – on the role of the State in public enterprise. I thought that was rather strange coming from such a person because it was disclosed to me in a Dáil question last week that that body got £6m to £7m in taxpayers' money to run their outfit in the past decade."

The inference, which has wider implications than my outfit at the time, was that, if you take the emperor's shilling, you may not point out that he has no clothes.

We never went so far as to incur Iago's contempt for the

> ... duteous and knee-crooking knave
> That, doting on his own obsequious bondage,
> Wears out his time, much like his master's ass,
> For nought but provender ...

But listen to this:

> You believe in private enterprise and individual responsibility. So do I. But, if private enterprise is to survive as the governing factor in industry, it must learn to stand on its own feet. It has nothing to gain, and it runs grave risks, by leaning too heavily on the State; by asking the Government to do this thing or that thing or the other, when many of the propositions broached in such requests are properly ventures for private enterprise. Give the State the excuse in such matters to encroach upon your proper sphere, and you will find that the ultimate outcome will be the practical expropriation of your interest in your own business. Wise businessmen will refrain from encouraging the State to do for them in their own businesses what they ought to do for themselves.

That was Seán MacEntee in 1940, a Fianna Fáil Minister for Industry and Commerce.

In the dismal early '80s, as I got angrier and became increasingly vocal, I provoked what I believe to be an Irish phenomenon: verbal violence. I've looked through all the press cuttings. I can't find one that was *ad rem*, that took my arguments to pieces. Instead the tone was that "some businessmen" felt I had gone too far, that I had become shrill. The arguments were universally *ad hominem*. They reached a peak when Tomás Mac Giolla of the Workers' Party described me as "the most dangerous man in Ireland".

Heady stuff. I can't say I was displeased to make headlines or to be the centrepiece of the *Late Late Show*, but that wore off quickly. The IMI was about change, and I was trying to encourage change – but it was from the sidelines not from the centre of the pitch.

The change for me came when I left the IMI, on March 31, 1983. I am indebted to UCD and its Presidents, Tom Murphy, Paddy Masterson, Art Cosgrove and Hugh Brady, for giving me the precious gift of freedom and a lair from which to venture into the world of praxis and to which to return to gather my thoughts.

The years in the IMI, apart from the last two, were happy and fulfilling, with several great colleagues. The recent years in UCD were even more satisfying, working with major international companies and, I believe, adding value to them.

Along the way, in my work, and in my membership of company boards, I have made many friends. At this stage of my life, I see with greater clarity the truth in Belloc's *Dedicatory Ode*:

> There's nothing worth the wear of winning
> But laughter and the love of friends.

My friends are mostly managers. They are the salt of the earth.

Ivor Kenny
Woodview
University College Dublin
September 2006

2

THE BEGINNING

Head of the Management Development Unit.

Maureen said to me, "You're working in Radio Éireann, you're teaching in St. Michael's and Blackrock, you're trying to do your doctorate, and if you go out in the garden for a breath of fresh air, you come in covered in guilt. Could you not get one job?".

I said, "Funnily enough, I saw an ad in the paper. The Irish Management Institute is looking for an information officer and editor of its magazine. I might have a go". Maureen told me the paper was in the bin and went off to do her shopping. I extracted the paper, brushed it down and applied for the job. I did not know what the Irish Management Institute was.

I was interviewed in the basement of 12 Leeson Park, in what was grandly called the Hunting Pink Room. The carpet was Hunting Pink Tintawn made by Irish Ropes where Paul Quigley, Director of the IMI, had worked.

I was interviewed by Paul and by Paddy Dillon-Malone whom I was to succeed. They seemed impressed when I told them my combined income was £1,000 a year. My subsequent letter of appointment said my salary was to be £1,200, something we had not discussed. I have not forgotten that touch of generosity.

The IMI's working hours were the standard 9.30 to 5.30 with an hour for lunch. On December 29, 1959, I arrived at 12 Leeson Park at 9.00 o'clock, in my good suit. The place was quiet. Eventually I found Des O'Brien in his tiny office in a return at the top of the stairs. He looked up. His greeting was, "Do you think you'll like it here?". Des was company secretary, an ex-army man like Paul Quigley.

The job as Information Officer and Editor of *Irish Management* was a doddle. As Information Officer, I had to churn out the occasional press release and to be the boss of the Librarian, Inagh Duff. She did not need, nor, politely, would she tolerate, a boss. She was a self-trained librarian whose work laid the foundations of the finest management library on this island.

I looked at the cover of the *Irish Management* "journal", posher than "magazine", and wondered what the "Irish" was for. I did a mock-up with the title *Management*, brought it along to the Executive Committee and that was that. Well almost, there was a small demurral from Sir Charles Harvey.

In later years, John Marsh, head of the British Institute of Management, called me to say they were selling their magazine to Michael Heseltine of Haymarket Press, which he built up before entering politics in 1966. Heseltine was going to call it *Management*. I told John I would pillory him for plagiarism before every management centre in Europe. He shrugged and said it was now out of his hands. Tom Cox, a Kerryman, then editor of *Management*, went to London to see Heseltine and returned with an agreement that we would retain our title and the Heseltine publication would be called *Management Today*, which it still is.

In 1960, Hugh MacNeill was Head of the embryo Management Development Unit, on a two-year secondment from the HR department of Aer Lingus. Amicable, bright and relaxed, he was a great coach for seasoned managers. When I joined the IMI, I did not know there had been a competition to replace him. Nor did I know that the candidate who came first in the competition, Hugh Munro, had proved too independent-minded for some members of the interview board. There was an impasse.

Paddy Dillon-Malone, one of the finest people I have met, had left me to my own devices after a week. He was off with his young wife to a job in the shipyards in Malta. Not many years later, he collapsed in Paris and died too young.

About a month in the job, I had an in-depth discussion with Paul Quigley as he was going up the stairs and I was standing in my office door. I said, "Paul, I can do this job in two days a week. Is there any way I can help out with what seems to be the key work of the

Institute, management development?". Paul said, "Oh", and continued up the stairs.

I was sent as a full-time participant in the Institute's longest programme, a two-week management course. After a good dinner each evening in Power's Hotel at the bottom of Dawson Street, we would adjourn to a lounge and each of us in turn would lead a discussion on a chapter of Peter Drucker's *The Practice of Management* (1955). I can still remember the yellow dust-jacket. Never having managed anything, except the UCG Boat Club as Captain and the UCG Dramatic Society as a very bad Director, I enjoyed every bit of the management course and particularly the fellowship of the other participants.

In later, more exalted years, when I was Chancellor of the International Academy of Management, Peter Drucker became a friend of both myself and, particularly, Maureen. Tom Cox had invited him to Dublin back in February 1969 to give the inaugural Laurie Lecture (so-called for Tom Laurie, one of the earlier Presidents of the Institute). The concert hall of the Royal Dublin Society, the largest available venue, could hardly contain the audience. Eighteen years later, he came to Dublin in 1987, to be awarded the Chancellor's Gold Medal of the Academy and to be made a Life Fellow of the IMI. Although I was five years out of the IMI, I organised there a Morning with Peter Drucker. Something like 15 CEOs booked and 10 turned up. *Sic transit ...* Peter died at 95 as these words were written, Friday, November 11, 2005. May he rest in peace.

I was with Hugh MacNeill at an IMI do in the Shamrock Lodge Hotel in Athlone. We walked out to get some night air. He told me I had "done well" on the management course, that I had proved "acceptable". He said I was being considered for the job as Head of the MDU. I was gob-smacked. I was hardly a wet week in the place and had damn all management experience. I could not wait to get back to the hotel bedroom to call Maureen. With her quiet wisdom, she said it was a bit early to count chickens.

In 1960, Paul Quigley announced his imminent departure. We thought the sky would fall. Paul *was* the IMI. He had been seduced by that persuasive man, Brendan O'Regan, aided and abetted by Garret FitzGerald, to head SFADCo, the Shannon Free Airport

Development Company. Brendan had started the first duty-free airport in the world. It was subsequently to become a duty-free zone and several international companies located there.

(At Brendan's invitation, I gave my very first seminar to the SFADCo senior management. It was scary to have Paul Quigley sitting in front of me, however briefly and benign a boss he had been. I must have begun with an apology for myself. Paul gave me a piece of advice I never forgot. "If you begin by saying you're going to give a poor talk, people will believe you ...".)

Before he left, Paul had called me into his office and apologised for the fact that I had not been considered as a possible successor. I had already been gob-smacked at my appointment as Head of the Management Development Unit. Being even mentioned as a possible candidate for Paul's job was a bridge way too far. He told me he was being succeeded by a James de Valera Mansfield. He saw my reaction at the "de Valera" and said his successor had been told to drop it, at least while he was Director of the IMI.

There was a helpful (for me) ambiguity about my reporting relationship with James Mansfield. As Head of the MDU, I kind of reported to him and also to what was called the Consultative Board, of which Michael Dargan was Chairman. He was the founding honorary secretary of the Institute and its most committed member. The MDU had a dual role. It ran short executive development programmes and it also had a role in encouraging business education, which was then rudimentary, in the universities and technical colleges. Hence the title "Consultative" – the Board was representative of the educational institutions with a leavening of businessmen. It was not until 1969 that Michael MacCormac started Ireland's first MBA in UCD and then only after a prolonged struggle with the college hierarchy.

Michael Dargan saw to it that I got as much business/management experience stuffed into me as was possible in as short a time. I was sent first to Aer Lingus. There were three maintenance shifts, discrete teams with their own bosses. Between the three, they covered the 24 hours. The maintenance men (no women) were highly-qualified, with certificates from the relevant authorities. You don't let any old guy with a screwdriver loose in an aircraft.

My mission was to find out why one shift team was superb, one more than adequate, and one less so. I was given six weeks. It took three days. I waited until each team was on night shift. This did not intrude on my day job, and it was a good time to gain confidences.

On my first night, I looked for the boss and was told, with a grin, that he was in his office. His office was a glass box. He was attired in a well-cut tweed jacket and cavalry twill trousers. He was known as "The Squire". I asked him how he got on with his men. He told me he was interested in human relations.

Another night, I asked for the boss of the next team. Several people told me they did not know where he was, until one spotted a small man moving like a train down the aisles. I caught up with him and, a bit breathless, asked him how he got on with his men. He said, "What do you mean?". I gave a woolly reply. He said, "I dunno. I have me tea with them, if that's what you mean". He was an ex-NCO in the Air Corps and he ran the best shift.

Next stop was the Pressed Steel Works in Cowley, Oxford. They made car bodies, from small Fords to Rolls Royces. It was like hell. Workers would throw sheets of steel onto a huge press. The press would come down with a deafening hammer blow to form a piece of car. I was told the workers – there were many Irish – spent their time working and getting drunk. Who could blame them?

Then there was Slough for a six-week management course with the consultants Urwick Orr and Partners. The course was to train their own consultants. I was the only blow-in, a privilege. I was asked to give the speech at the concluding dinner. I've no idea what I said, but two things I won't forget. At the beginning, I cracked one or two jokes. The man sitting directly in front of me burst his breeches laughing, which was fine. What was not fine was that he thought the rest of the speech was hilarious and he continued to laugh all the way through. On the other hand, the old guru, Lt. Col. Lyndall Urwick, OBE, MC, MA, kept looking directly at me, stony-faced. He had a word with me afterwards. Perhaps I had conveyed the smart-assed arrogance of youth. He said, "When you're interviewing the chief executive of a large company and you wonder how such an unintelligent person got to such a high position, remember the evidence of his unintelligence is the Rolls Royce parked outside". Louden Ryan, in one of his Loudenisms, said recently to me,

"Nothing gives the illusion of intelligence so much as personal association with large sums of money".

What I got from that enjoyable course was a set of notes I reduced to PLOC – Planning, Leading, Organising and Controlling. These four traditional pillars of wisdom neatly formed a two-day seminar that I launched in the early '60s on the unsuspecting and tolerant managers of Ireland. One came up to me at the end of the second day and, in his refreshing innocence, said, "Mr. Kenny. What has oft been thought but ne'er so well expressed". The market for management courses in the '60s was virgin territory and the IMI was the only significant supplier.

However, during the '60s, the myth of the manager as rational decision-maker was exploded. Managers, in common with a lot of people, do not always live in reality. In an Irish poll in the late '80s, 52% of the chief executives interviewed believed the economy would decline, while 36% thought it would improve. When, however, they were asked how their own companies would fare, the percentages were almost exactly reversed: 53% thought their own companies would do better, while only 33% thought they would decline.

There is an echo here of the work done by Paddy Dillon-Malone in his book, *An Analysis of Marketing*, published by the IMI in 1970.[1] He found that what is perceived at the general level is not always related back to the individual, who tends to see himself as an exception to the rule. Many Irish firms, faced with free trade, believed they themselves would survive in the 1970s. The others would go to the wall. They were, unfortunately, wrong. This euphoria is like the bravado with which soldiers go into battle, knowing that some of them are going to be killed, but none of them believing it will be himself.

And managers subscribe to an enduring myth: "There is light at the end of the tunnel". This is the Blue Lagoon Syndrome – the belief that, when we have sorted out present difficulties, we shall find a tranquil haven. In their hearts, managers know this is a myth, but it keeps them going.

Years later, working in Western countries, and in the erstwhile Soviet Union, I made a point of asking managers the penetrating

---

[1]   0950032751.

question, "How's business?". The answer invariably was, across those different cultures, "Next year is going to be difficult, but after that we should be all right". The universal hockey-stick.

The longer I work with managers, the more I am impressed with our inability to forecast the future. The future is not some fixed entity that awaits us in time. The only real thing is the present. Peter Drucker said: "The question that faces the strategic decision-maker is not what his organisation should do tomorrow. It is, what do we have to do today to be ready for an uncertain tomorrow?". By focusing our concern on present issues that have long-term consequences, we deal realistically with the long term.

The fact that a single, fixed future does not exist means that leaders can change how that future unfolds by influencing which future possibilities can become realities. Successful leaders know that the future isn't found – it is invented. It is shaped by people with the vision, courage, and wisdom to think beyond the boundaries of the familiar.

That the future is mouldable is a powerful concept. If an organisation does not try to shape its future environment, it will be overtaken by others that shape the future to give themselves a competitive advantage.

(A clear example was Tony O'Reilly in 1973 ,when he took over what is now known as Independent News and Media. There were then seven titles, all in Ireland. Today, INM publishes 175 titles in five countries and has added radio, TV, outdoor advertising, distribution, contract printing, and the Internet. The point is that Tony O'Reilly nailed his visionary colours to the mast as far back as 1973. His original letter to the shareholders, August 27, set out clearly the vision that has now been achieved. Or the courage of Denis Brosnan in 1988, when he bought something Kerry's own size. Kerry was valued on the Irish market at £120m. He bought Beatreme in the US for $135m at a conversion rate of 1.20.)

I settled into a non-relationship with James Mansfield. It must have been more difficult for him. He was head of the Institute and yet he had this cuckoo in the nest who was the only revenue-earning member of staff and who did not really report to him.

James had been appointed at the urging of Denis Hegarty, Chairman of the IMI, 1959-1961. James had been Secretary of RGDATA, the Retail, Grocery, Dairy and Allied Trades' Association.

I may have been Head of the MDU, but I was not the boss. The Institute became directionless. I was at an IMI course lunch in Powers Hotel. James, white-faced, was at a table with Michael Dargan, stony-faced. I saluted them but passed on quickly. Afterwards, Michael Dargan called me and said it had been decided to raise my salary to £3,000 – James was on £3,200 – and that James was instructed to "leave me alone".

Not long after, he left the IMI for Germany where he had laid foundations for himself. There he became a successful consultant, earned a doctorate, and married.

It is not possible to predict with certainty how a person who has not been a chief executive, or who has worked in a different culture, will perform in the top job. It is different in kind from any other job in an organisation. However, when someone turns out to be unsuitable, those who selected him/her bear a heavy responsibility.

A mistake I made a number of times was to be misled by a candidate with a high IQ. People with a high IQ are often so talented at arguing with and criticising others that they focus on that rather than on arriving at constructive solutions – they justify their wrong decisions. People with a high IQ don't necessarily make good decisions – otherwise we'd all be hiring mathematicians. A high IQ can be trumped by a high EQ – emotional intelligence: getting to know your own emotions, learning to manage those emotions, and learning to recognise and deal with the concerns of others. You bring your emotions to work with you.

I thought I would walk into the job to replace James. I was wrong.

3
THE TOP JOB

The Executive Committee was reluctant to offer the job to someone as young and inexperienced as myself.

The job was advertised. I applied and found out subsequently that I had headed a shortlist of three. The other candidates were Brian Farrell and the late Jack Agnew, head of AnCO, the forerunner to FÁS. AnCO gave 50% grants to encourage companies to send their managers to IMI courses. In later years, Jack and I became friends. Jack, as an Assistant Secretary in the Department of Labour, had drawn up the legislation for AnCO and, I'm afraid, gave away the sovereign right of the board to appoint its CEO. Instead, it was to produce three names for the Minister. This practice was subsequently followed in legislation for other State companies, already hog-tied by the infamous "Red" Devlin Report on the remuneration of State company CEOs. I never talked with Jack about his interest in the IMI job. Perhaps he saw it as giving him more freedom and maybe a bigger salary.

It took a long time to get rid of the prurience of the Devlin Review Body. Its antics were tailor-made to ensure a level of demotivation in the management of State-sponsored bodies such as to cause the further intervention of the ultimate masters. For example, in an orotund paragraph, the Review Body described the qualities necessary for the Director General of RTÉ:

> Despite the most careful and sympathetic consideration, we are not satisfied that the burdens falling on the Director General as "editor-in-chief", or the inherent complexity of the problems with which he has to grapple in that role, or, for

that matter, the degree to which he is personally exposed – given the Authority above him and the structure down to the broadcasters below him – are surpassingly great in the context of the public sector as a whole. The decisions he has to make in this capacity may be immediate and of a sensitive nature, politically and otherwise, but, in our view, they are not of such profundity or long term consequence, or so beyond the realm of what should be comprehended by reasonable ability, care, integrity, commonsense and experience, as to warrant uprating the post in advance of a general review.

As the penny catechism taught us about baptism, in case of necessity any lay man or woman can do it.

However, this Review Body – or super-board – was merely a gross manifestation of a deeper malaise. The government had submitted to an iron-clad pecking order from which it could not extricate itself. It was bedevilled by relativities and had lost administrative flexibility. It is reminiscent of the Victorian joke about six to a bed: when father says "Turn", we must all turn.

My remuneration practice for the IMI staff as the Institute grew was to pay as much as possible tax-effectively. We were competing with industry for the best and brightest. The staff got an excellent pension scheme, where there had been none, and the great perk of a car (before BIK). This freedom to pay well was regarded with mild envy by AnCO staff with whom we had a lot of interaction. Joe Brennan from Donegal was the Minister for Labour. His office overlooked AnCO's back yard. One day, he saw it full of shiny new cars. He made enquiries. Days later, the cars were gone.

I did not know Brian Farrell at all. I had met Marie Thérèse (Dillon), his wife, when, with the Irish University Players in 1949, we took Synge's *Playboy* to Oxford and to Cambridge for a week in each place. Years passed and, with both families living in Dundrum, we became family friends. Brian, at the time of his interest in the IMI, which he has now completely forgotten, was on the admin staff of UCD in Earlsfort Terrace and also lectured. Eventually, as we know, he became professor and a leading political commentator, best known for his work on RTÉ public affairs programmes, where he was an iconic figure, complete with bow tie, like the late Robin Day on BBC.

My appointment as Director was not plain sailing. The Executive Committee, having had their fingers burnt once, were reluctant to offer the job to someone as young (33!) and as inexperienced as myself. Strong resistance came from John Leydon, then the formidable Secretary of the Department of Industry and Commerce, with Seán Lemass as Minister. John Leydon's word was law. He had been involved in the founding of the Institute. Time changes perspectives. John was present at the opening of the National Management Centre on September 25, 1974. He put his hand on my arm and said, "I supported you very strongly when you were appointed Director".

Stairways seem to have played an important part in my life – for example, the conversation with Paul Quigley on the stairs. John Masser, head of Masser Waterford Ironfounders, Chairman of the Institute, met me on the steps of Leeson Park and told me it had been decided to offer me the job of Acting Director. My heart sank. What the Institute needed was strong direction. An Acting Director was the wrong sort of animal. I told John this and said I would have to think about the job. If that sounds courageous, it was not. I was shaking inside.

My advantage was that I knew the Institute. I had worked, however briefly, on the membership side of the house and then as head of the Management Development Unit. After a week or so, they decided to take a chance on the callow youth.

When I vacated the Information Officer position, I strongly recommended Tom Cox to Garret FitzGerald, Chairman of the Editorial Committee. (The Institute started as a voluntary body. It retained for a time several of its voluntary committees, such as the Finance Committee, which diligently examined the petty cash book, and the Editorial Committee, which was a good sounding board for the journal. Garret was an active member of the Institute's Council.) While in Radio Éireann, I had worked alongside Tom, one of the best announcers I have known. I knew he had exhausted Radio Éireann's potential for him, as it had done for me. It was a pleasant and convivial existence, but you quickly tire of the mindless task of reading a script into a microphone. This was before television, when announcers became celebrities. Tom took the job, transformed it and, in years that followed, became Secretary of the Institute, as well as Head of Membership. His masterpiece was the annual Killarney Conference.

Tom gave me two pieces of advice to which I have adhered. I would seldom let anything out – papers, serious letters – without showing them first to him. His advice about a strong letter or an OTT paper was to write it, sleep on it, and tear it up the next day. The other piece of advice came when he put his head into my office and said, "You're coming to the funeral?". I said, "Tom, I really am too busy". Tom said angrily, "What's happened to your values?" and left.

Tom retired from the IMI not long after I did and became chief executive of the Dublin Chamber of Commerce, which he transformed. In an active retirement, he wrote *The Making of Managers*, a splendid history of the IMI.[2] Tom's wife, Nóirín, a teacher, whom he met while she was singing on radio, was at school with my wife.

While I'm against nepotism and cronyism, there is something to be said for people whom you both know and trust – you can't have one without the other. The danger with nepotism is you can exclude good people. The danger of cronyism is that you may never be told the truth. The late Frank Sherwin TD once said in the Dáil, "Like everything else, nothing is perfect".

I have found that chief executives who volunteer that they can't abide yes-men are the most likely to be surrounded by them. Similarly that hoary phrase, "Management is not a popularity contest" is a licence for unpleasant, and ultimately unproductive, behaviour.

---

[2]   ISBN: 1860762409.

4
GROWING OUR OWN TIMBER

The Four Horsemen of the Apocalypse.

The MDU meanwhile was buzzing. Michael Dargan was a great Chairman. We set up a "review committee" to look at both the MDU itself and at the development of management education in Ireland generally. I was lucky to get on the final European Productivity Agency Programme for study in the United States with added funding from the Scholarship Exchange Board. There was no cost to the IMI. What I proposed was:

♦ To have tested by eminent authorities the preliminary suggestions on the growth of the educational activities of the Irish Management Institute;

♦ To establish personal contact with management teachers in the US to ensure a continuing supply of specialists to the IMI.

The academic atmosphere I met with in the States was radically different from my experience in the early '50s as a postgrad at the London School of Economics. When I went to my first seminar at the LSE – seminar was not then in the UCG lexicon – I was dismayed to find myself in a group of about 15 people, all of whom were expected to talk. I made some clod-hopper statement. I was immediately turned on: "Why do you say that, Kenny? What evidence do you have for that?". I wanted to go home. When I first applied for a place at the LSE, the correspondence began, "Dear Mr. Kenny". When I was admitted it was, "Dear Kenny".

The welcome from distinguished US business academics was heart-warming. They listened. They were always positive. As the days progressed, I felt my confidence and convictions grow. It was intense and intensive. About three o'clock every day, an image of soft pillows and white sheets would float before me. I hope it did not show.

The purpose of the EPA mission was to restore in a war-ravaged Europe the spirit of get-up-and-go that is still characteristic of America. It taught me that we create our own boundaries, a fact of which I have been trying to persuade companies (and chief executives) for much of my life. I would go so far as to say *all* boundaries to the success of organisations are internal. You can't blame market forces. Who chose the market in the first place?

As soon as I got home, I wrote a note that was incorporated in the Report of the Review Committee. The core proposal was that the Institute would buy a house "on some acres of land", and would "grow its own timber" – the latter a phrase that echoed down the years in the IMI. We had been relying on visiting American firemen and the occasional local. I recommended that we recruit four full-time specialists with experience in marketing, finance, production and personnel, the original four disciplines of management. The men who got these jobs came to be known as the "Four Horsemen of the Apocalypse": Martin Rafferty in Finance, Eddie McDermott in Marketing, Dermot Egan in Organisation and Personnel, and Noel Mulcahy in Production. Brian Whelan was the first person appointed to the MDU after myself. When I became Director, he became Head of the MDU. More of him later.

I knew Noel Mulcahy only by sight and did not like him because he was a senior engineer in steam radio while I was there. We announcers felt the engineers strutted down the long corridor in Radio Éireann in Henry Street as if they owned the place. We did not know that they, in turn, regarded the announcers as a stuck-up bunch.

Noel presented himself before Brian Whelan and myself for the interview. A letter of recommendation preceded him. It was from Donogh O'Malley, the Minister for Education who introduced "free" second-level schooling. I produced the letter. I had honed my statement. "Mr. Mulcahy, I have here a letter supporting your candidature. It's from the Minister for Education. Did you send it because you felt your candidature was weak and needed support or that you felt the Institute was vulnerable to political influence?".

Noel gave me an old-fashioned look and said, "I thought it would do no harm". He waltzed into the job and ended as deputy director general of the IMI until he went to the new University of Limerick as a Vice-President.

He was cheerful, clever and eternally optimistic. He could carry a class of managers with his exuberance and undecipherable diagrams. Jack Lynch made him a senator. He decided to go for the Dáil. Maybe it's as well he did not get elected. He had too much to offer Irish managers.

He came with Maureen and myself to a European Foundation for Management Development Conference that I was chairing in Turin, May 1974. We hired a car and took a few days off afterwards. With no real plan, we found ourselves in the beautiful coastal town of Santa Margherita Ligure. On the way down to it, we had driven under a Venetian bridge spanning the road from, on the one side, a grand hotel to, on the other side, a swimming pool. We went back to the hotel and asked tentatively whether we could stay. We were welcomed and shown to rooms with huge beds and with ceilings covered with classical couples in questionable postures. We walked across the Venetian bridge to be greeted at the pool by Elio, with sculpted hair and a pristine white jacket. There were a number of Germans draped around the pool. They changed their swimwear every hour while they slowly sipped Campari. Noel arrived in flip-flops and a Foxford wool dressing gown that he must have had in school. The Germans looked at him in horror. He saw with delight a children's slide and, with his snow-white skin, hurtled down it, sending a tidal wave over the Germans and their Camparis. They departed in disgust – to the delight of Elio, who invited us back to his house that evening.

I drove and Noel was pilot. We nearly reached the snowline, turned back and found Elio standing at the door of an old and lovely farmhouse. He was a different person. He showed us his guns, his vineyard and his olive trees. He brought us to a lower room where Mamma was preparing supper – flat bread she baked in front of us on the open fire, Elio's home-grown broad beans with a touch of oil, onion and garlic, and Elio's own white wine. It was a noble meal. Afterwards, Noel, who has a great tenor voice, sang in the firelight. Mamma was enraptured.

The opening address at the Turin Conference was given by the Chairman of Fiat, Giovanni Agnelli. Tall and distinguished, he arrived in a standard dark blue Fiat accompanied by a slew of bodyguards. I welcomed him to the stage. He ignored me and started immediately to read his speech as if he'd rather be somewhere else. He hardly waited for the applause and was off, without acknowledging my thanks. The conference continued. The EFMD had gone all participative that year and divided the participants into discussion groups. At noon the following day, they deposited their reports on my desk. I had to summarise them and report back to the final assembly at 2 o'clock.

Charles Handy stuck his head in the door of the tiny office I was using, saw the pile of reports and said, "Would you like a gin and tonic?". Whether it was panic, the prospect of a gin and tonic, or Charles's support, I had an inspiration. I realised that none of the working groups had shared their reports with any other group – they knew only what was in their own report. I had a gin or two with Charles, took a bowl of nuts back to the office and was on the stage at five to two, the reports arranged on the desk as a stage prop. I had glanced through them. Where I saw a memorable phrase, I copied it for quotation and authenticity and then wrote some headings. Afterwards – it was the end of the conference – several people came to shake my hand and tell me it was the best summary of a conference they had ever heard, they could not figure how I did it.

That evening, the Mayor of Turin was to give a reception and address in the beautiful town hall. I was to respond. The mayor knew no English but could speak French. My French was OK but rusty. Jean-François Poncet, the Director General of EFMD, came to my hotel room to rehearse me. We raided the mini-bar and had a glass of whiskey for lubrication. We had 10 minutes to get to the town hall. We had one for the road, and arrived to find the crowd – and the mayor – had been waiting for 15 minutes. I looked down from the high stage at the assembly and felt great. *"Monsieur le Maire ..."*. I was a Renaissance figure, speaking perfect French, complete with expansive gestures.

Dermot Egan tells how he was dismayed when he saw who was at his final interview with us. A psychologist, we recruited him from Aer Lingus. He did not expect to meet at the interview his Aer

Lingus boss, Michael Dargan, who greeted him with a wry smile. Dermot, in turn, recruited another psychologist, Liam Gorman, the first PhD to join the Institute. They worked closely together and were the initiators of research in the IMI. When Dermot left the Institute, he joined AIB where he reached the number two spot under Gerry Scanlan. In retirement, he was Chairman of the National Concert Hall and is still a member of the board.

After I first interviewed Martin Rafferty, I went to Dermot and told him I knew less about Martin than I did before the interview. Martin was cheerfully impenetrable. Dermot said, "You should have done a stress interview. Hard cop, soft cop – that will get you through to any candidate".

I did the stress interview with Martin. It went something like this: "Tell me about your early successes, Martin". Martin would launch forth. I would interrupt rudely with something like, "Would you say you are a conceited person?". And so on, hard cop, soft cop. The only one who ended up stressed was me. When I told Dermot, he laughed, "But there should have been two of you".

Martin became the patron saint of small, particularly retail, businesses in Ireland. He worked with a distinguished American retailing lecturer, Walter Channing, who was trying to persuade Irish retailers to get their act together by showing them pictures of dogs lifting their legs on the vegetables, then sold off the floor. When he told the shopkeepers that "supermarkets" were inevitable, they scoffed.

When the excellent Walter could no longer be with us, he recommended a successor in the shape of a roly-poly man in a pork-pie hat. Because the recommendation came from Walter, we had no hesitation in letting his successor loose, sight unseen, on a conference room of retail managers who had paid good money. I can't remember his name, which is just as well. He came from Baton Rouge, Louisiana. He started by saying, "I wanna talk about pilferage. I saw this big nigga woman in the store. I knew her game. I said, 'Nigga woman, I saw you hide that hayam under yo' skirt. You take it out and be off with you before I call the po-lice'". At the coffee break, I led him gently away and went back to face the wrath of the participants, who were looking for their money back.

When Martin left the IMI, he joined AIB where he started their merchant bank, AIIB. He then went on to do so many things that, in the index of my concluding book about Irish business leaders, the only succinct description of him I could think of was "serial entrepreneur".

Eddie MacDermot, the marketing man, was the first member of the IMI staff to own a Mercedes. I borrowed it when I wanted to make an impression. He and Fred Copeland, our gardener and caretaker, were enemies. The premises in Orwell Road had a narrow entrance and a beautiful lawn, Fred's pride and joy. Most civilised drivers would give way to avoid driving over the edge of the lawn, but not our Eddie, who did not even see it. I looked out of my office window one day to see Eddie driving the Mercedes round and round the lawn followed by Fred waving a shovel.

We had a conference for Major Religious Superiors, as they were then called, in the Woodlands Hotel in Greystones. Eddie bounced in the first morning and asked, "What are you guys selling? Happiness?". Eddie died young.

In 1961, the Four Horsemen were joined by the redoubtable Nóirín Slattery as "Secretary/Stenographer to the Management Development Unit". This sonorous title was to avoid having Nóirín called "my" secretary, an appellation I have tried to avoid. The distasteful "my" arises in different contexts – for example, "my" organisation, as if we owned our colleagues. Nóirín went on to become Admin Manager, in succession to Des O'Brien. I came back to the IMI in 1986 for her going-away party. I said, "If I was head of the Institute, Nóirín was its heart". Nóirín went forward for election for Fianna Fáil in Rathmines in 1977 and gained a respectable 1,500 first preference votes. She subsequently joined the Progressive Democrats, where she is a trustee.

Not only was the recruitment of that nucleus of specialist staff accepted and implemented but so was a key recommendation in my Report following the EPA mission to the US that: "the MDU undertake an investigation into Irish managerial resources with the object of recommending ways for the development of those resources in the light of the existing knowledge on education for business and the future development of the Irish economy". This wordy recommendation was implemented by Breffni Tomlin, a young UCD economics graduate who joined the Institute in 1962. He wrote the magisterial 420-page book, *The Management of Irish Industry*,[3] the first ever study of the standard of management practice on a national scale. It showed that, while Ireland had several large companies that were well-run and entrepreneurial, with a handful that had the potential to become internationally competitive, there were many SMEs. In Tomlin's words, quoted in Tom Cox's book, "the Institute was teaching SMEs that were not viable how to be better at not being viable".

Many of the Institute's short "courses" – two days – were remedial, the daddy of them all being "Finance for the Non-Financial Manager", superbly taught by Ciarán Walsh and Ray Fitzgerald. Ciarán's book was translated into several languages, including Russian. I don't believe he ever got the roubles. Finance for the Non-Financial is alive and well. I got in today's post a flier from no less a business school than the University of Chicago, £4,200 sterling a head in London.

My Report had been in two parts, reflecting the Institute's dual role: to supply a service to its members – to be a resource in the development of practising managers and, secondly, to encourage business education in the universities and technical institutes. Looking now at the business schools even in Dublin alone, it's hard to recall the battle there was to establish the legitimacy of business studies in the traditional universities. Michael MacCormac of UCD was the pioneer.[4]

This is part of what I wrote in the Report about the role of the universities. I believe it is relevant. Please excuse the unfashionable male pronouns.

> The university cannot be concerned solely with the needs of today. What is true for all university education is equally true for business education offered by the universities. The business school must offer far more than training in specialised areas to meet the current needs of business. It must educate the individual for the problems of tomorrow. The business school should develop a flexibility of mind, and

---

3   No ISBN, IMI, Dublin, 1966.
4   He tells his story with meticulous accuracy and recall in *Achievers*, ISBN: 1904887031.

an openness to new ideas and to new environments, an historical perspective, and an ability to develop new ideas. It is this type of education which marks the university person off from the technically trained. Only this type of education will enable him to meet the challenge of the future more effectively. Flexibility of mind can be developed in many areas of knowledge. The contribution that the university business school can make is that it provides an opportunity to develop along the lines of the student's interest. It will equip him with a knowledge consistent with the needs of his business career.

The essential difference between pure training techniques and education, which is the function of the university, lies in the objectives. The technique-oriented course trains for the present. The university course should use techniques only as an aid to a broad understanding of the subject matter. Narrow specialisation destroys the essential value of the university educational process. Too often the university wastes resources in a multiplicity of detailed courses. Technical specialists train more technical specialists who in turn perpetuate the breed. The whole process becomes ingrown and deviates farther from the university's concept of its role of education.

In 1989, that splendid polemical historian, Joe Lee, wrote harshly: [5]

Most Irish businessmen were simply not interested in ideas ... The Irish Management Institute (IMI) strove to change this attitude after 1953. Supply ran well ahead of demand. A long-serving former director of the IMI, Ivor Kenny, could detect as late as 1984 'a suspicion of the intellectual process and the value of ideas' among businessmen. Kenny attributes this primarily to the pervasive anti-intellectualism of Irish culture. Even this may be too generous. Much of the suspicion may be more sub-intellectual than anti-intellectual. Anti-intellectualism is too intellectually demanding. The IMI depended heavily on support from a handful of big

---

[5]   *Ireland 1912-1985*, ISBN: 0521266483.

businessmen in the private sector, with a more capacious perspective than the vast majority, and on the enthusiasm of the chief executives in the State-sponsored sector. The bulk of Irish businessmen provided no market for business ideas, much less for ideas in general. A variety of factors have contributed to the poor performance of native Irish business, but sheer intellectual inadequacy counts among the basic weaknesses. A first-class business mind could be a joy to behold. There were too few of them in Ireland.

I have left till last in the story of those early days, Brian Whelan, who was, as I mentioned, the first person I ever recruited. For once, I got it absolutely right. You could say that people don't get fired – they fire themselves. Conversely, Brian recruited himself.

I asked Hugh MacNeill to give me a hand. He said that for a job that required social skills a group interview was helpful. We got the consent of the short-listed candidates. They arrived at Leeson Park and chose their seats at the table. Brian came in last, sat at the head of the table and chaired the discussion.

Brian is a big man, a champion swimmer and golfer (captain of Milltown). He is also a person of total, even overpowering, integrity. A qualified accountant, he came with a background in banking. He is a missionary, which is probably what caused him to leave a solid job for an embryo institution with no certain future. He came initially as a finance specialist. When I became Director, I relinquished the position of Head of the MDU and Brian replaced me.

What I did not see, and with a little more foresight should have, was that I was sowing the seed of the same conflict I had with James Mansfield. Only in very special circumstances, such as large multinationals, should organisations appoint a chief operations officer. The COO, if he or she is any good, will end up running the company and become increasingly impatient with the CEO. The CEO for his/her part will begin to wonder what they are for. "Managing" the environment? Responsible for high strategy while the COO does the grunt work? Rubbish. The CEO could end up talking to Rotary clubs. The best structure is where the CEO manages a strong team, each member with clear responsibilities. Only in that way is the CEO firmly anchored in the realities – the operations – of the organisation.

Only in that way can the CEO take informed decisions on strategy, his/her most important role.

Reg Revans was the father of Action Learning, the single most enduring influence on the IMI's work. On his first of many visits, he said to me, "You're teaching?". I told him I didn't really have time for that any more. He said, "Then you'll be lost".

Separating operations from strategy was the classic error made by the "Green" Devlin report on the reform of the civil service. There was to be an "aireacht", a bunch of senior servants whose job was to think beautiful thoughts and formulate strategy, while the troops were there to implement it.

When will we ever learn? We are awash with consultants, commissions, working groups, task forces, all of which produce "strategies", none of which is implemented.

This blinding insight was to shape the work I did from UCD in the second half of my life. It is the main theme of this book.

Brian was a leader and he managed well his growing team of specialists. I was comfortable enough with this for a while, until I began to wonder what I was for.

It was Brian who broke the ice. We decided to go off for a day to sort out our relationship. We took a flip chart down to a small room with green walls in the Downshire House Hotel in Blessington. There was no animosity in our relationship. There was affection and respect. But there was natural frustration. We were trying honestly to find out what was best for both of us and for the Institute.

At a point where we seemed to be getting nowhere, Brian said, "What do you *want*?". I blurted, "I want to manage the bloody place". Brian went silent. Two of us could not manage the bloody place.

Brian became increasingly interested in European management development initiatives. He was elected founding President of the European Foundation for Management Development (EFMD) and subsequently its full-time director. He and his family moved to Brussels. When he came back to Dublin, he was appointed to a senior position in AIB.

Brian represented the best of what the Institute was about – its missionary role. If the IMI were to lose that, it would have lost its soul and would become just another competitive management centre. (See also **Chapter 36**.)

5
GAELTARRA ÉIREANN

Subsidy has been a blight on the Western spirit.
- The Irish Times, November 27, 1969

Colm Barnes got to know me when he succeeded Michael Dargan as
Chairman of the IMI Consultative Board. We became friends. He
invited me somewhat opaquely to lunch in the Stephen's Green Club
with the Minister for the Gaeltacht, Micheál Ó Móráin (*anglice* Michael
Moran). We had finished the main course before I knew what the
agenda was. I was asked whether I was sympathetic. An innocent
abroad, it took a while for the penny to drop. I said I was politically
neutral, that I had voted in different ways at different times, and that
at the last election I had voted Fianna Fáil. I passed a test.

They knew I had fluent Irish, having had my secondary
education, including learning French, through Irish. I even took it as
a filler for First Arts in UCG.

They told me Gaeltarra Éireann was being reformed, new board,
new mandate, new powers. Colm was joining the Board. Would I
like to be Chairman? I was delighted and immediately said "Yes", no
need to think about it.

Some time later, Michael Moran showed me mischievously a
telegram he got from a Fianna Fáil worthy on my appointment. Did
he not know "that this man's father [who died in 1940] condoned the
execution of republican prisoners?".

I was shocked when I found Gaeltarra's headquarters in a dismal
building with a dismal history in Westland Row, Dublin, *ceartlár na
Gaeltachta*. I was met by a functionary who addressed me throughout
as *a Chathaoirligh*, though he did not speak Irish, and showed me to
my desk in a huge depressing room. He came close to my ear and

told me there was a charge account in the Shelbourne that "could be used *anytime*".

The first thing to do was to find at least an interim chief executive. I was lucky that Colm Geary was available. He had worked as a marketing specialist for a brief time in the IMI and left simply because he could not abide teaching. We moved quickly – while the going was good – and pensioned off some diehards. Colm's father was the inimitable Roy Geary, Director of the Economic and Social Research Institute.

Fate smiled on us when we got Cathal MacGabhann as chief executive. He had worked previously for Gaeltarra as an accountant, then briefly for Dunnes, until he discovered it was an autocracy under (old) Ben Dunne. He had fluent Irish – a *sine qua non* – and was devoted to the Gaeltacht. He had worked in Italy, was young, bright and devoured work. He died in 2005.

He had Terry Stewart as his indefatigable number two. Terry eventually joined the European Commission, rose quickly to senior rank and attained his heart's desire as head of the Commission's Irish office. In retirement in Dublin, he has completed an MA and is going on to a doctorate.

Cathal and Terry made a buoyant and optimistic team in the face of many discouragements.

We moved the headquarters to the Gaeltacht. We chose Barna, five miles from Galway, because it was equidistant from the Gaeltachts north and south. We disappointed a local architect who came back to us with costs double the budget we had set him. State companies were seen as soft marks, open to political pressure. He protested to the Minister, who told him it was a matter for the Board. On Cathal's recommendation, we appointed the distinguished Dublin architect, Arthur Gibney (who designed the award-winning IMI building). Arthur brought the Gaeltarra headquarters in on time, on cost, and in harmony with the rocky landscape.

Early in my time, the Board suggested I acquaint myself with developments in other countries. I went first to the Highlands and Islands Development Board in Scotland. I took my new car. At the Devil's Elbow on the mountain road up to Inverness, my brakes failed. I'd hate to think what would have happened coming down. Maureen came with me. We flew from Inverness to Stornoway and the Western Isles. I could easily understand the Gaelic on the signposts but not as it was spoken. We were given a warm welcome everywhere. I was surprised to find they thought highly of our Irish efforts. We had an elegant sufficiency of herrings in oatmeal.

Maureen and I were friends of Paulo Canali, the Italian ambassador. At a party in our house, Paulo sat on the floor eating his supper. When people asked him who he was, he told them, "Connolly from Meath". He was to arrange the Italian leg of a Gaeltarra trip to France, Germany and Italy. The French and German sections were programmed to the last minute. Nothing seemed to be happening about the Italian section. The day before I left, I called Paulo for the umpteenth time. All he said was "Don't worry. You'll be met at Fiumicino".

As I crossed the tarmac, the loudspeaker boomed, "Would Mr. Kenny from Dublin please make himself known". In the terminal building, I was met by Lieutenant Imbalzano of the Italian navy. He explained that I was a guest of the Italian government. He would be my aide throughout. A car and driver were provided. There were two drivers. He apologised for the fact that the No. 2 driver's English was not very good. We drove to the Hotel Hassler, where we parked on the pavement, a prominent Ministero sign on the windscreen.

My finest hour was to drive to Frosinone, south of Rome, in the Mezzogiorno, one of Italy's long-depressed regions. As we reached the town, we were escorted by two motor-cycle outriders, greeted at the town hall by the Mayor of Frosinone and brought to lunch. Glasses of prosecco and toasts. Lunch began with a large plate of antipasto, followed by pasta. I thought we had done until a huge *bistecca alla Fiorentina* arrived. I was flattened. My hosts ate merrily away, casting an occasional eye at the slow progress I made with the excellent steak.

Before I left Dublin, I had asked Father Joe Dunn, whom we shall meet later, if he could arrange an audience with the Pope. Joe did not know how, but asked the Archbishop of Cashel. The Archbishop, a kindly man, did not know either. Joe finally contacted a friend in the Irish College and said he thought it would be all right. I heard nothing and gave up on the idea until I had a visitor in the Hassler. A small monsignor arrived with tickets for Castel Gandolfo, the Pope's summer residence. He told me I would have a good seat but no *bacio di mano*. The audience took place in a large modern theatre. The Pope greeted the crowd in several languages and was cheered by the different nationalities. It was not very inspiring.

When I came home, I called Paulo to thank him and told him about the papal audience and no *bacio di mano*. He said, "Did no one tell you? The way to get a private audience is through the concierge in the Hotel Hassler".

Back to reality. In 1966, Gaeltarra was manufacturing tweed knitwear and toys in small and widely-scattered factories. We were losing 50p for every £1 we paid in wages. The new board decided that management must be given a single objective: in the short term, to reduce loss and, in the longer term, to make a profit. We made it clear – or thought we did – that we did not regard profit as an end in itself and that we were not out to abandon any of Gaeltarra's social objectives. We also declared our belief that, if the people of the Gaeltacht were given a chance to grow and develop in profitable business undertakings, they would do so and would stay in the Gaeltacht and continue to use their mother tongue.

The use of that word *profit*, however carefully we set it in context, proved explosive. For many people concerned for the Gaeltacht, my appointment and all I appeared to stand for as Director of the IMI, represented an alien culture that would pursue profit and efficiency at the expense of social concern. This suspicion could only add to our frustrations in attempting to reorganise plants, to bring in new industries and to seek out and encourage young Gaeltacht entrepreneurs.

Was it a record that *The Irish Times*, November 27, 1969, had a leading article with the heading in Irish: *Brabús?*

> Gaeltarra Éireann's fairly confident prediction of a profit by 1971 makes it necessary for its chairman, Mr. Ivor Kenny, to repeat that his board does not regard profit as an end in itself. Ever since Gaeltarra was severed from the Civil Service and given the managerial resources it needed, its critics – mainly urban Gaeilgeoirí – have been vigilant for signs that efficiency would be won at too high a cost to the people and language of the Gaeltacht.

Within Gaeltarra's own operations, this certainly does not seem to be the case. Even with rising overheads and a wage bill of more than half a million, Gaeltarra has improved its performance while increasing the number it employs. And however essential to the self-respect of the board and management may be the trend towards profit, its impact on the Gaeltacht's morale can be nothing but good. Subsidy has been a blight on the Western spirit. Profit may not – perhaps should not – be its salvation, but the feeling of having earned its way can certainly do it no harm.

Regional development of any kind cannot be conducted by remote control. We had compelling reasons for being where the action was. We needed to improve our own cultural rapport with the region and to put a full stop to traditions of remote administration. We had to be seen clearly to be part of the Gaeltacht.

But even with this move, we were left with mysteries of Gaeltacht behaviour. Why, for example, were people so reluctant to take promotion within a factory, or to have a local man as manager? Why would a smallholder hesitate to replace with a steady factory wage a rag-bag of income and sources, all adding up to a subsistence living? Why were so many young people determined to emigrate whether there were local jobs or not? Why were young local entrepreneurs so difficult to find and foster?

We had our fragmentary insights, but what we needed was a coherent picture of the Gaeltacht culture as a whole. A three-year study, carried out between 1967 and 1970, produced an eight-volume report. The study was directed by Dr. Eileen Kane, an anthropologist who was Director of the United States National Science Foundation Training Programme in Behavioral Sciences, based in Ireland.

Dr. Kane:

"Culture" is the common, learned way of life shared by members of a society, consisting not only of the arts and sciences of that society but also of its tools and techniques, the small habits of daily life as well as the large patterns of community organisation. Culture is not an accidental collection of customs and habits; it is a logical, functioning whole, in which each part is related to all other parts and each draws on the others for its form and existence. Each reflects the pervasive value system of the whole culture. Because this value system is shared by the members of the society, it enables them to classify and integrate unfamiliar items in such a way that they become part of the functioning whole. Culture thus makes possible the reasonably efficient and predictable interaction between individuals which is a prerequisite for social life.

What did that mean on the ground? In the Gaeltacht, it meant, for example, that workers leaving the farm for the factory were faced with learning not only new skills but also new economic concepts. The idea of time as money was not as necessary to subsistence agriculture as it was to industry. The industrial practice of divisions of labour was foreign to the versatility of skills and the co-operative effort of family farming.

There was also "the fallacy of the limited good" – the belief that all desirable commodities exist in limited supply and that, if any one person gets some of them, there are that many fewer for everyone else. This helped explain the rural secrecy about individual wealth and what could appear to be begrudging attitudes to individual enterprise and success. "The working class can kiss my ass, I've got the foreman's job at last" was not in the Gaeltacht's rubric.

For example, while 65% of Gaeltacht factory workers believed that a local person was fully capable of becoming a manager, just over half of the same group did not want to see a local man in the position.

Or again, why the reluctance to exchange a complex pattern of family subsistence for a straightforward factory wage? A cultural experience with roots as far back as the Famine had bred the fear of pinning one's material support to a single source. Full-time factory work would mean that a man could no longer go out after a storm and gather seaweed for the local alginate factory, or take off the fine spring days to cut his own turf for winter fuel. The first meant loss of one source of income; the second a loss of self-sufficiency. The traditional cultural system of the Gaeltacht was so carefully integrated between cash and non-cash services and products that decisions on which parts of it to sacrifice could be difficult, if made at all.

In the Gaeltacht, we saw that economic success of a kind might be possible without the responsible involvement of the people, but it would be achieved at the expense of the culture and the language.

There were, however, signs that the traditional Gaeltacht passivity was at an end. Community councils, local development associations and co-operatives were beginning to release energies. There was even a Gaeltacht civil rights movement. Its agitation was politically abrasive, but it expressed cultural ambition.

But, slowly, I had doubts. I persuaded Michael Brown, Bishop of Galway, to bless a new factory in Rosmuc. He was known as Cross Michael or Plus Michael and was not half as black as he was painted, but he had a short fuse and had a public spat with George Colley, then Minister for Finance and the Gaeltacht. The Bishop had lunch with the board in the Great Southern Hotel in Galway before we set off for Rosmuc. After a few hospitable glasses of wine, I asked him why he had exploded with Colley. He said, "I had to, Ivor, I had to". George Colley did not turn up for the opening. It was attended by Pádraig Faulkner, Parliamentary Secretary to the Minister for the Gaeltacht.

When we arrived, the factory was shining and perfect. A few days before, the door handles had been wrenched off and the walls covered with faeces. That caused for me the beginnings of disenchantment. I remember things like visitors being described as *na cuairteoirí mallaithe*, the cursed tourists, presumably because of the Gaeltacht's dependence on them.

A separate cause of disenchantment was a change in the way the board worked. The Secretary of the Department of the Gaeltacht, Liam Tóibín, was appointed to the board. When you took Gaeltarra out of his Department, there was not a lot left. Liam and I got on well at the beginning. The two of us toured all the Gaeltarra factories. I remember a grown man in a Crolly doll factory near Spiddal spending his day trimming pink plastic piggy-banks with a pen-knife.

When Liam joined the board, he behaved as the other board members did. Then he gradually became more interventionist. Following a discussion, when a decision had to be taken, the board would look to me as chairman to articulate it. Then, almost unwittingly, they began to look first to Liam to see whether he approved. I felt I was becoming a cipher.

But a more fundamental reason for my alienation was that I lost faith. It was the opposite of St. Paul's vision on the road to Damascus. The trivial incident that crystallised it was George Colley on a visit to a Gaeltarra factory. In his careful Christian Brothers' Irish, he said to the receptionist, "*Go mbeannaí Dia dhuit*". She replied, "Hallo" with a rich Connemara double L, while the factory loudspeakers blared Radio Luxembourg.

Vain wisdom all and false philosophy. We have had at least three national objectives: full employment, which we have attained not only for the mere Irish but for thousands of immigrants; the restoration of our six sundered counties – well ...; and the restoration of the Irish language as a vernacular. A key element in that last objective was to maintain Irish-speaking Gaeltachtaí. That meant to make the Gaeltachtaí sufficiently attractive for the natives to continue to live in them. That meant there had to be worthwhile jobs in the Gaeltacht, jobs with a future. That meant in the '60s and '70s (before the service sector took off) bringing industry to the Gaeltacht. But the language of industry or business in the Gaeltacht was always English. George Colley said in the Dáil on March 22, 1970, "I have set as an objective full employment in the '70s for Irish speakers". That was a bit of a cod.

Then I was hijacked by Brendan O'Regan, who had developed a burning concern for the language. On May 3, 1971, a "Working Party" was set up on the recommendation of Comhairle na Gaeilge by the Minister for Finance and the Gaeltacht, with the approval of the Minister for Industry and Commerce and of the Minister for Transport and Power in respect of the involvement of SFADCo. Its purpose was to formulate a co-ordinated set of development policies for the Gaeltacht areas. It was opposed by Liam Tóibín.

The members of the Working Party were Cathal MacGabhann, Terry Stewart, and myself as Chairman, with Brendan O'Regan, Paul Quigley and Tom Callanan of SFADCo. Paul wrote the report. That was an uncomfortable relationship for me. Paul had been my boss. Now I was in a superior position, which I did not much like and, more fundamentally, did not want.

In any event, we recommended the establishment of a State company – Údarás na Gaeltachta – to take over Gaeltarra Éireann and the developmental functions of Roinn na Gaeltachta. The report was presented to George Colley and Údarás na Gaeltachta came into being on January 1, 1980. Roinn na Gaeltachta was eventually absorbed into the Department of Community, Rural and Gaeltacht Affairs, which is responsible for, *inter alia*, the Government's drug strategy.

Údarás na Gaeltachta has soldiered on with a board of 13 members: seven elected, the chairman and five members appointed by the Minister.

The idea of the elected members was Brendan O'Regan's dream of the involvement of "the people". I asked that decent man, Thomas Morris, Archbishop of Cashel, why he had not, following Vatican II, established a diocesan council. He looked at me kindly between puffs of his pipe and said, "No sooner would it be established than it would split between Fianna Fáil and Fine Gael".

I had got on famously with Michael Moran. He had an enormous office opposite what are now Government Buildings. As I made the journey across the carpet to pay my *ad limina* visit, he'd look up and say, "Ye made a loss again".

George Colley, on the other hand, was The Minister, formal and condescending. My few meetings were almost in the army fashion of "Put your heels together and we'll have a chat". I went to see him and told him (in Irish) I wished to resign. For the first, and only time, he came out from behind his desk and we sat at the coffee table. I had not realised that the resignation of a State company chairman, even of one as far down the pecking order as Gaeltarra, was unusual. Chairmanship of a State company was a coveted office and opened doors.

I did not want to bleed over Colley's carpet. I told him I had been chairman for seven years and that was enough. And I did not want to let down a friend, Brendan O'Regan, even though I believed the language in the Gaeltachtaí was a lost cause.

6

JOE DUNN AND THE BISHOPS

*The bishops were drowning in reports to which they could
not respond.*

As we go through life, we accumulate a small number of close
friends, people with whom we've shared good times and bad, people
we trust totally.

Father Joe Dunn was such a friend. I half-heard on the six o'clock
news that he had died. I did not know who to call. Eventually, I rang
Archbishop's House and was told, yes, he had died. Maureen wept.
We had not even known he was ill.

Memories came flooding. Christmas Day, he would unfailingly
arrive with a Dunn's smoked salmon. Parties he gave in Pranstown
House with elaborate games. Times he had the two of us to dinner in
the Radharc house in Blackrock. He fancied himself as a cook. We
would be the objects of his experiments, like duck with peaches, the
last dinner he gave us. After that dinner, we both had a feeling about
it because the three of us had pored over photo albums, the story of
his life. He had been treated as a coeliac. He died of cancer.

Joe wrote three great books, *No Tigers in Africa*, *No Lions in the
Hierarchy* and *No Vipers in the Vatican*.[6] His personality shone through
them, forthright and honest.

I first met him in 1966, when he asked me to join the Catholic
Television Interim Committee. The story behind the Committee is
hilarious.

RTÉ decided to have a religious adviser. John Charles McQuaid,
far-sighted as he was, had sent Joe Dunn to England to be trained in

---

6   ISBNs 0948183314; 1856071006 ; 1856071677.

television. John Charles let it be known to Kevin McCourt, the director general of RTÉ, that he, John Charles, would make the appointment. Kevin said the appointments in RTÉ were his prerogative, not the Archbishop's. He would, however, go so far as to accept from His Grace a short-list of three trained nominees from whom he would make the final choice. His Grace was not well pleased. His list of three had Joe Dunn at the top, with strong indications that he was his preferred candidate which, if merit were the only consideration, Joe well deserved. At the bottom of the list was Father Romuald Dodd, a Dominican. Kevin McCourt did not want anyone who would be under the archiepiscopal thumb. To some consternation, he chose Rom Dodd.

When I joined the CTIC, they were in limbo. Rom was supposed to report to them. Though a delightful gentleman, he was independent and frequently missed meetings of the committee. After all, RTÉ paid his salary.

My membership of that small committee, which soon dissolved itself, was to lead me down an unanticipated path.

First was an appointment as Chairman of a Communications Council that was set up on November 29, 1967. Archbishop Morris was President, Joe Dunn, director. We were, *inter alia*, responsible for the spanking new Communications Centre in Booterstown that Joe begat. It was a lively council. Among its founding members were Jerry Dempsey, formerly head of Aer Lingus, John Horgan of *The Irish Times*, Louis McRedmond, soon to be editor of the *Irish Independent*, Gus Martin of UCD, Bill Murray of the then Roadstone Ltd., and Tony O'Reilly, then general manager of the Irish Sugar Company and of Erin Foods.

At the press conference to announce the Council, I said, "Charismatic communication will no longer suffice for the church. A younger, better-educated population, accustomed to the practice of democracy, will not willingly accept decisions handed down. Patient and detached diagnosis of each situation must become the norm when the option of enforcing one's views is no longer open".

I worked closely with Joe. The first thing that struck me was that the Church had no research function. At that time, no one knew even the number of priests and religious in Ireland.

The Communications Centre, while physically located in the archdiocese of Dublin, had the independent status of a Washington DC. It reported, not to John Charles, but to the Irish Conference of Bishops (familiarly, and inaccurately, known as the Hierarchy). This gave us unique freedom. I suggested to Joe that we could not plot our course until we had a map of the territory. Could we appoint some one in charge of R&D? Joe was several steps ahead. He knew a priest in London, a dynamo, Eamonn Casey. He was director of the Catholic Housing Society, which he had founded, and was chairman of SHELTER. We floated Eamonn's name with Archbishop Morris and got his imprimatur.

I was despatched to London to interview Eamonn. A day or two beforehand, I was sitting with Archbishop Morris in my car outside the Shelbourne Hotel waiting for his own car to take him back to Thurles. He said, "I wonder if you should be going to London at all. Father Casey's name has been mentioned as Bishop of Kerry". Then he said, "I suppose I should not have told you that". Whether it was a genuine indiscretion on the Archbishop's part or whether he was trying to save me from a fool's errand, I shall never know. I said nothing.

Maureen and I met Eamonn in a shabby office in London. He drove us in an old car to a tiny Italian restaurant for dinner where he was embraced by the proprietor. I said I had heard he might be made Bishop of Kerry. Eamonn's huge laugh echoed around the restaurant. The diners smiled.

Maureen and I went to Eamonn's ordination in the cathedral in Killarney. Father Peter Lemass did something never done before – he gave a quiet commentary throughout the ordination. It was moving and brought the congregation right into the ceremony.

Afterwards there was a reception in the Great Southern Hotel, wine and sandwiches. There was a regal reverend mother attended by a flotilla of young nuns. Her glass was never left empty. She spilled some red wine on her white wimple. Like Queen Victoria, who sat down wherever the humour took her in the sure and certain knowledge that a chair would be put under her bum, the reverend mother, without looking, stretched her hand out for a hankie. Carl O'Sullivan, the Chief of Staff, took a pristine one from his breast pocket. She received it as her due, without acknowledgement.

Joe and Peter had dinner with Maureen and myself. Joe said, "Let's go over to Eamonn". I was shocked. I thought he would be alone in the bishop's house, deep in prayer. Instead, there was a helluva party going with lots of young people who had worked with him in London. The bishop's old house had never seen anything like it. In an upstairs room, the floor was sagging with the crowd and tall book-cases were in danger of toppling over.

We were lucky to get Father Jim Lennon as head of R&D. Jim eventually became an assistant bishop in the archdiocese of Armagh.

The Communications Institute grew. The bishops agreed to the merging with us of the Catholic Truth Society. Archbishop Morris left it to me to break the news to the honorary officers of the CTS who saw it as a crude take-over. We had a difficult meeting.

Critically, the bishops decided to have a church collection for us on Communications Sunday, May 10, 1970. Whether or not a church collection works depends absolutely on the quality of the homilies at the Masses. We raised £150,000.

Meanwhile, the Council had been strengthened by the addition of Seán Lemass, the former Taoiseach, by Brian Farrell of UCD, Liam Healy of Independent Newspapers and Rom Dodd.

Joe relinquished the position of director and was succeeded by Peter Lemass, who, in turn, was succeeded by Bunny Carr.

Bunny had been involved in the training courses from the start. I felt I had to give good example by participating. Obviously, I didn't need a course. Had I not had five years' training as a staff announcer in steam radio? Had I not chaired several television programmes in both Irish and English, including the popular *That This House*, an inter-university debating series? At the end of the course, we were asked to give Bunny a choice of three topics. He would choose one as the subject for an interview. My subject was Gaeltarra, about which I knew more than Bunny Carr. I was crisp and forthright with a touch of humour. At the end, Bunny turned his big eyes towards the camera and summed up, "There you have it. A State company unclear about its objectives and using our money in pursuit of them".

I was succeeded on July 6, 1972 by Declan Costello, SC.

(I was to see Declan again when, for the first and only time, I had to appear in court. My car had been stolen from the IMI, for a raid on Brereton's pawnbrokers, where my umbrella was used to beat Mr.

Brereton brutally. I identified the broken, blood-stained thing from the engraved ferrule. We all stood when Mr. Justice Costello appeared on the bench. He spotted me. Afterwards he said, "I was afraid you'd say 'How'ya , Declan'".)

I had got to know several of the bishops. In that quieter age, when the bishops gave you trust, they gave you total trust. Eamonn Casey was a dynamo in London. He was also a dynamo in the Conference of Bishops. I worked closely with him. The friendship grew.

When the bishops returned from Vatican II, they implemented in full the Council's recommendations. As a result, they ended up with an intolerable number of committees and commissions with chairmen and secretaries and notepaper. The bishops were drowning in conscientious reports to which they could never respond.

Eamonn brought Bill Murray, Joe Dunn and myself to his house in Inch. The Archbishop of Cashel sat quietly in an armchair while we papered the room with flip-chart paper. We managed to get the commissions down to 12. On paper. Selling that to the incumbents was a different problem. Archbishop Morris said the only one who could do it was the Cardinal. Four of us drove up in my car to Ara Coeli, Cardinal Conway's residence in Armagh.

He was a tall commanding presence with a warm humanity and a sense of humour.

We had dinner with him and were to stay the night. As he carved the joint, he told us about giving lunch to Terence O'Neill, the Northern Ireland Prime Minister. He had been persuaded to use an electric carver. It tore the leg of lamb to flitters. He kept stamping on the bell-push under the table which took that moment not to work.

He made our recommendations his own.

I was given a huge bedroom with vast wardrobes. I could not resist taking a peek. They were full of purple bishops' cassocks. No. I did not try them on.

Some years later, I was standing with the Cardinal on the steps of the Shelbourne. I said, "Eminence, everything I've recommended has been accepted by the bishops – and I can't always be right". "You know why you say that, Ivor? Because you think we're old fools."

I suggested the bishops needed a finance committee. That was agreed. I asked Ken Whitaker and Martin Rafferty to join, Ken as an establishment figure and Martin who was creative. I stayed on it myself for a brief while but it was not my bag. Eamonn Casey was chairman.

I always kept in touch with him and stayed once or twice in his house on Taylor's Hill when he moved to Galway.

Maureen and I were with our eldest son, Dermot, and his wife Geraldine at their home in Milwaukee, when Dermot came into our bedroom and said Helen, our daughter, wanted me on the phone. Your first thought is something bad has happened to the family. I have taught them all never to preface a conversation by saying, "I'm afraid I have bad news". Helen got straight to the point. She said, "Eamonn has had a son and has left Galway". It was a kick in the stomach.

Eamonn is at last back in peace in Shanaglish in the Galway diocese.

On August 8, 2002, he presided in Québec at the wedding of our youngest son, Mark, to Nathalie Desbiens. The wedding took place in the Cathedral with its stunning gold baldacchino. Eamonn spent hours preparing his homily. It was a masterpiece. Uncompromising on truth, yet clothed in a warm understanding of the human condition. The young people were captivated.

The reception was French-style at small round tables, no top table. Speeches were few and lasted no longer than three minutes. Mark was the last to speak. He looked directly down at Eamonn, who was sitting at our table. He said, "Bishop Eamonn, there is a picture in my bedroom of you blessing me in my pram. Eamonn, you are a great man".

A man who paid more than the price.

Years ago, Conor Cruise O'Brien wrote that post-Catholic Ireland would be worse than Sicily. It is painful to see church leaders in denial as the cover-up of serial sexual abuse is stripped away. Good priests like Joe Dunn and Peter Lemass would have been profoundly betrayed, as are the many good priests who continue to bring us the Christian message. However, despite the few courageous voices, there is depressingly little sign of the reforms necessary to address the causes, not just the manifestations, of the corruption. Faith without works is dead (James ii 20).

7

THE NATIONWIDE IRISH BUSINESS ORGANISATION

A second-rate society ... promotes the unspoken conspiracy where everybody instinctively combines to ensure that nobody rocks the boat.

- Charles McCarthy, 1924-1986

In the early 1960s, the Government established an advisory body, the National Industrial Economic Council (NIEC), on which Government, trade unions and business, private and State-owned, had an equal number of seats. On the whole, Government accepted the Council's proposals. The emphasis of NIEC deliberations had shifted since 1965 from economic planning to such matters as education, emigration, and full employment. This was made necessary, in part, by the move toward free trade.

In 1966, the Government proposed to formalise the tri-partite planning discussions on an industry-by-industry basis in Development Councils. Government would provide the necessary staff.

Government policy supported private enterprise. State companies were confined to areas where private enterprise "could or would not engage". Their goals were openly stated as partly economic – profits, efficiency, exports – and partly social – employment and regional development. State company management were mainly young and aggressive, following "modern management principles". State company managers said they were often blocked by interference from the civil service and Government. They also felt that they were strong enough themselves to exert influence in the opposite direction and to widen their room for manoeuvre.

In April 1966, some 50 Irish companies raised funds and commissioned Harbridge House Europe, a US-based consulting firm, to undertake a study of business representation in Irish national affairs. This group of companies, which called itself the 1966 Business Conference, included most of the largest Irish manufacturing companies and some medium and small companies. Together, they accounted for one-half or more of the total private industrial production of the country.

The initiative stemmed from growing concern about Government pressure to engage private business in tri-partite economic planning, both at national and industry levels. At a meeting of the Federation of Irish Industries, of which they were members, the companies had concluded that (a) they had no adequate organisation to participate in such a planning task, and (b) even if they were organised, they were not sure they wanted to sit with trade unions in so-called Development Councils to plan the future of their industries. At the time, a Free Trade Agreement between Ireland and the UK had been concluded, virtually without consultation with business, and there were recurring rounds of national wage negotiations and long and bitter strikes.

In February 1967, the consultants submitted a report to the 1966 Business Conference: Irish business was ill-equipped to deal collectively with free trade, economic planning and mounting trade union pressure. The many existing voluntary business organisations suffered from lack of professional staff, active members, policy planning and co-ordination between organisations. Among a total of more than 100 trade and employer associations, only four had any permanent staff at all. Between them, these four had a membership of some 3,500 companies, annual budgets of approximately $350,000 (1967), and a staff of about 30 professionals. Since their membership and functions were largely complementary, any attempt to strengthen the representational power of Irish business should best start with these four organisations and, at a minimum, would have to build on the Federated Union of Employers (FUE) and the Federation of Irish Industries (FII).

The FUE and FII were singled out, not only because of their national importance, but also because dissatisfaction with their performance was widespread among their membership. Members of the FUE felt that it acted mainly as a fire brigade reacting to trade union pressure, and that the National Council of the organisation was composed of too many men who viewed labour relations as a battle rather than a search for constructive solutions. Members of the FII felt that their organisation was a protectionist club for young Irish manufacturing companies and did not have enough qualified staff to maintain an intelligent dialogue with Government.

The consultants recommended that the two, and possibly several more organisations, should be integrated into a single new body that would represent its entire membership in all matters, including economic planning and labour negotiations. They proposed the name, Nationwide Irish Business Organisation (NIBO).

The members of the 1966 Business Conference unanimously accepted the recommendations and expressed their determination to bring about NIBO. But rumours about the project were spreading. Rivalries would make it difficult for the 1966 Business Conference to implement the recommendations because it was too closely associated with one particular organisation, the FII, whose President was among its members. The group decided to raise additional funds to retain the consultants for another few months as independent outsiders to help implement a merger of FII and FUE.

Although the 1966 Business Conference was a powerful group, critically it had no formal authority to dissolve existing organisations and form a new organisation. There were heated discussions. The revolutionary initiative of the 1966 Business Conference was deeply resented by many. You could expect powerful resistance to the death of any organisation, particularly from those who had served it for long years.

A good arms-length relationship had been worked out between NIBO and the IMI:

♦ IMI's function was an educational one. It was significantly different in its objective and its work from NIBO.

♦ IMI would require continuing Government subvention and it would be undesirable for a branch of NIBO to be subvented by Government.

The "special position" of the IMI as the principal educational resource of NIBO was to be established. As a result, I was put on a

Feasibility Committee to implement the NIBO proposal. I was really there as an observer, though I remember stopping the show when I mentioned the number of IMI staff and our income – far in excess of any of the other bodies represented. However, I was enthusiastic about the NIBO concept, not so much for the absorption of the FUE, as for a much stronger voice for business facing Government.

Not being in the inner circle, when I went to a final meeting of the Feasibility Committee, I thought it would be only a formality: NIBO would be established.

I was shocked when Hugh Lennox of the FUE, flanked by the Director General, Charlie Cuffe, dropped his bombshell. The following is an extract from the FUE's "Policy Statement":

1. The Committee congratulates the 1966 Business Conference on securing such a valuable, critical appraisal of the present state of employer organisation in Ireland. The Report indicates the main areas in which employer organisations are lacking in effectiveness.

2. Insofar as FUE is concerned, this proposal requires (a) the dissolution of the FUE and (b) the creation of a new organisation, NIBO, which would represent employer interests in the fields of industrial relations, economic planning, commercial affairs and general employer representation. The implications of these deserve close study.

3. It is the considered view of the Executive Committee that it would be extremely difficult to arrange for these collective bargaining groups to be transferred en bloc to a new organisation which would have "mixed" functions.

4. They are in membership of the FUE in order to avail of the labour relations services provided by the organisation and for collective protection against the power of trade unionism.

5. The Executive Committee accepts, notwithstanding the above-mentioned reservations and hazards, the desirability of the existing employer organisations accepting as a principle [sic] objective the development of a comprehensive national employer body ...

6. These measures would lead to the establishment of two fully-representative employer organisations working in clearly defined and separate areas. Continuous liaison between the two would be established by the formation of a joint council which would ensure a continuous process of rationalisation and development.

NIBO was dead.

In 1992, it merited only one short paragraph in a booklet celebrating the 50th anniversary of the FIE, successor to the FUE.

Last word to an old friend, Charles McCarthy. It is from *The Distasteful Challenge*, published in 1968:[7]

We are aware of the challenge that is upon us. But it is so difficult for many to accept the challenge; there are many who wish to be left in peace. A second-rate society has the virtue of tranquillity; it rewards those who conform; it aims at preserving itself in accordance with its own standards. It promotes the unspoken conspiracy of the second-rate where everybody instinctively combines to ensure that nobody rocks the boat.

---

[7]   ISBN: 0902173308.

8

THE IRISH NATIONAL PRODUCTIVITY COMMITTEE

There was talk of a bitter split in the Institute.

In my early days, the executive staff – all four of us – would attend the meetings of the Executive Committee of the IMI. Denis Hegarty was Chairman. He would take up a large part of the meeting telling us about the Irish National Productivity Committee (INPC), of which he was the founding Chairman as the Institute's representative, together with the IMI Director, Paul Quigley.

The INPC had a difficult birth, in the delivery of which the IMI had played a key role. The initiative had come from the European Productivity Agency and was seized by Hegarty, then Vice-Chairman of the IMI. Hegarty had access to Seán Lemass, Minister for Industry and Commerce. Lemass's enthusiasm for the INPC waxed and waned.

However, Hegarty persisted and the INPC effectively was formed on July 1, 1968. [8]

When I was appointed IMI Director, I became with Hegarty the second IMI representative on the Committee. I found the meetings dreary. There was the usual tension between the trade union and the employers' side, especially the FUE, who were forever watchful of encroachments on their territory. My frustration came from (a) the fact that it was a talking shop and (b) from a wariness that, if and when the Committee decided to "do" something, it would conflict

---

[8] The INPC's story is well-told in a chapter by Peter Murray in *The Lemass Era*, ISBN: 1904558291.

with the IMI. Organisations that are talking shops make people fed-up. To survive, they have to find something to "do".

The INPC decided to set up a consultancy aimed at small businesses. This would be directly competitive with the IMI, which had been mentioned several times as the proper home for such a service. A committee was formed, representative of the INPC and the IMI. It met several times. The arguments for locating the service in the IMI seemed to have been accepted. At the final meeting, Ruaidhrí Roberts, a trade union representative who had succeeded Hegarty as Chairman of the INPC, simply said, "No". I was shocked. I asked him naïvely why he had not said so in the course of the lengthy discussions. He smiled.

Hegarty had been Chairman of the IMI when it was emerging from being a voluntary body run by committees to being a professional institution with a relatively large staff and income. The Executive Committee changed the representation on the INPC to the Director and the incumbent Chairman. Jerry Dempsey, General Manager of Aer Lingus, was then Chairman. Hegarty legitimately felt that the INPC was his baby and was bitterly disappointed.

At a Council meeting, he rightly blamed me: "I believe the Executive Committee has not been in sufficiently close touch with the matter and has allowed itself to be influenced by the exaggerated fears of the Director and by the, perhaps, unconscious promotion of a 'staff' policy, which is not in the best interest of the country, or indeed of the Institute".

Dempsey told Hegarty I had the full support of the Executive Committee.

Hegarty did not let go.

When I was appointed Director, the first question I had been asked was what changes I would like to make. Up to then, practically anyone who attended the AGM would get elected to the Council of 24 members. I suggested a secret postal ballot of all the members, following proper nominations and administered by the Institute's auditors. The eight members of the Executive Committee would then be elected by, and from, the 24 elected Council members by secret postal ballot, again administered by the auditors. This was accepted and is still, I believe, the Institute's practice.

However, I had another objective besides openness and accountability. From a widespread ballot, only known business leaders would get elected. Council was, in effect, a *Conseil de Haut Patronage*, with the Executive Committee fulfilling the functions of a Board of Directors. (In the IMI today, there is now a formal board of directors working in conformity with good corporate governance.)

The Chairmanship was a different matter. It was agreed by Council that a Chairman-designate would be *selected* from the Council by the Executive Committee and endorsed by the Council to serve a two-year apprenticeship as Vice-Chairman. This worked well. Only practising managers were selected. The last thing a chief executive wants is a chairman who has little else to do or, worse, someone who seeks the office for self-promotion.

The Institute had not had much success with the building industry. Gunnar Larsen, a Dane, and managing director of Cement Limited, was persuaded to go forward.

Hegarty, contrary to the agreed practice of selection, put forward Tommy Hogan, a founder member of the Institute, to run against Larsen in an election. This led to ructions at a Council meeting. I had been advised to keep my mouth shut. I could not take sides. As was usual, I sat beside Jerry Dempsey. I remember his writing one word on his note-pad: xenophobia.

Gunnar Larsen never uttered a word.

The Executive Committee's decision was endorsed by the Council and, as an emollient, Tommy Hogan was appointed a second vice-chairman (an apprenticeship of four years!). Looking back now, for Hogan this was more patronising than emollient. In any event, he failed to get re-elected to Council, as did Hegarty. He confided to me in later years that he had been made a patsy of.

There was talk of a bitter split in the Institute. This was probably true for a few individuals whose *amour propre* was hurt. The work of the Institute was unaffected. The staff cared little about what they saw as the shenanigans at Council level, which to them was remote and hardly relevant to their day-jobs.

Gunnar Larsen was an effective Chairman. I had never spoken with him until after his appointment. We would meet over lunch in his well-furnished office in Fitzwilliam Square. Lunch was preceded by a generous scotch. It was an effort of will to keep my wits about me. If I banged on with a loosened tongue, Gunnar, in his heavy Danish accent, would say, "That is not material, Mr. Kenny".

9

INTERLUDE: BRUSSELS

Word came from Garret FitzGerald, then Minister for Foreign Affairs: would I accompany a senior civil servant to Brussels to review the list of Irish applications for the job of A3 in the European Commission. The two of us were to come up with a short-list. I was flattered – and delighted when I heard my companion was to be Denis Maher. Denis retired as a Second Secretary in the Department of Finance in 1976. He was the key man in our negotiations for entry to the Community and wrote the definitive account in *The Tortuous Path*,[9] completed shortly before his death, aged 68, in December 1984. In 1973, the Taoiseach, Jack Lynch, presented him with a silver medallion as a member of the negotiating team. The President, Paddy Hillery, who was Foreign Minister in the negotiations, in a foreword to Denis's book wrote:

> The value of providing a written record of the evolution of significant events in our history cannot be overstated ... The recollection of details, however clear it may be close to events, soon becomes less reliable.

I had met Denis regularly at Tadhg and Sheila Ó Cearbhaill's Christmas parties with Michael Murphy, Secretary of the Department. Denis had a fund of stories and a fine bass voice. He took little persuasion to sing.

Denis and I were given an office over a long weekend in the Berlaymont, February 25/26, 1973.

---

9   ISBN: 0906980453.

Denis was the more meticulous. I would finish my pile of folders before he did. I fiddled around in the desk and found a big bar of Belgian chocolate. Denis and I ate it and were overcome with guilt. We replaced it on the double next day.

Our job was not so much to choose worthy candidates as to eliminate the unworthy. I was surprised at how many senior Irish people had applied, including a handful of judges. It must have been the money, which at that time compared favourably with Irish salaries.

Denis told me that, at the start of the negotiations, he was accompanied by a young civil servant who had never been out of Ireland. There's a park in Brussels with a shallow pond crossed by a concrete path. At that time, see-through blouses were fashionable. A delightful young lady came bouncing along. Denis heard a splash. An abashed junior civil servant wondered whether he had damaged his career (knowing Denis, he may well have enhanced it).

Denis knew Brussels intimately, spoke fluent French (Tadhg Ó Cearbhaill and he translated *The Bould Thady Quill* into French in one of the inevitable *longueurs* of negotiations), and took charge of the trip. We'd have a Kronenbourg in a bar after work and adjourn to *Aux Armes de Bruxelles* in the old town, where we'd have *moules vin blanc, frites* and a bottle of Sancerre. The décor of *Aux Armes de Bruxelles* was public lavatory with a clattery black and white tiled floor. The mussels were brought to the table in buckets. When you finished, they brought unasked another bucket.

Denis told me there was a party in Brussels to celebrate Ireland's accession. Jack Lynch decided, unusually, that the negotiating team should bring their wives. New dresses were bought and hair-dos arranged. At the last minute, Jack Lynch disappointingly changed his mind.

At the party, Denis found himself momentarily alone and noticed a man in a grey suit also standing alone. Being sociable, Denis decided to join him. He knew he had seen him somewhere before but could not recall the circumstances or the name. He was about to use a standard Irish greeting, like "I know you but you don't know me", when he drew himself up, gave a slight bow and said, "*Votre majesté*". In the nick of time, it had struck him that where he had seen the face was on a postage stamp.

10
THE COMMISSION ON THE GARDA SÍOCHÁNA

The style and structures by which the police are managed will have to be changed radically.

Between 1955 and 1970, most of the founding members of An Garda Síochána were retiring: 7,000 vacancies had to be filled over a 15-year period. The younger gardaí were rebelling against rigid authoritarianism and a stifling bureaucracy.

The dam broke in 1961, when a pay award was agreed by the Representative Body. Gardaí with less than three years service were excluded. At that time, the Representative Body represented all ranks. In practice, it did not represent the younger gardaí.

The vacuum was filled by a number of younger officers, led by Detective Dick Keating. A meeting was called for November 4, 1961 at the Macushla Ballroom, Amiens Street, Dublin. Charge notices were served on 160 gardaí who had attended; 11 other gardaí were fired by Commissioner Costigan. The matter was resolved just 10 days after the Macushla meeting, through the intervention of Archbishop McQuaid and Father Tom Fehily, the Archbishop's secretary, whom we shall meet again later. They contacted Charlie Haughey, the Minister for Justice, and the 11 gardaí were reinstated.

A result was a strengthening of the power of the Representative Bodies, in particular the new Representative Body for Guards, as distinct from superior ranks. It was skilfully led by Jack Marrinan, who wielded influence at least equal to the Minister or the Commissioner.

Jackie would talk to me occasionally about management matters. He was always eager to learn. He called to tell me a Commission was being set up: would I be willing to serve? From my coaching the Garda Boat Club, I had a lot of affection for the guards, and willingly agreed.

The Commission first met on September 27, 1968. Its members were Charlie Conroy, Chairman, the senior Circuit Court judge in Dublin; Patrick Noonan, a solicitor from Athboy and President of the Incorporated Law Society; Gerry Quinn, a UCD economist; Willie Quinn, a former Garda Commissioner; and myself.

I have served under distinguished chairmen. Charlie Conroy was one of the best. He was irreverent, determined and independent. Charlie, who was a free spirit, told us a story about a young barrister rambling on. Charlie stopped him and told him that, for every five minutes he continued, he would add a week to his client's sentence. (Years later, I asked a judge if Charlie could really do that and was told, "It was his court".)

We met to hear submissions in the old Land Commission Court, now part of the Merrion Hotel. The five of us sat like the Supreme Court on an elevated platform and were addressed as "Mr. Commissioner". You could get to like it. I thought I had discovered a way to have a nap during the more tedious submissions but a kindly guard told me I had been rumbled.

The Department of Justice offered us a Secretary from among their staff. Charlie Conroy gracefully declined. We were lucky to get Joe Chadwick, a Higher Executive Officer in the Department of Labour. Joe was intelligent, politically-witful and committed.

Charlie Conroy should have died of carbon poisoning. During the submissions, he left the questioning largely to Gerry Quinn and myself, kept the head down and took extensive notes with bits of pencils, which he moistened by sucking on them.

We visited some police stations in a couple of funereal Austin Princess limousines. On occasion, the sergeant would have the troops lined up to meet us. Charlie got a rocket from Peter Berry, Secretary of the Department of Justice, saying this was ostentatious (which it was), never mind expensive. Charlie ignored the missive and told us that, if he got any more, he would find irrefutable reasons why we had to visit the Hawaiian police. It must have got back – we got no more rockets.

When it came to writing the Report, Charlie brought us to a private room in the Royal Marine Hotel in Dun Laoghaire and was merciless. He would not let us out for a pint until we had agreed on a chapter. (He did not drink himself but loved his food. We were a well-fed Commission.)

We made one mistake in our recommendations. We introduced overtime into the Garda Síochána. It would have come eventually. We hastened its advent. Now it is institutionalised and seen as an entitlement, a corruption of its original purpose.

However, our reasoning at the time was thus. An inspector who was charged with mustering a number of guards to cover a match in Croke Park would have them *in situ* at 10 or 11 in the morning, assing around, nothing to do and demoralised. We got the brilliant idea of having the inspector responsible for paying them through overtime, forcing efficiency and accountability. Some of the commentary this caused was a cartoon of a bank robber being chased by a copper who was looking at his watch and giving up the chase – until overtime arrived.

Before we broke up, Charlie, knowing that we would not get even a letter of thanks for our work, decided that we'd blow what was left in our official float on a good dinner in the Russell. Joe Chadwick reported that we had a little over £20. We had a good dinner but, after the oysters and pheasant, we all had to dig deep.

On the final night in our room in the Royal Marine, we were chatting with a feeling of completion and nostalgia. It had been a rewarding experience and gave us an understanding of one of the most important arms of the State.

I turned to Charlie and said, "We've solved nothing. Most of the problems stem from the relationship between the Garda Síochána and the Department of Justice". Charlie said, "You write a Concluding Comment and we'll put it in as a final chapter".

This is it *verbatim*, emphases included:

> 1262. At the outset of this report we said we were satisfied that there is serious and long-standing discontent in the Garda Síochána.
>
> 1263. We have dealt with the principal matters raised by, or on behalf of, the members of the Force and which were

suggested by them to be the root causes of the discontent. We believe that the recommendations we have made will, if accepted, go a long way towards removing the causes of the discontent.

1264. Because of our terms of reference, our recommendations are almost exclusively about pay and conditions of service. We have not had an opportunity, nor were we asked, to look at other factors influencing the morale of the Force.

1265. However, we are satisfied from the evidence that pay and conditions are only part of the problem. The objective is an effective police force with high morale, fully accepted by and integrated with the community it serves. This objective will certainly not be fully attained merely by paying the Force fairly and by looking after their physical conditions of employment.

1266. **We would be failing in our duty to the Minister if we did not strongly urge that an examination be carried out by appropriately qualified people into the role, organisation and personnel policy of the Force and, in particular, its relationship with the Department of Justice.**

1267. For example:

(a) There was evidence of an unclear definition of roles as between the Department of Justice and the Garda Síochána. Specifically, there was a vagueness, causing uncertainty and ineffectiveness, about the relationship between the Department and the Commissioner. There seemed to us to be a lack of delegation from the Department to the Force. This lack of delegation permeated the Force. Authority – particularly in relation to financial resources – was not commensurate with responsibility, causing an unhealthy "them and us" attitude.

(b) There was no comprehensive planning based on research. No one was specifically charged with this function. The result was reaction to circumstances and ad hoc decision-making.

(c) There was no clear personnel policy. We found it disturbing that, in a Force of this size, there was no one with specific responsibility for developing an on-going personnel policy, including training and re-training.

1268. These are some of the areas requiring further examination. They are akin to the weaknesses found in the Public Service as a whole by the Devlin Group.

1269. However, despite organisational shortcomings, we were left with the abiding impression of the Garda Síochána as a Force whose members were men and women of integrity, dedicated to a job of increasing difficulty and complexity, a job that is frequently thankless. Since its foundations as an unarmed force in 1922, the Garda Síochána has served the country well. We believe that, if our recommendations are implemented and if the matters to which we have drawn attention are put right, it can serve the country better.

The way in which the Report was made available both to the press and to the Garda representative bodies could not have been handled worse. It got extensive publicity. The best account was in the *Irish Press* of January 26, 1970. It was headlined with my best Freudian slip, when I called the release "flat-footed".

A member of the Conroy Commission, Mr. Ivor Kenny, Director of the Irish Management Institute, yesterday criticised what he called the "extraordinarily flat-footed" attitude of the Government in relation to the Commission's report on the Garda.

The Commission, he said, accepted that there had been widespread and long-standing discontent in the Force. In a highly-charged situation like that, he would have thought that the report would have been issued with more care.

"I think the way it has been communicated has been extraordinarily flat-footed. There has been no indication of the Government's attitude.

"As far as I know, the report was issued to the press with only a few hours in which to prepare comments on it, with the result that what has got across to the young gardaí has been a very attenuated version of what is contained in a 250-page report."

Mr. Kenny, who was being interviewed about the report on radio, also criticised the Sunday newspapers for what he termed irresponsible reporting of the gardaí's reaction to the report and he criticised the gardaí as well for expressing an opinion about a report which, he claimed, they had not even read.

He said he thought the Sunday newspaper headlines were irresponsible, because the reports seemed to contain "little enough substance" for their claims about the strong reaction of gardaí against the report.

Mr. Kenny said the Commission were dismayed by some of the physical conditions under which the gardaí either worked or lived. "I would even go so far as to say that, in some of the places, if prisoners were kept in the same conditions in which gardaí had to sleep, you would have pickets outside."

The Commission's report, he added, started from the premise that a garda was unique in the community, because his authority came by virtue of his office and not from superior officers. "In other words, a young, just qualified garda has the same amount of authority, essentially, as the Commissioner has."

Questioned about the pay recommendations, Mr. Kenny said the increases would also be pushed up by the imminent 12th round and the Government's 7 per cent, all of which would add an average of about 30s to a garda's weekly wage. "If that is not fair, you go through the roof", he added.

He asked what the gardaí who wanted to reject this did, in fact, want. "Would they be satisfied if they got £10 a week? You have to draw the line somewhere.

"I say to the younger gardaí, who seem to be a bit hot-headed about this, if they want to push it that far perhaps they have reached a point where they should ask themselves if they have chosen the right profession."

Mr. Jack Marrinan, general secretary of the Garda Representative Body, who also took part in the programme, was asked about the general feeling among gardaí. He said that, for the last two years, there had been an extraordinary amount of pent-up feeling, anger and frustration in the Force.

Of the call for his resignation by gardaí in the Dundalk area, he said this amused him, to say the least. "I did not write the report", he added. If the gardaí as a whole were dissatisfied with the submissions from the Representative Body, this attitude would have been indicated earlier.

Mr. Marrinan said he thought that, in the rush to make limited copies of the report available both to the Force and the general public, the Government had overlooked the need to indicate its attitude to the report at the time its contents became public.

The reaction of many gardaí to the pay recommendations was influenced by what employees in industry were being paid. But, he pointed out, police forces generally, in common with other public servants, enjoyed other benefits such as pension, sick pay and early retirement benefits.

In a further report, the *Irish Press* pointed out that the Gardaí would now "be the best paid police in England, Scotland, Ireland or Wales" and be better paid than the Royal Ulster Constabulary "across the Border".

The Department of Justice cherry-picked the Report and concentrated on our recommendations on pay.

Conor Brady, a former editor of the *Garda Review*, then Features Editor of *The Irish Times* (he was subsequently Editor), wrote a long scathing article in *The Irish Times*, October 18, 1977. His father was a Garda Superintendent.

In 1968, the Government set up a full-scale commission of inquiry and it came up with a whole range of improvements. The commission was initially seen as the panacea to all ills.

It did have one beneficial effect. It improved the lot of the working Garda. In 1968, he lived a hard and miserable life, badly paid, rigidly disciplined, living in dark, damp barracks if he was single. He had two days off a month and he could be forced to work endless hours without compensation of any kind. Conroy changed all that.

The Garda Síochána needed more than a papering and plaster job. It needed a full-scale reconstruction.

What has emerged in the post-Conroy era is a Garda Síochána which is well paid and well equipped but which lacks dedication and professionalism.

On November 2, 1978, a Committee of Inquiry on pay up to the rank of Chief Superintendent was established. Jack Marrinan called me to see whether I'd be interested in chairing it. I said I would. Nothing came of it. I was told subsequently that, so far as the Department of Justice was concerned, I was *persona non grata*: they knew who wrote the final chapter of the Conroy Report.

I suggested Louden Ryan to Jack Marrinan. Louden, an old friend, was as distinguished a chairman as could be found. He had joined the Court of Directors of Bank of Ireland, where he was subsequently to become Governor. He was Professor of Political Economy in Trinity, Chairman of the National Economic and Social Council, Chairman of a Committee to recommend on teachers' pay – *inter alia*. I was delighted when he took on the task, knowing that whatever emerged would be objective, authoritative and quick. In fact, he reported in six months, April 1979. The only link with the Conroy Commission was Gerry Quinn, who was also a member of Louden's Committee.

More hopeful was the report published February 10, 2006 of a review group charged with overseeing the first stages of the implementation of a new Garda Síochána Act, an Act that dealt with many of the issues raised in the report of the continuing Tribunal of Inquiry into the actions of certain gardaí in the Donegal Division, the

Morris Tribunal. Judge Frederick Morris's rapier recommendations pierced a cloud of unknowing. His findings related exclusively to Donegal. However, they came at a time when there was a public perception of general indiscipline such as the "blue flu" and truculent resistance to a reserve police force, the latter agreed practically unanimously by Dáil Éireann.

The review group was chaired by Senator Maurice Hayes, a friend and colleague on the Board of Independent News and Media. Maurice played a key role in the Patten Report, which led to the formation of the Police Service of Northern Ireland, successor to the Royal Ulster Constabulary. It is a terrible cliché, but he is a renaissance man: deeply cultured and informed, his influence on Northern Ireland affairs inestimable, an elegant and warm author, and with unquestionable integrity.

It took 38 years to move from the concerns of the Conroy Commission to the Hayes group's recommendations:

♦ The Department of Justice should recognise the implications of the transfer of the Accounting Officer function, which effectively ceded control of the Garda budget to the Commissioner.

♦ The Commissioner should place more power in the hands of Regional Assistant Commissioners.

♦ Civilianisation of posts across the force needs to be accelerated in order to get as many gardaí as possible on frontline duties.

♦ A €10 million budget for the Ombudsman Commission is adequate but, in the long term, the budget should be determined by the number of complaints it decides to investigate. Workload should never be dictated by budget constraints.

♦ The €115,000 salary for the Chief Inspector to head the Garda Inspectorate should be increased to attract a high-calibre candidate.

♦ Joint policing committees made up of gardaí and representatives from local authorities and other agencies need to operate in a way that does not overburden gardaí.

♦ Department of Justice officials should consult with the UK Police Standards Unit in drawing up mooted performance targets for the Gardaí.

♦ Younger gardaí should be promoted to senior posts. Applications for senior positions should be invited from overseas to bring in new ideas.

♦ A major programme of training and consultation needs to be undertaken if changes under the Act are to be realised.

I am also hopeful about the Garda Síochána Ombudsman's Commission. I believe it would have been better with a single Ombudsman, but I know well two members of the three-person Commission, Kevin Haugh and Conor Brady. Kevin Haugh is a next-door neighbour, no airs and graces, with a forensic and humorous intelligence. Conor Brady is an old friend, his biography in my book on Irish editors, *Talking to Ourselves* (1994).[10] He was the historian of the early Garda Síochána.

The appointment in May 2006 of Kathleen O'Toole, a former Boston police chief, as head of the new Garda Inspectorate, is encouraging.

The Garda Commissioner, Noel Conroy, said he looked forward to the changes ahead.

The recurring theme in this book is the gap between intentions and actions. The Commissioner and his senior team will now have a tight group of four to advise them and to drive change. Headed by Maurice Hayes, the group are skilled people, used to change. Their mandate is to last one year. I should be surprised if it is not extended.

The world, and with it the critical job of the police, has changed radically in the 38 years since the Conroy Commission. The Morris Tribunal illustrated clearly a problem endemic with bureaucracies – outdated systems and sanctions failing to cope, not changing until they are up against it and have no choice.

Things came to a head on August 18, 2006, when subsequent reports of the Morris Tribunal were published. Judge Morris painted an appalling vista. His conclusions were no longer confined to Donegal. He said:

> The Tribunal has been staggered by the amount of indiscipline and insubordination it has found in the Garda

---

[10] ISBN: 090631240X.

force. There is a small, but disproportionately influential, core of mischief-making members, who will not obey orders, who will not follow procedures, who will not tell the truth and have no respect for their officers ...

It is wrong to suggest that the people of Ireland are getting value from every Garda employed by them ... Discipline is necessary to bring out the kind of energy and optimism to make a real difference: that shone out in the evidence of Sergeant Fergus Trainor and Deputy Commissioner Peter Fitzgerald ...

Without structures of strict accounting, and without a swift method of disposing of those who are causing real problems ... a terrible and costly waste of talent will occur.

The Minister, Michael McDowell, responded with draft new disciplinary regulations, long overdue. In place of the lengthy, ineffective and bureaucratic regulations, the Garda Commissioner would have the power to dismiss a member summarily "on the balance of probabilities". The Minister warned members that threats of non-cooperation by them or, significantly, their representative associations, would not be tolerated, a reference to, *inter alia*, the associations' opposition to the Garda Reserve, for which the number of individuals who expressed interest far exceeded the initial recruitment of 900.

The Garda Síochána, like other police forces, is a self-reinforcing priesthood, resenting outside "interference". Mahatma Gandhi struck the balance: "I do not want my house to be walled in on all sides and my windows to be stuffed. I want the cultures of all lands to be blown about my house, as freely as possible. But I refuse to be blown off my feet by any".

The Review Group quoted Commissioner Michael Staines, 1922:

The Civic Guard will succeed not by force of arms, or numbers, but on their moral authority as servants of the people.

That is precisely the spirit that needs to be restored.

11

THE NATIONAL MANAGEMENT CONFERENCE

At their best, the Conferences were at the heart of the
raison d'être of the IMI.

Tom Cox was the architect of the National Management Conference. It was held mostly in Killarney, because Killarney was the only place that, in the '60s and early '70s, had an adequate conference centre (in the Great Southern Hotel) and, at least as important, an adequate number of bedrooms.

The Conference had plain beginnings. The first one I attended in 1960 was held on hard chairs in a room in the Great Southern Hotel, where bedrooms were shared by the participants. The conference then had little social dimension. A key decision in later years was to invite wives. Several had been coming privately to the Conference, but were not invited to any of the functions. They were left unchivalrously to lurk in the corridors. The form of the eventual invitation was an evolving social commentary: wives, spouses, accompanying persons, partners.

1963, a conference was held for a change in Galway. Des O'Brien was coming down in the lift with the Institute's President, Tom Laurie. Having been up all night, Des was not feeling well. He'd had a military shave – to the bone – but, as he himself said, "You can't shave your eyes". Tom Laurie buttonholed him.

"Des, you know I'm a man of the world."

"Yes, sir."

"I saw Ivor last night."

"Oh God", thought Des, "What's coming? What has he been up to?"

"He was taking a woman into his bedroom."

That's all right, sir," said Des, "That was his wife", to what, I am sure, was Tom Laurie's disappointment.

Brian Collins was the manager of the Great Southern Hotel – then by far Galway's leading hotel. It was he who introduced showmanship to hotel management. As we sat for lunch, there was a skirl of pipes. A piper entered the room followed by two waiters carrying shoulder-high on an oval platter, a dead woolly lamb. It took strong stomachs to face the roast.

The lunchtime speaker was Seán Lemass, who from the start had been a good friend of the Institute. He used the National Conferences as a platform for important speeches. In 1963, he said:

> There is a signpost to the future that our industrial leaders must read very clearly. Obsolete procedures or equipment, defects of management or operative training, or restrictive practices bolstering up costs will no longer be made possible by protective tariffs. While we have proceeded in this year and also in 1964 by non-discriminatory across-the-board tariff cuts, there may be need for more selective action to force a change in the situation in any industry in which high cost procedures are maintained, or where evidence of effective action towards modernisation and improvement is not clear. In view of the financial aids which the Government are making available in all cases where development and improvement plans involve new capital expenditure and in view of the wide range of services and facilities extended to industry, there can be no sympathy for any unenterprising concern which spurns these measures and contents itself with relying on the tariff, diminishing and temporary though it will be, to maintain higher prices.
>
> All this has been said before, but it may have to be restated many times before the message is heard in some quarters. It is one of the difficulties of the situation that the firms who are represented at Conferences like this are usually those least in need of exhortation to efficiency, and

those who need the advice are often hardest to contact. Now the sentiment prevailing in industrial circles usually has a great influence on the policies of individual firms, and I hope that all present at this Conference will repeat these exhortations and warnings to all their industrial associates so that the right response to our situation will be generally forthcoming, and forthcoming soon.

At another conference, this time in Killarney, it was my job to go to the Taoiseach's room and escort him to the conference hall. Seán Lemass called cheerily for me to come in. He was just finishing his breakfast and was stirring his tea with his fountain pen. Miss Chapman, the legendary manageress in the hotel, would have been mortified.

Seán Lemass resigned as Taoiseach, November 10, 1966, to be succeeded by Jack Lynch, whom he described as tougher than himself.

I was delighted when, not long following his retirement, Sean Lemass gladly agreed to come to Orwell Road and talk informally with the staff. He had accumulated quite a number of non-executive directorships. When asked why he had accepted them, he said he wanted a reason to get up in the morning and, secondly, he could use the money.

I drove him home that night to his modest house in Churchtown. He said to me, "If you haven't your shoes laced by nine o'clock in the morning, you're in trouble".

In Killarney, we had on the Friday evening before the concluding half-day what was laughingly known as a working dinner for the Taoiseach and speakers. It was a chance for the chef in the Europe, Frederick Lösel, to show his paces. There was an elegant buffet. There were little penguins fashioned from hard-boiled eggs and olives, huge crayfish carved and then put together again.

When I worked with Smurfit UK, I was based in their UK headquarters in Windsor. The office was on the banks of the Thames, which was fine, but was overshadowed by the depressing pile of Windsor Castle. In the meantime, Frederick had moved from the Europe to an hotel in Maidenhead. It was a relief to get back there in the evening, to Frederick's cuisine.

The 1969 Conference, April 24-26, was on *Leadership*. I gave my first talk to a conference. Reading back over the 40-minute talk, I can't imagine how I held the participants' attention. But then, all the talks were about that length – perhaps it was before we were dumbed-down by instant-tell television.

In summary, I said:

> The 70s will be a time when change will not merely be an academic subject to be discussed at management conferences. It will be something that will be happening at an increasing pace to all of us. It will require change – sometimes painful change – within ourselves: change in our attitudes and in our behaviour. It will involve a process of continuing learning, not just for managers, but at every level in an organisation. It will require a willingness to experiment with new and untried forms of organisation. It will require leadership that is flexible and adaptive. It will require constant and open communication in an open society.
>
> But, more than this, it will require also the unchanging qualities of enterprise, realism, courage and determination. Enterprise that can see beyond what is to what might be, enterprise that sees the opportunities and not merely the difficulties, enterprise that does not suffer from the Irish disease – resolving problems by talking about them.

I had invited Cardinal Conway to the conference. When he arrived unceremoniously at the door of the Great Southern Hotel, I burst out laughing. He was not amused. He looked raffish. He was unshaven. His shirt-cuffs, *sans* cufflinks, flapped around his wrists. His luggage had gone astray on his way from Rome. The barrister, now Judge, Dermot Kinlen, came to the rescue. Dermot and I had acted together as undergraduates in Synge's *Playboy* in Oxford and Cambridge (*q.v.*).

The hotel went into overdrive with a Prince of the Church and insisted that he dine in his suite. He seemed to enjoy his fillet steak as officers of the Institute sat in a reverential semi-circle around him.

In his introduction to the Conference, the Chairman, Gunnar Larsen, quoted his successor, Frank Lemass, who said, "Business is now everybody's business in society".

J.G. Bavinck, of Philips, Netherlands, the opening speaker, said:

> The freedom of action of management, where free enterprise exists, is restricted by an almost endless number of laws, rules and regulations and by different pressure groups. However there remains a vast area of free activity for management, though I am convinced that it will have to be tuned more and more to the concept of tomorrow's society. Changes and demands in many areas of human life are so clear that management's attitude, to preserve the essentials of free enterprise, can neither be an attitude of wait and see nor an attitude of saying no and fighting rear-guard actions".

Bravo, Dr. Bavinck.

David Rockefeller, head of Chase Manhattan Bank, was persuaded by Ian Morrison to participate. He said:

> There is a lesson here for all of us who occupy managerial jobs in private enterprise, regardless of our nationality. We must continue to be profit-oriented, for it is upon profit that the survival of our enterprises – and, in my view, of our free societies – ultimately depends. At the same time, though, we must keep in close touch with men who are not essentially profit-oriented – that troublesome but creative minority of academics and intellectuals who can help us to identify emerging social problems before they reach crisis proportions. Above all, we must factor social considerations into every decision we make, for only thus can we hope to preserve the kind of stable social environment which is essential to the preservation of free enterprise.
>
> For the modern manager, in short, it is no longer enough to respond to the revolution of rising economic expectations. Today, if we are to perform our function fully, we must also respond to an infinitely more complex revolution – the revolution of rising social expectations.

The last word to Cardinal Conway:

> Even if all our world problems were solved tomorrow, life
> would still be utterly inadequate to satisfy the soul of man.
> Suppose that hunger and disease and ignorance and war
> were banished from the earth, that there was "middle-class
> comfort" for everyone, would that satisfy us – or would not
> the utter pointlessness of such an existence, as the only
> existence, eventually lead to utter madness? This is
> something which the existentialist philosophy of our day has
> rediscovered for itself – that there is in man, very often in the
> sub-conscious, but it is there, a yearning for a "foothold in the
> infinite", a reaching-out for an absolute which he feels lies
> beyond the horizon of the mind but which atheistic dogma
> tells him is not there. It is this tension between man's appeal
> for something beyond the closed circle of a finite life and "the
> world's irrational silence" that gives rise to the agony of a
> Camus, a Beckett or a Kafka and leads to the conclusion that,
> as they put it, life is essentially "absurd".
>
> And it is this too which makes ultimately meaningless
> those noble causes, such as social justice and the brotherhood
> of man, with which, in the first spring of the Enlightenment,
> man hoped to fill the vacuum left by the decline of religion.
>
> What is the ultimate basis for the brotherhood of man in
> materialist philosophy? Is it some kind of herd instinct, with
> a more high-sounding name, and, if so, what claim has that
> on man's noblest efforts? Nothing is more striking than the
> way in which the bright élan of an H.G. Wells or a Zola has
> been replaced by a creeping pessimism and despair. A
> hundred years ago the great German philosopher, Nietzsche,
> cried aloud with joy that man was now alone in the universe
> because God was dead. "I am alone and free – alone with the
> blue ocean and the clear sky." In our day, his words find a
> chill echo in Jean-Paul Sartre, "I am alone and free, but my
> freedom is a little bit like death".
>
> I am suggesting that managers – and all of us – should be
> continually asking ourselves the basic question: what kind of
> place do we want Ireland to be? You will agree, I am sure,

that we do not want to simply reproduce here the kind of society which leads into the cul-de-sac of mere affluence. We want to produce a society of free men. We want to cultivate a soil where the human person can grow.

Tom Cox and I were in the front row close to the Cardinal as he gave his address. He never seemed even to glance at his script. He explained to us that he had a photographic memory and could "see" the script without looking at it.

Seven years later, he was diagnosed with terminal cancer. He wrote a sad letter to his fellow bishops to tell them. He died at his house in Armagh on April 17, 1977.

David Rockefeller had never been in Ireland before. He said he would love to see Kerry. Jack Lynch offered to have Máirín (Lynch) take him on a trip in the State car. Jack smoked a pipe. Máirín Lynch and my Maureen, together with Jack's long-term driver, brought the car to a quiet *bóithrín* where they would not be seen and cleaned the inside as best they could.

Douglas Gageby once said to me that editors of *The Irish Times* were expected to write, particularly leading articles. At a working dinner, I asked Jack Lynch what he thought of that day's leading article. It could have been written only by Douglas. It ended, "This is a bloody awful government". The Taoiseach said, "If I was to be concerned at that kind of thing, I'd never do my job. Water off a duck".

A while later, he and I were standing side-by-side in the men's room. He turned and said, "That bastard Gageby".

In 1983, Brian Patterson was concerned that the Conference was attracting unfavourable publicity at a time when the Government grant was in danger. Its social image – junket, jamboree – was attracting as much media attention as the important messages it was delivering. He asked me what I thought of moving it to Dublin as a one-day event. I told him he would never know until he did it. It did not work out. It was too easy to go back to the office. Killarney was a commitment. The Conference returned there the following year.

Tom Cox had an unbroken rule: he would never break faith with the participants. The speakers named in the brochure would be at the Conference come hell or high water. Hell and high water arrived in the shape of Jean-Jacques Servan-Schreiber, author of *Le Défi*

Américain (1968) and co-founder of the *Mouvement Réformateur* (1972). A matter of days before the Conference, Tom got a note to say, "JJSS regrets ...". Tom sat at his desk, eventually got through to JJSS's secretary and painfully extracted from her Servan-Schreiber's location in Nancy. JJSS agreed to come only if we supplied a private plane, almost unheard of at that time. Tom got onto a small Irish airline who said of course they could do it – in about five hops. Tom had to hire a Lear jet from Air Ural at a price that wiped out the Conference surplus. No matter, we had kept faith.

JJSS took advantage of the transport to bring his wife and child. He appeared on the platform in a light blue sweater – Killarney was always business suits – and gave an excellent performance.

The planning for the Conference – first the theme, then the speakers – would begin with Tom and myself in early autumn. Tom says in his book, *The Making of Managers* :

> Spanning a half-century, the conference themes are like benchmarks in the maturing of Irish management, from early discussions on the simplest management techniques to the latter-day complexities of competing in a global marketplace. When *The Entrepreneur* was proposed as the title of the 1970 conference, some council members demurred on the basis that few would know what it meant. This was sufficient reason, said others, to go with it. It was one of the landmark conferences, helping to define for the first time the characteristics that distinguish the entrepreneur from the manager. It sparked interest in the need to identify and nurture this attribute found sparingly in the population but crucial to the development of innovative, indigenous enterprise. Because of the demand, the executive committee even considered rationing places per company.

1970, I was unknowingly on the fringe of what was to be high drama. Jack and Máirín Lynch came to the working dinner on the Friday night, April 24. It was followed by an opportunity for Council members to have a drink with the Taoiseach. Jack and Máirín left the Europe quite late to go back to the Great Southern. I stayed dutifully until the end. Before leaving, I saw that Máirín Lynch had left her coat behind. I brought it to the Great Southern where they were staying. I asked the porter where the Taoiseach and Mrs. Lynch were. He told me they were in Frank and Moll Lemass's room. Without thinking, Maureen and I made our way there. When we knocked at the door, Máirín Lynch and Moll Lemass were in one corner. Frank was sitting on a bed in animated conversation with the Taoiseach. We felt we were intruding, but were waved inside and prevailed on to stay until an unearthly hour. A fair amount of Paddy was consumed but, not by the blink of an eyelid, did Jack Lynch reveal what was going through his mind.

He gave his talk the next day and then came down to lunch. I asked him if he'd like a gin and tonic. He said he'd love one. We had the usual excellent lunch. After it, I asked him if he'd like a sauna and a swim. As we sat side-by-side in the sauna, he looked at the sweat dropping off us and said, "That's pure alcohol". He went for a swim. When he surfaced, I told him several people had invited him for a round of golf. He was attracted by the idea, but Máirín had arrived and said, "No, Jack, I think we'd better go home".

On May 6, he fired two ministers, Charlie Haughey and Neil Blaney, who were arrested on May 28 and charged with conspiring to import arms and ammunition. Blaney was subsequently acquitted and Haughey was found not guilty by a jury. He immediately demanded Jack Lynch's resignation and succeeded him as leader nine years later.

Once it had been planned and the speakers had accepted, a national conference for 500 required meticulous organisation and attention to a thousand details. That is where Nóirín Slattery shone. Over the years, she wrote a bible for the Conference – what, where and, most important, when everything had to be in place. She built a team, every member of which knew exactly what was to be expected of them. It was good to see how they handled cranky businessmen after the weary drive to Killarney. Tom Cox's words before every Conference were, "If there's a problem that can be solved by spending money, spend it".

The Conference has now moved to the Druid's Glen Hotel in Wicklow, a short drive from Dublin, but sufficient to discourage defections.

I had not been at an IMI Conference for 20 years when Tom McCarthy invited me to the 2006 one. In form, it was exactly like the

Killarney Conference, though the technology had improved. In content, it was light years from the 1980s. It was a measure, not only of the maturing of Irish management, but also of the problems they faced – and dealt with – in a world of global competition.

It's easy to be cynical about conferences – all talk. At their best, they were at the heart of the *raison d'être* of the IMI: anticipating the future and developing among the community of managers a collegiality that helped them learn from one another.

12

THE CONFEDERATION OF IRISH BUSINESS

With Government support assured, the CII Executive
unanimously in favour, it looked like plain sailing.

The short, sharp story of the Confederation of Irish Business began
on September 16, 1971. Ned Gray, Director General of the CII, came
to see me in Orwell Road. Gray sought visibility for his position as
chief spokesman for Irish industry. He felt the CII had reached the
limits of its potential. He told me he proposed to leave the CII: now
was a good time to talk about a closer integration of the
Confederation with the IMI. I said I had an open mind in the matter,
but that the case made for NIBO (see **Chapter 7**) was compelling. We
agreed to continue the discussions.

I wrote to him on October 1, 1971 saying that, whatever the
outcome of our discussions, "a principle will be to distinguish
between educational and representational activities", as was
proposed for NIBO. He agreed.

On December 31, 1971, Gray came again to the IMI for
discussions. To Gray's disappointment, our ardour, such as it was,
had cooled, since the overtures had come not from us but from the
CII. The meeting was inconclusive.

We both now had considerable doubts about a merger. We agreed
to have further talks. They were never held.

On Thursday, June 15, 1972, Gray and I, with our wives, stood
chatting happily on the steps of the new Dublin Sport Hotel near
Enniskerry, as we watched the Director General of Bord Fáilte
perform the opening ceremony. Gray said, "It is time we started the

talks again". Three days later, Sunday, June 18, 1972, he, Michael Sweetman, his close colleague and a great friend of the IMI, with 10 others were killed in an air crash at Staines near London. They were travelling to Brussels to discuss Ireland's entry into the EEC. At a stroke, the CII lost with them its President, Con Smith, its immediate past-President, Guy Jackson, its Economics and Trade Officer, Fergus Mooney, and Michael Rigby-Jones, a former Chairman and President of the IMI. Others who died were the President of the Dublin Chamber of Commerce, M.W. O'Reilly; the Chairman of the Irish Employers' Confederation, Ivan Webb; a former Vice-President and Deputy Chairman of the FUE, Melville Miller; a Vice-President of the Association of Chambers of Commerce of Ireland, Owen Lochrin; Hugh Kilfeather, Assistant General Manager of the Irish Export Board; and Edward A. Coleman, Deputy General Manager of Irish Steel Holdings.

Thirty-four years later, the shock of that Sunday, as the news came through bit by sickening bit, is still palpable. I heard it first while I was driving to Donegal for a Gaeltarra meeting. Colm Barnes was with me. He would have been on the flight had he not had the meeting in Donegal. I had nightmares that night.

In a *Requiescant* in *Management*, Basil Payne wrote:

> The headlined horror
> Sickens the stomach as it rips the memory
> The jagged odds-and-ends of reminiscence.

The horror was deepened as, the following weekend, we went from funeral to funeral and saw the wives and families. Their loss was immeasurable. The blow to Irish business representation was, literally, stunning.

It fell to Peter Keehan, then Managing Director of Unilever in Ireland, and Vice-President of the CII, to pick up the pieces.

He acted quickly. His priority was to get at least an acting chief executive. He turned to the IMI, of which he was a Council Member: it had by far the largest staff of any Irish business organisation.

On July 3, 1972, Liam Connellan, head of the IMI's Small Business Division, was seconded to the CII as Director General *ad interim*. His secondment was to be for six months only. Connellan was 36. He had worked in A.C.E.C. as Production Controller and was to be the first

Director General of the CII with direct experience of manufacturing industry.

On August 23, 1972, I met with Peter Keehan, then installed as President of the CII. There had been a tragic illustration of the scarcity of business leadership in a small community. Integration with the IMI seemed a shining – and rapid – solution. In a phrase that was to be used many times, it made sense.

Why did it now make sense, when in different circumstances, a few short months earlier, my feelings towards it, shared by my colleagues, were at best cool?

It is doubtful whether Ned Gray would have opened discussions with the IMI had he not already decided to leave. If he had planned to stay on, who was going to head up a new organisation. Was I to work for him? Or he for me? Or both of us for someone else?

I was not excited at the idea of relinquishing my position. Ned had asked whether my getting the top job in a new, merged organisation was a precondition of a merger. I replied that I would be interested. I told him also that I fancied my chances in a free competition. He said he would not be so optimistic. The IMI carried an academic tag.

What had changed? First, there was the emotional impact of the air crash. It left a feeling of vulnerability and impermanence. The reaction was a desire for renewal and strength and a belief that here was a new opportunity. At such a time, personal motivation would have been shabby. But, second, there was the fact that the IMI was now the organisation with which the initiative lay. The CII's President was the catalyst. That was critical. But the IMI was the stronger continuing organisation. The CII was wounded.

Against this background, arguments for a Confederation of Irish Business were developed. They were developed at a pace that was to be, at least partly, a cause of their failure, only eight weeks following my meeting with Keehan on August 23.

The day after, August 24, 1972, I discussed the possible integration with Ronnie Nesbitt, head of Arnotts and the IMI Chairman. He approved, provided the academic independence of the IMI was adequately safeguarded. He felt deeply about this.

The idea of a CIB now had the minimum necessary commitment of the chief honorary officers and the chief executives (albeit one of them acting) of both organisations. To this inner circle was added Michael Dargan, Chairman Designate of the IMI. He was also a member of the CII Council. His support was essential.

The first step, as we saw it, was to get together a small working group of CII and IMI senior staff to formulate outline proposals. A Timetable for Implementation was prepared, ending neatly with the first meeting of the new CIB Council on October 31 at 5.30 pm. There was little doubt in our minds that this timetable would be followed.

As the circle of consultation widened, confidence grew. Influential figures were impressed by the timeliness of the proposals and their decisiveness. The CII Executive Committee was to meet on September 11, 1972, the IMI's Executive Committee the following day.

Peter Keehan emphasised the urgency of the situation, the advantages of the new organisation, and the fact that it was in line with the objectives of those who had died. The Confederation of Irish Business would be organised to provide for effective and positive participation by Irish business in national and European affairs. It would have strong supporting services, including policy formulation, research and information. The Irish Management Institute, with its key role of management development, would be integrated into the Confederation, but would maintain the autonomy necessary for objective research and training. A staff of 156 in 1972/3 was envisaged, with an annual operating budget of £900,000. It was an attractive package.

The National Executive Committee of the CII seemed to think so. On September 19, 1972, they passed unanimously the following resolution:

> That the National Executive Committee of CII gives its
> support to the proposal to merge with the Irish Management
> Institute in order to form a Confederation of Irish Business
> and that it recommends this decision to the National Council
> for adoption.

The IMI, for its part, had to ensure that integration in a business representative body would not affect its Government grant. On September 19, 1972, Ronnie Nesbitt and I met with the Minister for Labour, Joe Brennan, and the Secretary of the Department, Tadhg Ó Cearbhaill. We came away with their support and an assurance that "the proposed organisation would not interfere with the present form of State subvention". The Minister mentioned that he had informed the Government of the proposals at their last meeting and would do so again. I saw the Secretary of the Department of Finance, Charlie Murray, and the Assistant Secretary, Michael Murphy. I got a slightly more guarded attitude from that Department, but "a possible formula was that subvention would be given to 'the Confederation of Irish Business for the Irish Management Institute'". Charlie Murray said there was a need for a strong business organisation that did not indulge in "tip and run" comment: the CII had, for example, recently criticised the "proliferation" of State bodies and had never followed through on the criticism. Murray had spent many frustrating years in the early stages of economic planning dealing with business organisations that were not effectively representative and seemed to make up policy as they went along.

With Government support assured, the CII Executive unanimously in favour, it looked like plain sailing for the IMI Executive Committee meeting. There were letters of support from all those who could not be present.

J.P. Hayes, Managing Director of Ford and a subsequent Chairman of IMI, raised in his letter what might be considered impolite to mention too openly: "Would some people regard it as the pursuit of vested interests by Ivor Kenny?". He answered his own question: "I have discussed all these aspects very frankly with Ivor Kenny – the advantages should outweigh the disadvantages". The Executive Committee decided unanimously to recommend the proposals to the Institute's Council.

Two critical hurdles had now been cleared. It would have been quite unusual for the Council of either body to go against the considered recommendations of its Executive Committee. Only once had the IMI Council thrown out a recommendation of its Executive Committee, and that, oddly enough, was a proposal for a merger – with the Institute of Public Administration in 1959. The way was clear for wider consultation.

Nesbitt wrote to the IMI Council members:

> I have regarded it as my prime responsibility as your Chairman to ensure that the Institute retained its essential characteristics of relevance and independence: I am satisfied

that the proposals before you achieve that end and that I shall have discharged my responsibility. I shall now be happy to stand down to clear the way for whatever new appointments are agreed for the Confederation of Irish Business.

You will agree that the Institute has responsibilities wider than merely ensuring its own integrity. The proposals before you present us with an opportunity to serve Irish business with a new, strong, outward-looking organisation. Some of our colleagues, including our past President, Michael Rigby-Jones, died in this service and with this vision.

At a time of change, I believe we owe it to their memory and to Irish business to take this initiative and to act decisively.

I am sending this letter to you personally and confidentially as a Council member. I know you will understand the necessity for strict confidentiality until the Councils of both organisations have taken their decisions.

The confidentiality was shattered a week later by an article in *The Irish Times*, September 29, 1972. The article, by Andrew Whittaker, *The Irish Times's* Business Editor, dealt with "this extraordinary proposal" and said:

Since the CII, compared with the IMI, is much younger, much smaller, less well-financed, and much more in need of an injection of men and money to take account of such expanded areas of importance as EEC developments, the talk of a merger looks very like an IMI take-over bid.

Peter Keehan saw the Minister for Foreign Affairs, Paddy Hillery, because of the EEC dimension. Hillery welcomed the proposal, as did the Secretary of the Department of Industry and Commerce, J.C.B. McCarthy. Michael Dargan (for the IMI – Nesbitt was away on holiday) and Keehan saw the Taoiseach, Jack Lynch. He was officially neutral, but expressed personal approval. They saw the Minister for Finance, George Colley. He had been concerned about the question of subvention but, following the meeting, seemed to them to think his argument had been adequately answered.

I met again with the Minister for Labour on October 5, 1972 and, at his request, prepared a note for him for a meeting of the Government. He was to let me have a final word about the Government's general attitude in time for the key Council meeting.

I met with the Officer Board of the Irish Congress of Trade Unions on October 4, 1972. My note of the meeting was that "they were benevolent".

The IMI Council members were overwhelmingly in favour. Dr. T.K. Whitaker said that the merger was "likely to lead to a strengthening of Ireland's position in the critical EEC transition period and beyond". Sir Basil Goulding, Fitzwilton, wrote: "We missed the NIBO bus – it moved too quickly and passengers were half asleep, or drugged, at the bus stop. Now we are called for again and must not miss again".

Connellan sounded the first sombre note. Some members of the CII Council, particularly the sector members, did not favour the proposals. Haste, secrecy and an IMI take-over were the currency.

A joint CII/IMI memorandum to the Taoiseach and the relevant Ministers said that "The Councils of both the IMI and CII – comprising over 60 chief executives of Ireland's principal businesses in the public and private sectors – have given serious consideration to the merger of the two bodies. The unanimity of support for the merger is impressive ...". This was premature.

The case for Government support for the proposal was made thus:

> Government support for the new organisation is important, not because of the subvention to IMI, but because the Confederation of Irish Business can be effective only if it starts out with and develops a working relationship with Government and its agencies. Co-operation rather than criticism will be the keynote of the relationship. This is not to say that the Government with its much wider, and ultimate, responsibilities will always see eye to eye with a Confederation representing one sector of the community. It is to say that Government policy for business will be that much more informed if it has a strong business organisation with which to consult in the formulation of policy and a genuinely representative body to participate in the consequent implementation of that policy.

There was spin in my phrasing.

The crucial Council meetings were carefully arranged for the same day, Tuesday, October 10, 1972. The plan was that the CII Council would meet in the morning and take its – the critical – decision. The IMI Council would meet in the afternoon and give its blessing. Then a joint press conference would be held.

On the Sunday before, events took an unpleasant turn. The front page headline in *The Sunday Press* read *Crash Widows Slam Plan*. Under this ghoulish banner, an obviously heartfelt letter from Una Gray and Barbara Sweetman was published:[11]

> It was with great concern that we learned of the proposed merger between the CII and IMI to form a new Confederation of Irish Business and feel we would be failing our husbands if we did not make our voices heard. We know that neither of them would have supported this merger because it goes against everything they worked for within the Confederation and would not be in the best interests of Irish industry. For this reason we are very disturbed to hear that their names are being used to support the merger.

Peter Keehan was interviewed on RTÉ radio that day:

> I would, of course, regret if any distress was caused to the relatives. I am not certain I would agree with what their husbands might have recommended. For one thing, the situation is obviously so different from what it was before their husbands unfortunately died.

On that Sunday also, Colm Rapple, Business Editor of the *Sunday Independent* wrote, without knowledge of Mrs. Gray's and Mrs. Sweetman's letter, a cool and well-reasoned article. It was unequivocally against the merger.

Press comment reached a peak on Monday, October 9, 1972, the day before the Council meetings. Andrew Whittaker quoted freely from the documents that had been circulated. He embellished them

---

[11] It was published also in the *Sunday Independent* and in all Irish daily papers the following Monday.

with some facts and some fiction. There was an emphasis on secrecy and on personalities:

> It is an open secret at IMI headquarters in Rathgar [sic] that the job [of Director General of the CIB] would be given to Mr. Kenny ... A failure of the present proposal ... would probably mean the resignation of Mr. Keehan from the Presidency. The merger body would lack the hard, cutting edge that CII was developing in representing the private sector in the Irish economy.

In fact, the CII represented both private and State companies.

The following day, the day they were to meet, Whittaker wrote that the CII and IMI Councils had not received the same information about the proposal from their respective executives:

> The IMI, it became known yesterday, has sent to its council members a memorandum significantly different from the documents sent to the CII council ... The fact that the two different councils had not received the same information came as a shock, yesterday, to some members of each council.

The two Councils got precisely the same memorandum. Whittaker went some way to withdrawing the inaccuracy the following day when, under a heading, *Corrections*, he quoted from an interview with Keehan and myself. What was clear was that he got some documents at draft stage.

It is impossible to measure the effect of press comment on the events. Fellow journalists said: "Mr. Whittaker's early warning of the proposed behind-the-doors merger between IMI and CII was a very special sort of scoop. It was certainly instrumental in forcing a rethink of that whole proposition".

That judgment was at one end of the scale. At the other was my own, given in a radio interview the day of the Council meeting. Part of the transcript was published by Whittaker:

> Interrupted by Mr. Bowman and asked: "How good for instance was the coverage generally, the very extensive coverage in yesterday's and today's *Irish Times*", Mr. Kenny

answered: "The coverage was extensive and skilful and, in many serious respects, inaccurate".

"It seemed to be critical of the IMI handling of the affair, of your handling of the affair?"

"Yes."

"Do you think that was inaccurate?"

"Yes."

"Do you think it was damaging to the negotiations themselves as they went on?"

"I don't think so. I think that the Councils are rather more mature than to be stampeded by speculation."

At 11.30 am on Tuesday, October 10, 1972, the Council of the CII met in the Burlington Hotel, Dublin. The following motion was passed:

> It was unanimously agreed that the proposal to effect the merger between the CII and IMI in a new organisation to be known as the Confederation of Irish Business be examined further in depth and considered again by Council following consultation with the members.

The merger was dead, just like NIBO. The proposal for further study and consultation was face-saving, just like NIBO.

The decision was telephoned to the IMI. Its Council met at 3.00 pm. When a member asked if any other link-ups were considered other than the one with the CII, Nesbitt replied that "when contemplating marriage, you did not consider matrimony in general, you considered someone in particular".

In a radio interview that evening, I said: "It moved too fast and did not take into account that, towards the end of the process, there were many people who felt they had not been fully consulted". At first there had been "an absolutely overwhelming degree of support ... As we came nearer the shore, we found that some rocks began to appear".

In the October 1972 issue of *Management*, I wrote: "With hindsight, the curiously-titled Nationwide Irish Business Organisation was a mixture of objectivity and expediency". With a little more hindsight, so, too, was the Confederation of Irish Business.

Twenty-six years after NIBO, 22 years after the CIB, progress was finally made. IBEC, the Irish Business and Employers Confederation, was formed on January 1, 1993 from a merger of the Federation of Irish Employers (FIE) and the Confederation of Irish Industry (CII). The negotiations took place with a degree of secrecy after hours in the Smurfit Paribas Bank, of which I was Chairman. Mark Hely Hutchinson, a former IMI Chairman, chaired the discussions. Paddy Wright, then President of the CII, was a director of the Bank. I knew nothing about the discussions. Significantly, they took place at a time when Liam Connellan was to retire. John Dunne, the FIE CEO, was the first chief executive of IBEC. The CII staff moved to the FIE headquarters.

13

TEN THOUGHTS ON MERGERS AND ACQUISITIONS

1. The first question to be answered is what are we buying? Scale? Market share and/or route to market? Technology/skills we lack? Management? Enhanced positioning?

2. The broad-brush statesmanlike answer can be seductive and misleading. In acquisitions, the devil is in the detail.

3. Acquisitions damage the acquired company. You never get what you paid for.

4. Bankers can tell you a deal is (financially) doable. After that, their advice is useless. And they have a vested interest. If things don't work out, it's your fault. "Doable", in banking parlance, means subsistence level.

5. A company is not a set of inanimate numbers. It is a living organic thing consisting, oddly enough, of people. Once they have wind of the word, the good guys may be preparing their CVs.

6. A serious cause of enduring misfit is different company cultures.

7. There is no such thing as a merger. One company has to have management control. "We're all in this together" is a management myth.

8. If the judgment of the CEO of the dominant company is clouded with pride/ego/ambition – beware. He can wreck the

joint. The power of a chief executive, for better or for worse, is near limitless.

9.   For that matter, the motivation of the key players needs to be constantly monitored by a cool, experienced Board. An acquisition can develop an inner momentum (in pursuit of the glittering prize) and the still small voice of commercial logic be overwhelmed. The Jesuits say, "The Lord protect us from zeal".

10. Lastly, no Board should approve an acquisition until it sees clearly the end of the road – a detailed post-acquisition integration strategy.

Then there is always the black hole, something you don't discover until after the event.

14

A TURNING POINT

The Institute is now firmly set on a path of selectivity because the nature of its work requires that it apply itself to those firms and individuals who want to grow.

In 1972, there was a change in IMI strategy. There is an echo here of Seán Lemass's speech to the IMI National Conference 10 years earlier. I was accused of being élitist. If an élite is defined as people with social and technical skills, I'd willingly wear the badge. Faced with increasing competition, we had no choice but to move from *grá mo chroí* management and governance to a more selective hard-nosed style.

This is what we said at the time:

> Research by the IMI described the characteristics of the successful business leader. He is outward looking, has a good nose for ideas, an awareness of people's tastes and how they are thinking, is willing to take risks, and to lose if needs be. The picture is of an aggressive, restless, high energy, single-minded individual (or narrow-minded, if you prefer). He might not be a "nice" person in the sense we normally use the word.

> Business, like athletics or war, is a competitive encounter. Success depends on being in the right market at the right time with enough resources to exploit the opportunities and capitalise on the weakness of your rivals. And like war, God seems to favour the big legions. Big firms have a greater chance of long-term survival than small ones. Since all our firms by international standards are small and since we have

been locked mentally in the small home market [1972], then failures in Irish businesses will continue to occur, more especially as technology changes and scales of operations become critical.

In a country as poor as ours, we can survive only if we squarely face the choices: either we put our resources behind those firms and individuals who are successful or we continue as we have been doing, going a bit of the road with everyone.

If we want to reduce redundancies in the long-term, and achieve full employment, our system must reward the companies who show that they can grow. The hiving off of resources by taxation from the successful Peter to bolster the less successful Paul may be meritorious from some value standpoint. It is hardly a realistic strategy for long-term survival. This country owes nothing to the entrepreneur who didn't last the pace or the old firm gone arthritic – the Limited Liability Act was designed for their protection and is still working happily on their behalf.

Perhaps the time has come when we should consider channelling subventions and grants through some new instruments at one or two removes from pressure groups so that more objective and business-like decisions can be taken about where resources should go. This would be in line with some of the restructuring of Irish business which has already begun to take place. For what we need badly is a growth dynamic in our business scene – and that presumes a system which rewards it.

If our joining the European Economic Community helps us to face these realities in a more rational and optimistic way, it will be worth a lot. If it helps us to overcome something of our dependency complex, by shocking us into an awareness of how European businessmen behave, it will be worth even more.

Protection and dependency were useful cushions in the past but they have proved to be the enemies of growth, initiative and creativity. In this, as elsewhere, we are going to be pushed to make a choice. We can't keep on having it both ways.

The IMI itself had to make a choice. It did so in April of this year [1972], when there was a significant change in policy. We had to an extent accepted reaching every manager in the country as an ultimate target. An influence was that much of our policy was formulated in documents addressed to the Department of Labour looking for State subvention. We felt that, in asking for taxpayers' money, we had to relate to the total problem expressed as the total number of managers in the country. This approach was symptomatic of a deeper problem the State perennially faces: the compulsion to take grapeshot, lowest-common-denominator-type action, when what would be effective is rifle-shot, selective action.

We had in the past in the IMI been guilty of trying to be all things to all men, in a vacuum of management development filled by no one else. But we had been finding out, with increasing force, that a key factor – if not the key factor – in management development is the individual manager's wanting to learn. We had been finding out that management development may not be for every manager. While the classic measure of our training activity – participant days – is steadily increasing year by year, the proportion of managers in the total managerial population who participate in our work is relatively fixed.

The Institute, therefore, is now set firmly on a path of selectivity, not merely for philosophical reasons, but because the nature of its work requires that it apply itself to those firms and individuals who want to grow. We have learned, maybe too slowly, but at least now the lesson is well learned, that to do otherwise is futile.

Our job is, through the development of managers, to stimulate business growth with innovation and change involving more and different jobs, new products and markets, increased sales and investment.

We are also concerned with growth in another sense. We must continually try to enlarge our freedom to control our own affairs – not in a chauvinistic sense, but as a precondition for a healthy community. For example, we are concerned about the extent to which industrial development puts real control of business out of the grasp of managers in Ireland and consequently diminishes their creativity and vision. At another level, we expressed concern recently at the recommendation in the Devlin Report on Remuneration, which will lock the chief executives of State enterprises into an ironclad pecking order.

The IMI's job in the past was mainly to help managers with the technical tools of their trade. It will continue to fill this need and will continue to develop its skill so that it meets it better. But we must also help develop qualities of independence, creativity, enterprise and vision. The last statement would be a suitable bromide to end an after-dinner speech, were it not for the fact that, over the past five years, we have been developing on a basis of solid research ways in which we can encourage and give practical help to personal growth and creativity. We are beginning to understand better the many factors in Irish life which discourage initiative and risk. We are beginning to understand that there are few enough problems that can't be overcome provided the individual who faces them really wants to overcome them. And we know that that type of individual will always be in a minority.

15

ON MEETING HERMAN KAHN
(1922–1983)[12]

The world is too complex to be shown realistically by
"models" of academic precision.

I met Herman Kahn, the futurologist and director of the
Hudson Institute, last Sunday morning [March 25, 1973], at
his house in Chappaqua, 30 miles north of New York. (I went
to meet him the previous Friday but he had to see President
Nixon. I told him I did not mind.)

The first impressions were hardly Strangelovean. His
house was a modest one. The only touch of indulgence was
an indoor swimming pool. The house looked like a bomb had
hit it. The door was opened by a vague youth, who supposed
we wanted "Uncle Hoyman". The lounge was strewn mostly
with books, but also with two very big dogs: one, an Irish
wolfhound puppy, was called Evermore.

Uncle Herman, a man of generous girth, appeared in a
blue silk dressing gown and assured us he had been up and
about for hours. He left us to put on shirt and trousers, while
we found seats between the books and dogs and
gramophone records.

He talked about the Hudson Institute Study: *The Corporate
Environment 1975-1985* – his main theme for the IMI Killarney
Conference. It was refreshing to hear a futurologist begin by
saying: "No one can know the future". No one could make

12   *The Irish Times*, Friday, March 30, 1973.

certain predictions or projections. But it was possible to improve guesses – to understand general alternatives to the point where you could make more circumspect choices.

The aim of the Hudson Study is to help people understand better the big issues that seem likely to be shaping the environment in which business will be working over the next decade or so. It could also be thought of as offering snapshots of alternative plausible worlds. The pictures might not be clear or co-ordinated. They could easily mean different things to different people. But, taken together, they should give people a better insight into the likely problems and opportunities coming up, and how business might react to them.

The method of Kahn's study is typical of policy research done by the Hudson Institute. Its objective is different from academic research. Policy research is half-intuitive, wide-ranging and often uses information and theories that are speculative and shadowy, in an effort to develop a complex pattern of decisions.

The theory behind this is simple – that the world is too complex to be shown realistically by "models" of academic precision. To define the problem is often the key issue. Exceptional events and extraneous issues can be more important.

For example: in trying to hypothesise long-term or short-term prospects for a given industry, changes in tariff barriers, labour issues, technology, and the national and global economic situation are as important as supply and demand factors. In short-term calculations, you often assume these to be constant, or make arbitrary adjustments for changes that seem long-range projections. On the other hand, the non-quantifiable factors often become the most interesting and important things to study.

The difficult part of future-oriented policy research is not in coming up with some kind of projections – it is in trying to make them realistic, or at least useful. One important requirement is to have a good understanding of what is going on now – which are the important trends and real forces, how they interact, what their impact is over time, what are the countervailing forces and trends that may appear.

This means developing both a global viewpoint and a familiarity with important details. It means looking at "everything" at once, trying to understand context, isolated components, and the interactions – and, often most importantly, trying to avoid or at least account for, individual and/or professional biases.

Kahn in Killarney will follow two distinguished members of the Club of Rome, Bertrand de Jouvenel and Alexander King. The Club of Rome is a prestigious European gathering of people concerned with the future. [Paddy Lynch, Professor of Economics at UCD was a member.] They argue from the study *Limits to Growth* (1972)[13] that the depletion of non-renewable resources will, within 100 years, force the end of society as we know it today.

The argument, is simple: a consumer society is just that – it consumes resources so that more money and time are spent on producing raw materials and less on new plants and facilities. Investment in equipment falls behind the rate of obsolescence and industry collapses, bringing disaster also to the service and agricultural activities that have become dependent on it.

The study concludes that all growth projections end in collapse. The solution: end further growth by 1975. Equalise birth and death rates, replace only old plant, change consumer behaviour so that mind-satisfaction replaces materialism. This lack of growth, say some members of the Club of Rome, would not create stagnation or stop creativity, but just allow for it to be rechannelled:

A society released from struggling with the many problems imposed by growth may have more energy and ingenuity available for solving other problems ...

But Herman Kahn says: "The Club of Rome is dead wrong and provably so. I will demolish the Club of Rome in Killarney".

---

13   ISBN: 0856440086.

As a "futurologist", Kahn is essentially, if globally, optimistic. He believes that Europe will grow more slowly than the rest of the world but that Ireland will grow faster than Europe. He believes we shall solve our environmental problems. He believes [1973] that, in the coming decade, France will surpass West Germany in production and, 13 years from now, will be the most powerful nation in Europe. He believes the UK is in for a rough time and may even consider opting out of the EEC. [In Killarney, he predicted that oil would not go above $8 a barrel. Bliss was it in that dawn to be alive ...]

Ireland, says Kahn, is mad not to have diplomatic representation in Japan, which he sees as the country with the greatest possible future. He thinks we should concentrate more on sub-contracting for the large corporations than on offering them wholly-owned and controlled subsidiaries in Ireland as a policy for attracting foreign capital and know-how.

When I suggested that business exercised little real influence in Ireland, he had only cold comfort to offer. That, he said, was universally true.

*

Herman Kahn's talk in the Killarney was chaired by Sir Basil Goulding, who wound up the session thus:

> It is my pleasure and duty to thank you for the immense grasp which you have demonstrated so well to us today. I went so far in my own mind as to identify you with that well-known instrument, the Hoover. I thought of you as an intellectual Hoover, and wrote these four lines:
>
> > Factual omphaloskepsis
> > Visions of crisis from crux
> > Swept by the mind of a Hoover,
> > Who beats as he sweeps as he sucks.

16

TWO LITTLE PROBLEMS

It looked like we might fall flat on our faces.

When we were moving from 12 Leeson Park to the big house on Orwell Road, there was a gap between what we would get for Leeson Park and what we had to pay for Orwell Road. As Jerry Dempsey, then Chairman, stepped into his dark blue Rover following an Executive Committee meeting, he said, "You have a problem there, Ivor".

The saintly Jim Beddy called me to say, "We'll give you the money". Dr. Beddy – it would have been impertinence to call him other than doctor from an earned doctorate – was managing director of the Industrial Credit Company, a State body that no longer exists. Some Executive Committee members did not want to take on long-term debt, but we had more than exhausted the capacity of Leeson Park, even with four Portakabins in the back garden. People liked working in the Portakabins so much that we took them with us to Orwell Road.

The family from whom we had bought Orwell Road ran some newsagents. When we dug up the orchard to accommodate more temporary buildings, we found a cache of Dutch chocolate, probably smuggled in during World War II.

We celebrated the opening of Orwell Road in June 1965 with a garden party. It poured. We retreated to a marquee. Paddy Hillery, Minister for Labour, could not be heard with the rain drumming on the roof. The late Michael Biggs, the sculptor, had made two beautiful marble plaques for the gate pillars. A bearded giant, he made his way in the rain from the marquee to the main building, beard dripping, but with his hand carefully shielding a glass of champagne.

It was not long until I had another problem. The Institute quickly outgrew Orwell Road, even though we had bought the adjoining house and covered the available land with temporary buildings.

I suggested to Jim Darlington that he buy an Instamatic camera and visit the best centres in Europe and the US. In Aarhus, in Denmark, he came across a beautiful centre designed by engineers. It had all sorts of gadgetry. The conference manager told Jim the gadgets were never used. In America, he saw another beautiful centre and took many photographs. As he was leaving, the conference manager said, to Jim's dismay, "If only I could do it all over again".

We had a few strokes of luck. We commissioned that creative architect, Arthur Gibney, to design the centre in Sandyford, for which he was awarded the Institute of Architects' 1979 Triennial Gold Medal, its highest award. I called his office May 17, 2006, to check the date of the medal. I was told he was terminally ill. He died the next day, aged 73. It is sad to hear someone has died. It is sadder to hear they are dying.

Arthur and I worked well together. We consulted all the staff. The engine rooms were the classrooms. Some specialists favoured the Harvard-style tiered classrooms, where the lecturer would be the cynosure of neighbouring eyes. The more groupy-feely specialists wanted infinitely flexible classrooms with level floors. We decided on both.

The secretaries at first were reluctant to leave their cosy offices in Orwell Road. At Arthur's suggestion, we took them on a tour of new open-plan offices so they could talk to the incumbents. They were converted. I told Arthur we did not want a monumental building, one that would intimidate. We were not a lofty university. The building ended up slightly monumental. It is built on granite, on an elevated site, but its deceptive simplicity has stood the test of time and was a factor in Arthur's winning the Gold Medal.

The Institute received government subvention annually, championed for us by Tadhg Ó Cearbhaill, Secretary of the Department of Labour. Coming up to the Estimates was an anxious time. I would go to see Tadhg at his office on Mespil Road to ask about our grant. Tadhg would put on his mandarin face and say, "I can tell you 'No' now". Then he would look at his watch and say,

"It's after five. I'll see you in the Deerpark". Whichever of us got there first would have two pints waiting and Tadhg would unbutton just enough to ease my anxiety.

The Department of Finance agreed to fund our current expenditure and part of our capital borrowing, again from the ICC, for the Sandyford centre. The capital financing was a breakthrough, as it implied some long-term commitment.

I had a call from Michael Murphy, then Assistant Secretary, subsequently Secretary, of Finance. He said, "The idea of our subventing annually your payments to a State company makes no sense. Why don't we send you a cheque for the lot?". I swallowed and said levelly, "That makes sense to me too, Michael". He wrote me there's-a-£400,000-cheque-in-the-post letter. It was a high point to read it out to a Council meeting.

We still had to sell Orwell Road. At a glum Executive Committee meeting, Ian Morrison said, "There's nothing moving. If there was we [in Bank of Ireland] would have heard about it". We had been told by our auctioneers that the best we could expect was £300,000.

An Assistant Secretary in the Department of Foreign Affairs rang to ask whether he could come to see me. I said to such a senior personage that I would come and see him. He said, "No, no. Can I come and see you now?". I told Moya MacNamee to get out the good coffee cups.

He told me in strict secrecy that a foreign embassy, not hitherto represented in Ireland, was interested in purchasing the property. Representatives were coming from London the following day. I still did not know who they represented. It was two days before the auction. There was no sign of an offer. It looked like we might fall flat on our faces.

One day before the auction, at 12 noon, a red Jaguar drew up under my office windows and two young men got out. Seán Henneberry, Secretary and Financial Controller of the Institute, and an astute negotiator, joined me. The two young men were from the Soviet Embassy in Kensington. They were very polite, but with unsubtle English. They said they might be prepared to make an offer. There was no question of their having to inspect the property.

I told them we would be glad to consider their offer at the auction at 3.00 pm the following day. They recoiled, "No auction, please, for

Soviet Government". Seán Henneberry kicked me under the table. I said, "I'm very sorry, but we are a public body and we must be seen publicly to do what is right. The premises have been advertised for sale".

They said, with some concern, "We cannot have auction, please".

I made a little speech. I said the Institute would be very willing to encourage Irish-Soviet relations and to welcome them among us, but the only way we could do that would be if they were to make us an offer sufficient to justify our withdrawing from public auction. That would mean an offer substantially in excess of other offers we were considering. In any event, I would have to consult with my Chairman about such a serious decision.

The two young men were anxious.

I rang Metro Cabs as if I were talking to the Chairman. Metro Cabs thought I was a lunatic and hung up.

I said the Chairman was willing, in the interest of Irish-Soviet harmony, to withdraw from the auction provided they made an offer of £600,000.

They said, "That is too high. We do not have authority". Seán Henneberry kicked me again in case I'd weaken.

I said, "Why don't you consult your ambassador? You can use the telephone in another office". They came back to say the ambassador had gone to lunch. I began to see my dream of riches fading. Seán sensed I might be weakening and looked daggers.

We left them alone in the other office and counted the minutes. Finally, there was a knock on my door. I had hardly opened it when the young man said, beaming, "Ambassador says we are prepared to make offer of £550,000 but definitely no auction." I put my hand out to shake his but he said, "No, no. Is bad luck to shake hands across threshold". I said, to keep up appearances, "I shall, of course, have to consult once more with my Chairman, but I am sure he will approve your offer". Metro Cabs said, "Not you again".

When the two young men had gone, Seán said, "What'll we do next?".

Seán went off to make his fortune. He was succeeded as Financial Controller by Jim Byrne, who skilfully managed the Institute's finances for many years.

17

THE INTERNATIONAL ACADEMY OF MANAGEMENT

It was a mixture of elation and wonderment that I had somehow joined the ranks of management immortels.

Jerry Dempsey, head of Aer Lingus and a Chairman of the IMI, was the first, and at that time the only, Irishman to be elected to Fellowship of the International Academy of Management. When I walked up the steps of the IMI in Leeson Park just after Christmas, 1959, I knew nothing about management. It says a lot for the Institute and its learning capabilities that, 15 years later, I would be elected Chancellor of the Academy, in which capacity, like the Cabots of Boston, I would talk only to God.[14]

The International Academy of Management had its origins in the first international management congress held in Prague in 1924 at the initiative of President Jan Masaryk. At the congress, CIOS (*Conseil International de l'Organisation Scientifique*, the World Council of Management) was founded. CIOS established the International Academy of Management in 1958. The Academy is now independent of CIOS. Its objectives are:

♦ To honour excellence in management through the election to Fellowship of individuals who have made an outstanding international contribution to the science and art of management.

---

14   And this is good old Boston / The home of the bean and the cod, / Where the Lowells talk only to Cabots / And the Cabots talk only to God.

♦ To provide a forum for the exchange internationally of knowledge
and experience so as to contribute to the advancement of the
science and art of management and thus to human progress.

In the 1980s, the Academy had 218 Fellows from 34 different
countries. Election is by invitation.

I was invited to speak to a CIOS congress in Caracas on
November 13, 1975. Maureen and I had never been to South America.
We took a holiday on the island of Aruba for two weeks before the
congress. Too long and boring. Aruba, 30 km off the north coast of
Venezuela, was at that time still part of the Netherlands Antilles.
Beautiful beaches, lots of sunshine, banana dacquiris and that was it.
We were relieved to get off the island and to the companionship of
the congress, but with forebodings about the taxi ride from Caracas
airport on the coast up to the city: a dangerous mountain road with
macho taxi drivers trying to outdo one another.

Venezuela is a country of great wealth and great poverty. There
was a splendid conference centre but it was stiff with security
guards, some carrying machine guns.

I was nominated a Fellow of the Academy by Sir Walter Scott,
Australia, a former Chancellor, Erich Mittlesten Scheid, Germany,
President of CIOS, and Jerry Dempsey.

Meanwhile, I had to give my address to as prestigious and
informed an audience as I'd ever faced. I had sweated over the paper.

While the IMI had established a good reputation in Europe, it was
unknown to the rest of the world. For that matter, not much was
known about Ireland. (I was registered in a hotel in Washington DC
as being from Iceland and recently in the RAC Club in Pall Mall as
from Iran.)

The congress hall was packed. The Chairman introduced me and,
after polite applause, the lights went out. Caracas may have had a
splendid conference centre, but the electricity supply throughout
Venezuela was subject to vagaries. Having no electricity meant there
were no microphones. A few torches appeared. I asked the audience
in as loud a voice as I could muster whether I should go on. There
was a polite chorus of "Yes". Perhaps what they wanted to hear now
was not so much a paper as an athletic feat. A kind person brought
me a tiny torch. Fortunately, I had headings throughout the paper

repeated on the cover page. I got through the half-hour at the expense of a sore throat.

Then – as you might have expected – the lights came on. Erich Mittlesten Scheid stood up and said, "I, with some colleagues, have nominated Mr. Kenny for Fellowship of the International Academy of Management. His election is subject to ratification by the Governing Board at a meeting at the conclusion of the conference. I propose that he be elected by acclamation".

The applause was as much for the lights coming on as for my election. Douglas Gageby once told me it was difficult to get an appropriate photo for *The Irish Times* at a funeral – everybody was smiling at their own survival.

I was relieved and delighted. That night, we were invited to the home of Ivan and Josette Lansberg Henriquez. Ivan owned an insurance company, Segurosca. At the conclusion of the CIOS conference, he was elected President in succession to Erich Mittlesten Scheid. He was also elected to Life Fellowship of the IMI. We scraped up narrow streets in a bus to his house overlooking the city. A balmy night, I walked out into his extensive garden and looked down on the city of Caracas. There was a rustle and a man carrying a machine-gun appeared. I was trying to digest what had happened to me. It was a mixture of elation and wonderment that I had somehow joined the ranks of management *immortels*. I was from a small, relatively poor country, from a good but hardly world-class management centre, I had delivered a paper that would not influence the course of management history.

When I was a student in Paris at the *Institut d'Études Politiques*, I was lucky enough to spend a few hours with Père Leclerc at the *Institut Catholique*. He recommended the down-to-earth *La Vie Intellectuelle* by Sertillanges. It became a guide. Père Leclerc also said:

> *D'abord on obtient son baccalauréat, puis sa licence, puis son doctorat d'université, puis son doctorat d'état, puis si l'on a beaucoup de chance, on est élu à l'Académie, et puis on meurt.* [... and then you die].

Professor Harold (Howdy) Koontz, USA, was Chancellor from 1976 to 1981. He was a prolific and respected author and had written an acclaimed article, *The Management Jungle*. Up to then Chancellors had emerged, like leaders of the Tory Party. Howdy decided to have an election. A few colleagues in the IMI encouraged me to have a go. There were two candidates. The other was Dr. Bohdan Hawrylyshyn. Bob was born in the Ukraine, from which he escaped while it was still under Soviet rule. He was educated in Canada and, at the time of the election, was Director of another IMI, the International Management Institute in Geneva. His best-known publication was *Condemned to Co-Exist: Road Maps to the Future.*[15]

Harold Koontz wrote to say I had won, that I should appoint a Treasurer and four regional Vice-Chancellors. Ian Morrison became Treasurer, Bob gracefully accepted the Vice-Chancellorship for Europe.

*

My first engagement as Chancellor was in Moscow *via* Sofia, Bulgaria. It was also my first time behind the Iron Curtain, apart from a three-day CIOS conference in Prague, years before. That early experience was infinitely depressing. Wenceslas Square was dominated by a huge red neon star. Maureen and I were taken to a restaurant. A party of senior Soviet officers arrived with their wide-brimmed hats and jack-boots. They took over the best table without being escorted to it, called the waiter with a flick of their fingers and ordered bottles of vodka. Our Czech host was upset. We left quietly without finishing our meal.

We became friendly with the hotel manager. He drove us around Prague in an ancient auto. I ventured to ask him what he thought of the system. He said, "We would change it tomorrow" and swerved in time to miss an elderly pedestrian.

*

September 10, 1983, Sofia was sunny. I had stopped off there at the request of Professor Ivan Nicolov, director of the Institute for Social Management. We did not work too hard, spending a day at a seaside

---

[15]   ISBN: 0080261159.

resort. I quickly got used to consecutive translation, which has the advantage of giving you time to consider your thoughts, necessary in the repressed days before Gorbachev, *perestroika* and *glasnost*. There was a politeness and humanity about the Bulgarians, but still that wariness. You had to be – at least, I felt I had to be – careful of what I said.

Now the Irish are buying properties in Bulgaria. Moscow and St. Petersburg, the erstwhile Leningrad, are familiar tourist destinations.

*

September 15, Moscow. The purpose of my visit was to have a meeting of the Academy in the Soviet Union. I was met at Sheremetyevo airport by Mike Perov from the All-Union Research Institute for Systems Studies. Mike was to be my guide and mentor. Systems studies could be roughly translated as management studies, Soviet-style. I was the guest of Jermen Gvishiani, deputy chairman of the USSR Council of Ministers for Science and Technology and Chairman of the Systems Studies Institute. I was to have discussions with the Soviet International Research Institute for Systems Studies, the State Committee for Science and Technology and the Central Economics Mathematical Institute. In these splendidly-titled institutions, I was told about their work and responded, giving a Western perspective. I was careful to be non-ideological. Talking to young faculty was more enjoyable, but still careful. On one occasion, I casually mentioned the word Politburo, sometime Presidium. There was a frisson in the audience.

Mike brought me to my hotel, the Rossiya, off Red Square. It was huge, 2,000 bedrooms, and therefore did not work well. You surrendered your passport to the receptionist. It was kept until you were leaving. Mike brought me to my room, past the female dragon at the end of the corridor. She took note of everything. Russians had an endearing habit of coming right into the bedroom with you and looking on with interest while you unpacked.

Mike asked me if I wanted roubles. I said I supposed so and took out some dollars. Mike told me, so far as I can recall, that the official rate was four roubles to the dollar. He would be glad to give me eight. I began to count off the dollars and he went pale, shushing me and pointing to the television screen. I was staying in the bugged section of the Rossiya. On a subsequent visit, I was put in the same section. Even the KGB was incapable of bugging 2,000 bedrooms.

One benefit of a police state is that it is virtually crime-free. On the few occasions I had nothing to do, I walked alone across Red Square at night down to the Moskva River.

Mike and I took the Red Arrow express to Leningrad, departing at midnight. When we arrived at the station, I found I was to take pot luck as to whom I would occupy a sleeper compartment with. I stamped my chancellorial foot and said I was damned if I was to share a compartment with some ancient general who would snore his way across Russia. I can't remember if roubles passed but, fair dues to Mike, at either end of the carriage were single compartments and I got one.

In Leningrad, I was to visit the giant Electrosila enterprise. By contrast with the modern and ugly Rossiya in Moscow, I stayed in an old, beautiful and shabby hotel in Leningrad with the ubiquitous dragon guarding the floor.

I have three tourist memories. In a modern museum commemorating the 900-day siege, September 8, 1941 to January 27, 1944, there was a small piece of black Russian bread, the total daily ration of the besieged. One million people died. There was the Gold Room in the Winter Palace to which, as a VIP, I was admitted. In the centre of the room is a pillar with a glass dome. The dome is a huge magnifying glass. Beneath it is a pair of gold Etruscan ear-rings. On each ear-ring a figure is carrying a pannier with baskets. The baskets are woven as real baskets are. With all the aids of modern technology, they could not be replicated. Last memory: a senior official, to whom Mike had reported when we arrived, invited us to dinner before we got the train back to Moscow. There was beer at the table, but he produced a brown paper bag and poured vodka surreptitiously. Naughty schoolboys, but a forlorn commentary on life in the Soviet Union.

Back in Moscow, the Irish ambassador, Pádraic Murphy, gave a lunch at the unpretentious embassy for some senior Systems Institute officials. They in turn brought me on to one of the few decent restaurants, a Georgian one, in Moscow at that time. There was a long queue outside it. My host strode past, flashed a red card and we were escorted to the best table.

The visit bore fruit on the penultimate day, when I met Jermen Gvishiani in his elaborate office. Boris Milner, who became a good friend, was in attendance. He was the Deputy Director of the Systems Institute. I was told quietly that Boris was unlikely to get the top job as he was of Jewish parentage. While quite formal, the meeting was a done deal. Gvishiani said they would like to host a meeting of the Academy. Academicians would be responsible only for their flights to Moscow.

I had suggested a resort of some kind. They decided on Yerevan in Armenia, with a short visit to Moscow.

I had been wined, dined and travelled, had been at the Bolshoi ballet with its dining-room chairs, at a modern theatre inside the Kremlin, where Mike and I ate caviar at the bar before the opera. Mike remarked memorably, "You can have too much caviar".

On my last day, Mike asked me what I would like to do. I told him I would love to walk around the lovely Gorky Park one more time. As we walked, Mike said, "Would you like to buy a diamond?".

He told me he had a family heirloom, a nine-carat yellow diamond. The only way you could sell anything valuable in the Soviet Union was to sell it to the State for nothing like its worth. He would be prepared to sell it to me for $30,000. I asked him how I would know what it was worth. He said, "You bring your jeweller with you and the money in cash".

I said, "Mike, that would be totally inappropriate, particularly as I would be a guest of your country. And if it was discovered, it would be a major scandal".

Mike said, "No. No. You would be VIP. No danger of discovery".

Was I being set up? I talked to several knowledgeable people. The consensus was that I was not. The KGB thrived on the paranoia they engendered. I never bought the diamond.

One last frisson at the airport – a beautiful girl with shoulder-length blonde hair, which did not go at all with her smart uniform and her unsmiling attitude. She asked me about roubles (which I had bought illegally from Mike). I waffled. Fortunately, she had not good English. Mike came to the rescue and said I was VIP. I was happy when at last I sat in my wide Aeroflot seat, with stewardesses who looked as if they would be happier packing pistols.

But the memories of the Russians I met were warm. When they opened up, their irreverent and somewhat cynical humour was close to the Irish. In Red Square, Mike said to me, "You want to piss against the Kremlin?". There is a male urinal against the Kremlin wall. It is one way to register a protest.

*

It was the 25th anniversary of the Academy. Following on my meeting with Jermen Gvishiani, a conference was held in Moscow and Yerevan, October 6 to 13, 1984. There were 38 participants from 15 countries: the USSR, Nigeria, Greece, USA, France, UK, Denmark, Israel, Federal Republic of Germany, Italy, Spain, Brazil, Mexico and Belgium, with Pam Purcell from my office in UCD who acted as secretary of the Academy. Gay Haskins, a valued friend, who was to become Director General of the European Foundation for Management Development, was *rapporteuse*.

The journey from Moscow to Yerevan, the capital of Armenia, was interesting. We took a rickety bus to a scruffy little airport. There was a single toilet and no other amenities. Anxious babushkas sitting around holding their documentation. We took off in an ancient aircraft. One stewardess who did one round offering paper cups of water. A charming young Russian in the seat behind me was reassuring Pam Purcell: "Yes, good chance we arrive safely. Last time we ended in swamp".

Armenia was the smallest of the Soviet republics, with a population the size of Ireland's. It had known wars, occupations, massacres and deportations. It had its own language and alphabet. The alphabet was mounted inside a massive gold safe, which we were privileged to have opened for us. The Armenians were lively and humorous. At a state banquet given for us, we saw wonderful dancing. Meeting with the Prime Minister, Faddy (not Paddy) T. Sarkisian, I complimented him on the beauty of the Armenian women. He asked, "Did you get any phone numbers?".

Throughout a formal meal, Armenians would take nips of excellent brandy (which Churchill drank), in addition to good wine – just as Russians would take nips of vodka with dreadful wine. They also served jugs of buttermilk, a sovereign preventive of hangovers.

A word about the late Bill Exton. Bill was an indefatigable 77 at the conference. Small, white bearded, ex-captain in the US Navy. In my years with the Academy, he became a fast friend. He had an appetite for life – and for food. At lunch in the Harvard Club in New York, he piled his plate from the starter buffet, ate a large steak, followed by apple pie with a brandy. He was funny and irreverent and a distinguished New York management consultant. Foolhardy, he tried to fix a leak in the roof of his upstate country house, fell through two floors, survived but never fully recovered. May he rest in peace. As a tongue-in-cheek tribute to him, here is the title of the paper he gave in Yerevan. (It was not like that at all when he delivered it.)

A Preliminary Consideration of the
Nature of the (Conscious and Unconscious)
Psycholinguistic Processes Involved in the
Perception of Complex Problem-Situations
(With a View to Rendering Such Perceptions
More Effective in Achieving Satisfactory Resolutions).

Gay Haskins produced a comprehensive record of the proceedings, which the IMI printed and bound for us. What follows is a short extract from the proceedings in Yerevan, Monday, October 8, 1984, to give some insight into management under Soviet rule and the differences (and the occasional similarities) between it and the Western world. The Russians and Armenians who participated were more aware of Western practices than we from the West were of how the Soviet system worked – or, as happened subsequently, did not work, when the Union broke inevitably into its constituent and diverse republics.

Opening the seminar, I stressed the need for greater mutual understanding between nations and continents:

Today, as Fellows of the International Academy of Management, we come from many different parts of the world. We represent many differing ideologies. We shall strive, over the next few days, towards greater mutual understanding, frankness and trust.

Luther Gulick, USA: Over 2,000 years ago Yerevan was a busy trade centre, where caravans from East, West, South and North converged, not only to exchange their goods and treasures, but to manage both the transport and the exchange of valued goods, services, ideas and gossip. Historians and anthropologists tell us that money emerged to simplify these exchanges, except for the gossip. Thus it was the managers who invented money, not the economists, who came on the scene much later. We come with the same thirst and inspiration to advance the management of human affairs for the welfare of mankind. This is a quest which knows no national, racial or cultural boundaries or limitations.

Boris Milner, USSR stressed the need for peaceful coexistence, for participants both to obtain first-hand knowledge of the Soviet management system and to identify areas in which cooperation was possible. We would like to emphasise that the definition of profitability is practically the same here as elsewhere i.e. the difference between sales prices and production costs. These are very definite economic indicators which attest to the level of economic activity of any enterprise. The definition of profitability levels does not automatically require enterprises to be competing with each other.

Victor Starodubrovski, USSR: However, an enterprise never falls into bankruptcy, never disappears. An enterprise never gets to a position where its employees will find themselves out on the street. Naturally, this system breeds its own special problems. For instance, the incentive of unemployment (a cruel but effective one) does not exist here. As a result, we have to search for alternative sources of stimulation – not an easy task. Also, when we say an enterprise does not fall into bankruptcy, this should not imply that unprofitability is a societal goal. On the contrary, our aim is to restructure the unprofitable, even to get rid of some of them if necessary – but, if we do follow this route, we re-employ the staff elsewhere.

Ivor Kenny (Conclusion): I believe we achieved all that it was possible to achieve in the short time available. It would be quite naïve (and Fellows of the Academy by definition cannot be naïve) to expect that in three or four short days we could penetrate totally beneath the layers of conditioning that comprise our beliefs.

To summarise: Did the conference achieve its objectives? To test it, ask yourself one question: how different will it be when you come to Moscow the second time?

*

At a concluding meeting in Moscow, October 13, 1984, attended by the Irish Ambassador, Pádraic Murphy, Jermen Gvishiani was invested as a Vice-Chancellor of the Academy.

Jermen Gvishiani, USSR: My conviction is that this Academy might play a more important role. Let us, therefore, regard this particular event not as a climax of Soviet involvement, but as a beginning.

*

When the conference was over, back in Moscow, a number of us found a good restaurant in the basement of the Rossiya. It had all been a deeper experience than we expected. There was relief, laughter and vodka. Olu Akinyemi, from Nigeria, whose Paul Robeson laugh could be heard a block away, pinched the bottom of a buxom waitress, something for which he could now be jailed. The waitress laughed uproariously.

*

We organised another meeting of the Academy in Ashford Castle, Co. Mayo [1987]. It was not a success academically. It succeeded socially. It got off to an atrocious start. It was before nearby Knock Airport was opened. Most of the delegates arrived at Shannon. I had requested a luxury coach to take them to Ashford. Ian Morrison and Don Carroll arrived by helicopter, rather grand at that time. The coach was to arrive at 3.00 pm. At 4.00 pm, there was not a sign of it. At 5.00 pm, I was walking up and down outside the castle, looking anxiously up the drive. At 5.30 pm, a medium-sized van came over the bridge and debussed the academicians. I was mortified. To add insult to injury, the minibus was short of seats, so the driver had borrowed two hard metal chairs from Shannon Airport. For reasons known only to himself, he had taken them on the long scenic route by Maam Cross and the Maam Valley. The roof in the bus was so low that the academicians' distinguished heads were bowed for the entire journey.

It was, however, an enjoyable conference, with a solid talk by Ian Morrison on the role of chief executive. Ian had had a brilliant career as an accountant (first in everything) and as a banker. He was a graduate of the Harvard Business School and served subsequently on its Board. Here's a story he told for a private biography I prepared for his family as a labour of love.

> Harvard was tough, so were the professors. On my first day there, when asked my background in front of the class, I said, "Banker". The professor said, "I've nothing against bankers – it's just that I would not let my daughter marry one!". After three weeks, it was a Harvard custom for the class to elect a president. I was put forward, perhaps as a joke, as one of the younger members of the class, and had to stand a vote and the results of an election. That was not my forte. It did help that we had the worst snowfall in Boston for 70 years, with 200,000 cars buried and no access to restaurants or nightlife. I rang my friend Michael Dargan, then chief executive of Aer Lingus, and asked for a few hostesses – they would now be called cabin crew – for my election party and my speech for president. A bus complete with snow tyres and 15 girls in green arrived. With Irish coffee served by glorious Irish hostesses, my election as president, the first non-American ever at the Business School, was almost sure-fire.

But I paid the price later, when the Kent University shootings and strike spread to Harvard. The administrative buildings were invaded and a professor thrown out of a second-floor window and badly injured. The whole of Harvard, except the Business School, went on strike and I had to address 1,500 students in the ball-park in an attempt to prevent a Business School strike. [The Business School campus is on its own on one side of the Charles River, the main Harvard campus with the different colleges on the other.] I reckoned I could hold the audience's attention for no more than three minutes, by contrast with the long-winded diatribes, some of them very vicious, from the striking agitators from across the river. We won the vote. The experience stood me in good stead for the 36-week bank strike in Ireland the following year – but that's another story.

*

My final Academy conference was in Barcelona, September 20 to 23, 1987. The hosts were three business schools: IESE, Pedro Nueno, who was to become a successful Chancellor, opening up China for the Academy; ESADE, Xavier Adroer; and EAE, José de Orbaneja. The conference was sponsored by Irish academicians, including Tony O'Reilly, Michael Smurfit and Don Carroll.

The meeting was graced by the presence of a woman member of the Academy, Princess Gerarda de Orleans-Borbón, Gerry to her fellow academicians. Educated all over the place, ending up in Columbia University, New York, she was President of the San Telmo Foundation, Seville, a business school that offered top management programmes. She spoke five languages fluently and came to Dublin when we presented Peter Drucker with the first Gold Medal of the Academy. She unveiled a plaque in the IMI that commemorates the Institute's giving us a home.

There was a packed programme of good papers, subsequently published in books or reference journals.

Dermot Gogarty, the rowing coach, once said to me, "Life is a search for people who see the world the way you do". I was particularly taken by Tom Horton's paper, part of a book he was writing,[16] because it was what I was doing with Irish leaders. Here's part of what he said:

> A recurrent theme was the willingness to pay the price. This phrase implies intense motivation, a need to achieve, an inner desire to pay that price: not just long hours and longer days, but mental and physical stress, grinding travel schedules, a responsibility for the economic well-being of employees, loss of privacy, putting one's reputation at risk, guilt for neglecting spouses and children – and at times even risk to their safety. This price is high, but so is the willingness to pay it. Indeed, many compete for the privilege of doing so – they have a burning need to be the top manager.
>
> Some insist that CEOs are leaders, not managers at all. A United Technologies advertisement entitled "Let's get rid of management" says, "You can lead your horse to water, but you can't manage him to drink". (But then who says you can lead him to drink it, either?) Rear Admiral Grace Hopper of the US Navy has made the distinction that things and projects are managed, while people are led. Yet CEOs do more than lead. Hands-on leaders manage; CEOs of small companies must manage as well as lead; often, acquisitions are personally managed by CEOs of even the largest firms. So the argument that leadership and management are at all times mutually exclusive activities is not persuasive.
>
> Some suggest that "luck" plays a large part in success. Most of the chief executives mentioned the good fortune of being in a particular place at a particular time when, as one put it, "No one else is there". But was it mere luck that put them at the "right place" at the "right time"? Studies have shown that the person with a high need for achievement tends to show initiative in researching his or her environment, in travelling and searching for new opportunities. This factor may be related to luck or good fortune, since those who explore, who search and who visit

---

many places will naturally expose themselves to more situations – including situations of opportunity. Rosabeth Moss Kanter's study of opportunity within a large, hierarchical organisation stresses the importance of exposure and high visibility through movement within the organisation. Just as opportunity begets opportunity, so may mobility.

Mobility and exposure to opportunity, however, are not enough in themselves. Unless opportunities are recognised when they appear, they cannot be seized.

Tom Horton was President and CEO of the American Management Association. He half-knelt at his desk, specially designed for people with a painful back. He looked after my daughter, Helen, when she first went to New York on a student visa and worked in an attic over Burberry's, unpicking "Made in China" labels.

Tom Peters came to Barcelona. The *Economist* described Tom as "the uber-guru". His arrival was a story in itself. I had many telephone calls from his secretary asking me, *inter alia*, how long it took to get from the airport to the conference centre, from the hotel to the conference centre and so on. When he arrived, we had a quiet lunch apart from the other delegates. I asked him what all the questions were about. He said, "My primary resource is time. I don't expect my speaking and writing career to last forever. My office is there to make sure not a minute is wasted". In fact, his career has lasted. He was not, as so many gurus are, a comet who flashed across the sky never to be heard of again. As I write, his latest book, *Re-imagine, Business Excellence in a Disruptive Age* (2003),[17] is on my desk. We kept up a correspondence for several years following the conference, but it eventually faded as things do. I remember him fondly. He always mentions the Academy in his CVs.

However, he misjudged the Academy audience. They listened to their fellow academicians and questioned them closely. Tom made the mistake of haranguing them as he would an audience of managers in the Albert Hall. It did not go down well and, to coin a phrase, he petered out. I was sorry.

---

[17]   ISBN: 1405300493.

John Herring (UK) was the conference *rapporteur*. He described the conference as "a crashing of shibboleths, as dogma gave way to pragmatism".

There was a movement at the time in management literature from a directive, this-is-how-you-do-it approach to a humbler, more holistic one. It was brick on brick. Everything that had gone before was not a shibboleth and pragmatism did not now reign supreme. Contrary to Henry Ford's view, history is not more or less bunk. To believe that would be a true dumbing-down. In Barcelona, my distinguished colleagues may have fallen into the trap of false dichotomies.

Just as we need openness to new knowledge, so do we need to remember the lessons of the past. Put the other way around: effective strategies need not squander our heritage, but they have to be unchained from those traditions, values and behaviour whose usefulness has disappeared. Talleyrand said:

> In all one's actions, one must have in mind the future and the past.

*

I was succeeded as Chancellor by Jacques Maisonrouge, whom I first met in New York when he was Senior Vice-President of the IBM Corporation and Chairman of the Board of the IBM World Trade Corporation.

When I handed over to him in Paris, February 9, 1987, he invited me to lunch. Before we left his office, he took off his jacket and strapped on a shoulder holster with a pistol. At that time, a number of senior French businessmen, including Jacques, had been named for assassination by a subversive group. On our way to the restaurant, we were followed by an unmarked car. He told me he had to report weekly to a firing range to continue to carry the pistol the police insisted on.

18

THE CZECH REPUBLIC

*Management was considered superfluous at best and, at worst,
a threat to the system.*

My final foray behind the erstwhile Iron Curtain was in the Czech
Republic in 1994. The assignment from IMPAC Consultants was to
investigate the possibility of setting up a Czech Management
Institute.

At that time, the rotten legacy of communism was still strong. In
one-to-one conversations with chief executives of the larger Czech
enterprises, they were (sometimes startlingly) frank. When I brought
them together for a final dinner, they shut like clams and eyed each
other suspiciously. It was depressing.

This is a note I wrote at the conclusion of the study.

> An American professor said to me: "Teaching here can result
> in a positive experience. As our university is one of the best
> in this field, [at home in the USA] we tend to attract the rich
> kids who know a lot about business already and are likely to
> be successful anyway. They pretend that they are learning
> and we pretend that we are teaching them something they
> did not know before. Then we exchange our diploma for
> their fathers' money. Here it is different. I feel that what we
> do here makes a lot of difference, and the students respond
> much more enthusiastically. It is a special kind of
> gratification that I have not found anywhere else."

Management education under the old system was not impressive.
The infrastructure was scanty, the qualifications of the instructors

mediocre, and the scope within which they could operate was circumscribed. The political régime believed that Marxism had all the answers. Management, both as a theoretical discipline and as a practice, was considered superfluous at best and, at worst, a threat to the system. Far more attention was devoted to meticulous planning than to management. The communists hoped that state control would take care of all the nuts and bolts of the economy. People in the companies were expected simply to carry out the orders from above. The planners considered ridiculous the assumption that any education or training, let alone one in management, would help managers carry out their responsibilities or improve the efficiency of the economy.

After Communism, Eastern Europeans preferred to work with Americans as partners. Long- and short-term educational projects were launched, many with the support of the USAID or USIA and in co-operation with individual US universities. But educators, as well as managers, had to do their homework before they could expect to be successful in the Czech Republic. They were all welcome and there was nothing inherently alien between the two cultures that would prevent joint co-operative efforts from flourishing. However, anybody who planned to come to Central or Eastern Europe either to do business or to teach should be reminded of one fact. Regardless of the formal academic titles, what was taught there under the label of *steering* or *executive control*, and was then translated as *management*, was very different from what the Americans meant when they used the term *management education*.

The Czech Management Institute was not a runner largely because there was a plethora of half-baked indigenous initiatives and one or two promising ones, which, I hope, have flourished.

19

INTERLUDE: GALWAY[18]

I was not surprised to read that Galway does not have a city architect.

There are few enough things you can be really objective about. To be objective about Galway is impossible: I was born there, saw my parents die there, went to school and college there and married there. So Galway is in my bones. To sit down now and write for *The Irish Times* my personal thoughts on Galway brings crowding in memories, feelings, attitudes and prejudices. They are a dense undergrowth to hack a couple of thousand words from.

"Dear Mr. Kenny", said the letter from the Secretary of the Galway Chamber of Commerce and Industry, "if you would like to have a bar added to the President's Medallion for the late Mr. T.J.W. Kenny, who was President in 1925, 1930, 1935 and 1936, you might send me a cheque for £4-12-6, cost of 9ct. gold bar, connecting chain and engraving".

That was a fair old tug back across the years. 1930 was the year I was born.

And, in the end of all, the old man deserves better than a "9ct. gold bar, connecting chain and engraving". He did more than loose the town from the inertia that gripped it then and, for all I know, grips it to some degree now. [1969]

"For all I know", because I've been out of Galway almost as long as I was in it. And the impressions I have are only

---

18   *The Irish Times*, November 26, 1969.

impressions. There will be plenty of Galwaymen on my next visit to tell me how wrong I am.

There's no denying things are better, if you take care to define what "better" means. The old slums are gone. There are some newer and better slums. There is less overt poverty. By and large, the only people unemployed are the unemployable. The new industrial estate is exciting

Alexander Moon's drapery shop that used to dress the gentry has moved with the changes and now dresses the common people too. There's a Woolworth's and a Dunnes'. The university students – and the schoolchildren – are a lot better dressed than they were in my day. I got through college on a sports coat and a boat club blazer and the loan of a Christian brother's jacket for a dinner dance.

What's missing? Well, the physical character is being chipped away. It was a grey old city. It had winding streets that slowed the pace. It had the sea and it had the river. It was a city with texture.

They can't take away the sea and the river. But the greyness is being drowned in white concrete. Eyre Square has been raped. [1969] It had character and form. It is now a non-place. It rejoices incidentally in – amongst other things – a hilarious statue of Liam Mellows: nobody would have laughed at it more heartily than he – wasn't it he who said, "Solomon in all his glory was never in a raid like one of these?".

I suppose I could be persuaded that the new straight-roaded "prom" in Salthill is an improvement on the old, grey, winding road. But God forgive whoever bulldozed the Lazy Wall with its comfortable, desultory chat of blue-serged farmers on a warm September afternoon and the harvest in.

Saddest of all, the Claddagh is gone. Nobody is to blame. Who would have thought at the time that it wasn't a good thing to knock down all those unsavoury thatched cottages with their open drains and cobbled pathways?

Now, when there's hardly a thatched cottage left in the country – except the new ones Brendan O'Regan is building in Clare – now, we realise the thing we destroyed. A thing not primarily for the tourists, but for ourselves, to remind us that our roots go deeper than the council houses that replace the Claddagh.

There's still good stuff left (and still plenty of places that could be knocked down). There's an opportunity near the courthouse on the riverside that Dermot Gogarty, an architect, saw. He wanted to construct a civic centre on stilts over the river. Civic imagination, and, to be fair, civic money, didn't stretch that far. The cathedral nearby, for all its self-importance, is built of Galway grey limestone and, when it weathers, should be sympathetic.

My first intimations of mortality were in the cathedral. If you sit at the edge of the first row of seats behind the altar, you spend Mass looking straight into the faces of the main body of the congregation sitting in front of the altar. Galway is still small enough that, if you are a native, most of the indigenous faces are familiar. To be suddenly confronted with all those faces, all 16 years older – balder, fatter, more lined – was an interesting experience. I saw my own reflection next morning in a different light.

Up the road a bit, they have knocked down the old famine-built wall that, both symbolically and practically, separated the university from the town. In my day, the university's contribution to the town was culturally and scientifically zero. I hope it is better now.

I wonder if the old characters, or new ones, are there now. Shoots who looked like a member of the Mafia and who'd give you a burst of his imaginary machine-gun from a swerving bicycle. Ned o' the Hills, an enormous man sitting in contentment at the bus stop at Nile Lodge. Sweet Sixteen, who had the gift of eternal youth and invented the mini-skirt years before they thought of it in London. Mowleogs, and Gandhi, and Hairy Bacon ...

Is Galway too (God save the mark) sophisticated now to take these sort of people to its heart? Would they make Galway people slightly ashamed now, or would they be cherished as their own?

For all that I've said, I believe they would be cherished. There was always a warmth, a humanity, a directness, a freedom from the cant and side that seem to be an unavoidable feature of big city suburbia. Whether you've been a success or failure in the outside world, when you come home you're welcomed for one thing, the fact that you're a Galwayman.

The other night I met on the turkey-and-ham circuit in Dublin a Galwayman, a trade unionist who played a man's part in the maintenance dispute of unhappy memory. When we discovered we were both Galwegians, the relationship between us changed.

I reminded him of the time during the War, when his brother was playing in the Savoy Cinema on one of those mandatory variety shows before the film. This brother was courting (and subsequently married) a girl who was working in the rival Estoria Cinema. When he came to the microphone and crooned gently, "I wonder who's kissing her now?", a hoarse voice from the gods shouted, "The manager out in the Estoria".

*

In many historic European cities, the "old town" is jealously preserved, while the new town is built sympathetically. Some of old Galway has been well restored. The new Galway is a vulgar mess, epitomised by a squalid "G" logo that has replaced the elegant and ancient city coat of arms. Eyre Square has recently [2006] been doubly raped. I was not surprised to read that Galway does not have a city architect.

20

THE ATLANTIC
MANAGEMENT STUDY

We left Canada feeling we had done a good job.

The Atlantic Provinces of Canada are like the Gaeltachtaí. They consist of Newfoundland, a large island; Prince Edward Island, Canada's smallest province; New Brunswick and Nova Scotia, coastal provinces.

I was asked by John Dempsey (Irish-born) from the Department of Regional Economic Expansion (DREE) whether I would do a study of the Provinces "to identify the management training needs of the Atlantic Region" and "to make recommendations for an effective institutional framework" to meet those needs.

We agreed a substantial fee for the IMI. I put a notice on the board inviting any interested party to come and join me. Noel Donnellon, a senior IMI specialist, offered. I could not have had a more assiduous or companionable colleague.

We started well at Heathrow, by nearly missing our flight. When we arrived at check-in, economy seats were full. We were bumped up to first (not mere business) class. The nice girl at the check-in desk said, "Please don't disgrace me". She thought that, being Irish, the two of us would drink our way across the Atlantic and either burst into song or start a fight.

We were met in Halifax, Nova Scotia by Ken Hubbard, executive director of the Atlantic Management Institute. AMI was mainly a co-ordinating body. Nobody much likes being co-ordinated.

Ken, a former submarine commander, was to be our guide, mentor and friend. Weekends, we stayed with him and his young family. The study was to last from August to November, 1976. Among several pleasant interludes with Ken was a corn-boil party. When the corn was ripe, it was cooked in a huge pot on an open fire as we sat around and sang songs, including one written about Noel and me. I can remember only the chorus: "Drinking black rum and eating blueberry pie".

A Steering Committee was formed to keep an eye on us, but more important, to represent the Provinces. They are fiercely jealous of their autonomy. This was particularly true of Newfoundland which, being physically separated, referred to the mainland as "Canada". Their provincial flag was the Union Jack, unsettling when you see it flying for the first time. I was quickly disabused of the notion that this was an outpost of empire. When I arrived in St. John's, the capital, the taxi-driver said "Dis" and "Dat". I thought he was having me on, until I became familiar with the Newfie accent with its overtones of Ireland.

I was lucky to find Hopper and Sheila Mangan in St. John's. Hopper was at school and college with me. I knew Sheila in college. Hopper was now Professor Michael Mangan, a radiologist, at Memorial University Newfoundland; Sheila was an ophthalmologist with a lively practice. When she saw me squinting through the Newfoundland telephone directory, she brought me into her surgery and prescribed reading glasses.

Hopper's claim to fame was not so much his radiology as his ownership of Monksfield, called after his ancestral home in Salthill, Galway. Monksfield, a small horse, won the Cheltenham Champion Hurdle. I met Hopper at Dublin Airport in the depths of winter off a flight from Canada. The roads were icy. He said, "We'll go up and see the Monkey". With my heart in my mouth, I skidded to the trainer's stud somewhere north of Dublin. Monksfield, wild-eyed, wanted only to bite us, which delighted Michael.

Hopper had a bar in the basement of his home, decorated with Monksfield memorabilia. He and Sheila also had a mad cat. Some friends joined Hopper in the bar. On the way in, one of them stumbled over the cat. The cat waited in a corner in the bar, eyes fixed on the miscreant. When he moved to go home, the cat jumped, claws bared. I woke one morning in Mangans to find the cat on the foot of my bed. I was terrified. Fortunately, Sheila looked in before she went to work and the cat followed her.

The origins of the study were a conflict – between AMI and NIMAT, the Newfoundland Institute for Management Advancement and Training. Neither institution had sufficient resources to make a dent in their stated missions. Energy and initiative were drained away in institutional infighting.

There were a number of possible approaches to the problem. One would be to have management consultants do an "in-depth" study based on statistically valid interview samples, have a comprehensive range of international comparisons and take a year or more to complete. At the other end of the scale, was a suggestion that what was needed was an arbitrator between AMI and NIMAT.

In the event, it was decided that the IMI would do a short study and make recommendations under the guidance of the representative Steering Committee.

A short study has the disadvantage that it leaves some stones unturned. Not everybody can be consulted. Not every option can be explored. Elaborate statistical analyses cannot be adduced to prove that X increase in management training will produce Y increase in the development of the economy.

Our belief was that a long study would have added to the cosmetics of the report. It would not have affected the conclusions and recommendations. The strength of our recommendations lay in two factors. First, their internal validity and objectivity. This was based on the IMI's experience internationally and in Ireland. Secondly, the acceptability of the recommendations to key constituencies. The support the recommendations commanded in our consultations was more than sufficient evidence of acceptability.

We strongly believed there was an opportunity in Atlantic Canada to make a significant contribution to the development of its managers and to the growth of its business. We did not claim that what we recommended was the one right way. The structure we recommended would facilitate learning and adaptation and, given a few basic ground rules in our recommendations, it would develop its own paths for its own progress.

We recommended the setting up of The Atlantic Management Boards with the aim of accelerating the development of managers in the market sector of the economy.

The structure would consist of four Provincial Boards and a co-ordinating Atlantic Board. The Provincial Boards, composed of businessmen, would decide on Provincial priorities. The delivery institutions would be integrated through Provincial Councils for Management Development; Government Agencies through Government Agency Committees. The Boards would set up an Atlantic Management Foundation to redress the imbalance between Government and private funding. NIMAT, as the Newfoundland Management Board, would be part of the new organisation.

In November 1976, we presented to the Steering Committee a 165-page report for the Government of Canada in the person of the Honourable Marcel Lessard, Minister for Regional Economic Expansion.

In our covering letter, we said: "Readers of the report may be interested to learn that, at its meeting on 26 November, 1976, the Board of the Atlantic Management Institute expressed support for the recommendations, as did the Executive of the Newfoundland Institute for Management Advancement and Training at a meeting on 6 November, 1976. The support of these two key institutions, and the very considerable consensus we met in our consultations, particularly with senior businessmen, augur well for the success of the proposals".

However, we had also said that "the structure would not work unless it had the right people and adequate funding. If it did not have these, it would be better not to set it up".

Noel and I left Canada feeling we had done a good job. Subsequently, we came upon the same phenomenon NIBO and the CIB encountered. The proponents are carried along by the strength of their convictions. (In the case of this Canadian study, the convictions were well-founded.) Then, as the tide recedes and the consultants are safely despatched, the old rocks appear, just as they did with the Confederation of Irish Business. The proposals, while meeting with reasonable acclaim, never really sailed into port. The recommendations foundered as provincial loyalties reasserted themselves.

However, for Noel and myself there was, to coin a phrase, a lot of heurism. I don't know what I know until I'm asked or until I have to write something up. Noel and I found we had years of experience in the IMI to draw on, something we would not have thought of until we were confronted with a novel situation to which that experience could be applied.

I was subsequently invited back to Newfoundland for discussions with some senior businessmen. The agenda was obscure, but I think they wanted me to recommend an independent Newfoundland Management Institute. Discussions took place on a beautiful cruiser, so big the stateroom contained a piano. We skirted the shores of Newfoundland, ate fried cod's tongues (delicious) and sang bawdy songs around the piano. When I dimly discerned the agenda, I said "No". I had neither the time nor the inclination and, being Newfies, they were not too upset.

21

GOVERNMENT AND ENTERPRISE

There is no better yardstick of determining the acceptability of products and services than that of profit.

Following the failure of the Confederation of Irish Business, I felt a mixture of disappointment and relief. The relief surprised me. If the CIB came to pass, my job was at risk. That thought was buried under the righteousness of the cause and the red mist through which you can see only the shining goal. With defeat, the thought reasserted itself.

My immediate colleagues, including Liam Connellan, were also disappointed. We took ourselves off to Kilkea Castle to lick our wounds and to reassess. I can't remember anything significant coming out of the reassessment. I do remember that much alcohol was consumed, particularly when we (grown men) were told that one of us had been assigned the haunted room, the number of which was not revealed. Noel Mulcahy donned a sheet and roamed the battlements, knocking on windows and going "Woo!". Not all the rooms were occupied by IMI worthies. There were some honeymooners.

However, the Institute was growing at a rate of knots. There was much to do. Jim Darlington, who managed the building of our centre in Sandyford, said IMI stood for "Ireland, My Institute".

My concern with the increasing intrusiveness of the State and the ineffectiveness of business representation became an obsession. I used to wake fuming at 3 o'clock in the morning. I returned to the theme at the IMI conference in 1977. What follows is a short extract. The reader will judge its relevance to today.

Since the present Government took office, there have been at least six significant pieces of social/industrial legislation: on equal pay; on trade union amalgamation; on sex discrimination in recruitment and employment conditions; on collective redundancies; on dismissal procedures and unfair dismissals; on the election of workers to boards of seven State enterprises.

Where business representations were made on this legislation (and the representations were minimal), the emphasis was negative. What was sought was a watering-down of the proposals.

A recent book on the Confederation of British Industry was described as "the first major study" of the part played by that organisation in the British political system. Although the study might be major, the part it identified emerged, on even the most charitable interpretation, as pretty small. If a cool look were taken at business representation in Irish national affairs, would the conclusion be any different?

Business should avoid the loud-hailer approach. The air is thick enough with clichés, stereotypes, received ideas and mutual insults. The Minister for Finance has said that the first (and last) he frequently hears of "representations" made to him is in the newspapers.

We have an opportunity to study the nature and size of the communications gap between ourselves and the politicians, the civil service, the mass media, our own employees and the many people in the "caring" professions, the social services and education, who suspect business values. We have an opportunity for analysing the points of conflict and co-operation between business and politics. We have an opportunity to present practical alternatives to other people's ideas. We have an opportunity for anticipating social and political trends.

The alternative is to continue to be as we now are: dragged along, muttering darkly.

The Government share of the Irish cake has been increasing rapidly, from 37% to 55% [1977] in 10 years.

A genuine partnership between Government and business is needed.

The problem will not be solved by doctrinaire solutions either from the private or the State sectors. The private sector has no choice now but to play a positive part in formulating new social objectives. Irish business has not measured up to this task either at the level of the firm or at national, institutional level. Its posture, in a rapidly changing situation, has been conservative and ineffective.

*

In 1977, I took part in writing a report, *The Educational and Training Needs of European Managers*. There were nine of us – from London, Cologne, Barcelona, Lausanne, Rome, Götenborg, Aix-Marseille, Amsterdam and Dublin. The Chairman was C.C. Pocock of Royal Dutch Shell. I do not much like reports being given the title of the chairman, as many in Ireland are. It can be a put-down for the other members. However, what follows deserves the title the Pocock Report (as Charles Conroy's report on the Guards deserved his name). Charles Pocock did a memorable job of getting agreement from such a diverse bunch. It was a joy to find something written 30 years ago still fresh and relevant. Change is now so rapid and pervasive that we tend to look only to what is new to increase our understanding. The work summarised here was, from an eclectic bunch, far-seeing. No attempt was made to produce a consensus report that might emasculate individual views. We did not necessarily endorse each point, but we concurred with the general thrust. What we shared were *values*.

This is what we said.

We believed in the value for the individual and the general good of the free enterprise system, coupled with a democratic system associated with the mixed economy. We believed a system of decentralised decision-making was the best means of ensuring the far-reaching changes needed for the health of society. We believed there was no better yardstick for determining the acceptability of products and services than that of profit – surplus in public entities. We were aware that these values would be questioned.

Without profit, any corporation, including those in the public sector, would fail. But the social impact of business enterprise was now a necessary condition for its existence.

As social values change, business practices must adapt. It is difficult for business managers to accept that business is an actor and agent for social change. The hostility of groups to business can be partly explained by the unwillingness of corporations to look at the social repercussions of their actions. The status of women and the treatment of guest workers were, and still are, examples.

The first demand is that corporations should do more. Pressure groups demand that corporations go further than the law requires in social and employment policies, in the protection of the environment and the consumer, and even in corporate political behaviour.

On the other hand, there are pressing demands by all sorts of forces for corporations not to take actions that they may feel essential. Restrictions on rationalisation measures or closures is one: the corporate workforce should not be dispersed or manipulated at the sole will of management.

Legislation would become more restrictive as governments drifted further into economic *dirigisme*, in an effort to respond to social and political pressures. Managers would be faced with a seemingly inexorable growth of bureaucracy.

The manager's problem will be to achieve within this framework a degree of freedom, mutual co-operation and relative efficiency.

First, the challenge of contradiction. Economic ends must be responsive to social imperatives, but without putting the economic into jeopardy. But, on the other hand, without putting the economic in prime place, the social can be lost. Or, again, managerial power diminishes whereas managerial responsibilities grow. Thus, the tolerance and mastery of ambiguities increasingly will be a central feature of management for which no set approaches, let alone solutions, can be provided. Perhaps a searching mind, coupled with skills of analysis, will be more important than any portfolio of acquired knowledge.

Management, and particularly being seen to manage at the workplace, is a grind. Yet, if the manager opts out and starts to manage by remote control from his office, he is lost.

The future European manager will need real understanding of the emerging forces in society and must have the knowledge and capacity to cope with many demands, as examples:

- guiding constant innovation;
- working with changing organisations, which will increasingly have temporary structures where the co-ordination of semi-independent units will be critical;
- acting as an internal change agent, negotiating between conflicting interests and opposed value systems;
- acting in the political role of spokesman for the organisation.

We concentrated on the individual manager, but we also emphasised the importance of teams of managers with skills and qualities that complement and support each other. Much of the best teaching development in the business schools would be directed to team-building.

The most compelling need is for financial competence in the widest sense: managers must be numerate. The standard is fluency.

Managers need to be familiar with basic economic reasoning and with the conflicting arguments used by protagonists of differing schools of economics.

Not only must managers perform well, they must be seen and heard too. A successful mixed economy depends on understanding and co-operation, it depends on the pursuit of efficiency, and the acceptance of profitable enterprise whether public or private. Without such profits, the wider needs of society cannot be met. These concepts will always be attacked by antagonists of the system, and it is part of the manager's job to state his case and defend his beliefs with employees and union representatives, with government officials, with the political powers, and with the media and the public.

Business schools will no longer be able just to teach what they know. Schools should involve themselves even more with the real, messy world where managers operate, where the ideal solution is a theoretical luxury, where the important thing is to make decisions that are right enough (and right often enough) to get effective results, all within the time available. We recognised that it was the over-riding duty of management schools to address themselves to the future, to dedicate thought and research to what the management role would be some years ahead. But the schools would do this better and more credibly if their teaching staffs started from a deep understanding of what is today in the world in which managers work.

*

As I was summarising the Report, I got in the post the brochure for the IMI's 2006 National Management Conference. Some of the speakers were drawn from the National Competitiveness Council, the National Consumer Agency, the National Action Plan against Racism, the Equality Authority, none of them even thought of in 1977. The number of regulatory bodies that decide what businesses may or may not do increases, inexorably and expensively. All business representation can do is wring its hands and, if it's lucky, get some change around the edges, while commanding little public sympathy.

*

"What", Lloyd George asked the Labour leaders when he was forming his War Coalition, "is a government for except to dictate? If it does not dictate, then it is not a government ...".

Just over a year later, he told Lord Riddel: "It is no use being Prime Minister unless you can do what you want to do. It is useless for me to say I can, because I can't".

In these two remarks, Lloyd George travelled from the form to the reality of government in Britain.

Strategic Incompetence was the title of the first in a continuing series of papers I wrote just before the transition from the IMI to UCD, May 1983. Published in February 1983, it was the beginnings of the book *Government and Enterprise in Ireland*. It was given at an impressive conference, *Ireland in the Year 2000: Towards a National Strategy,*[19] organised by An Foras Forbartha and the National Board for Science and Technology.

The table overleaf, prepared by Brian MacCaba, then economist in the Confederation of Irish Industry, shows how bad things were in the early 80s. It would leave Celtic Tiger cubs unscathed, accustomed as they are to affluence.

Could it ever happen again? Pessimism is in poor taste – but nothing fails like success. The rivers of money flowing through the exchequer cover the underlying incompetences. We had whoopee economies before now – nothing of the scale or the pervasiveness of the present one. They gave us bad hangovers. It would be tempting fate to say we could never have them again. The economy can't continue to grow on the back of an inflated public sector and housing market and when we have forfeited to the ECB our ability to control our interest rates. On the one hand, there are [2006] some good things happening. On the other, we suffer from incompetent planning and execution, squandering the billions that are currently flowing through the Exchequer. There are clouds on the horizon. *Tout lasse, tout passe, tout casse.*

---

[19]   ISBN: 090612090X.

		1971	1972	1973	1974	1975	1976	1977	1978	1979	1980	1981	1982
1	Annual Inflation Rate	8.9	8.7	11.4	17.0	20.8	18.0	13.6	7.6	13.2	18.2	20.4	17.1
2	Annual % Change in Earnings	14.0	16.9	19.8	18.6	27.0	20.2	13.1	14.8	16.6	19.3	20.5	14.1
3	Government Expenditure as % GDP	40.5	39.0	39.2	43.7	47.8	47.5	46.4	46.5	50.5	55.2	58.0	58.8
4	Annual Increase in GDP%	2.4	5.4	3.6	3.2	1.5	1.6	4.8	4.6	1.4	0.9	-0.9	0.0
5	No. Employed in Public Sector '000s							220.7	226.7	236.5	240.2	244.7	
5	No. Employed in Public Sector as % of workforce (1960=16.5)							20.4	20.5	20.6	25.5	26.2	
6	No. Employed in Civil Service '000s	45.9	47.7	48.7	53.8	56.0	57.2	57.4	57.2	60.4	62.6	65.6	
7	No. Unemployed '000s	62.4	72.0	66.6	72.0	104.4	112.8	110.0	102.3	89.6	101.5	127.9	156.6
8	No. Employed in Manufacturing Industries '000s	196.4	197.4	204.2	210.2	197.4	196.7	202.8	206.8	215.1	216.4	206.0	200.3
9	Productivity: Manufacturing %	6.1	2.8	9.0	4.0	0.0	10.7	2.5	6.6	2.8	3.6	4.9	3.0

Sources: 1. CSO. 2. European Economy November 1982. 3. European Economy 1982. 4. European Economy November 1982 and Labour Force 1979. 5. Dáil Questions 24 June 1982. 7. Dáil Question 1 April 1982. 8. CSO. 9. CSO. 10. Central Bank Statistics 1981-82.

Back to 1983, my talk was about the gap between rhetoric and reality, between thought and action, between what we know and what we do, between planning and process. In 2006, we are equally incompetent at both.

In other words, if we were to get anywhere in 1983, never mind the year 2000, the subject of the conference, we would have to change our ways. And that was the hardest thing of all. How were we to get out of the recurrent situation where the State accumulated a stock of errors, nursed them to the point of infection and then wasted time and energy defending itself against deserved criticism? How were we to construct a State that provided its people with the power of adapting to the changes that constantly descended on it?

It is worth looking at some of the causes and manifestations of resistance to change, if only to see the height of the hurdle.

> The first is incrementalism. Democratic politics are incremental. To buy votes, politicians sell promises. Promises mean more. They certainly do not mean less, even if we were to judge by the last budget [1983], the harshest we had known. Current public expenditure increased. Criticism of this fact was met with weak rejoinders. One was "Nobody has suggested an alternative". This tedious statement was untrue. The general thrust of reductions in expenditure had been pointed out by many analysts. It was not their job to decide the fine print. As well invoke the argument that one must play the trombone to criticise the orchestra. Decisions are the job of government. This is where the sore thumb or beggar's sore technique is used – you don't want to hit or touch it. The skilled practitioner agrees to offer compensatory savings, but chooses items that are sure to reawaken painful memories of the political consequences that allegedly occurred the last time a cut was proposed in that area. Ministers are unlikely to agree to it. Then, there is a more pervasive form of incrementalism, the propensity of the system to throw good money after bad: when faced with a problem, to set up yet another agency or "scheme" with confused, frequently impossible, and always costly objectives, this in the face of a clear record of past failures.

A second cause of resistance to change was the nature of the public service. At a time [1983] when competitiveness was regarded as our first priority, the Deputy Secretary of the Department of the Public Service said that for most government managers there were "positive disincentives to productivity". The opposite of this turn of phrase must be "negative incentives". The problem has not gone away. The Civil Service is a closed priesthood, dangerously remote from its affected publics. As external social criticism continues to mass, abetted and armed with powers of information and communication, the Civil Service has a natural tendency to become more closed and to defend in lapidary fashion the indefensible.

A third cause of resistance to change was the public service trade unions, which, even in 1983, had penetrated up to the Assistant Secretary and Secretary General grades. Their vested interest was not only in the *status quo* of iron-clad relativities, promotion by seniority and dismissal impossible, but in the fact that governments crumble before their ranks. They combined an interest in increasing government expenditure with breathtaking unconcern about where the money was to come from.

The crisis was caused not simply by government's continually adding to the burdens that were then crushing the life out of it. It was caused also by Government's abdication of any effort at the long view and, more alarmingly, by its failure to deal effectively even with the One Damned Thing After Another phenomenon, damned things that were themselves caused by past failure of foresight.

What we were seeing was systemic resistance to change. This came not primarily from the tangled perceptions and reactions of politicians and civil servants but from the ineffectiveness of the system's capability to adapt to change.

The State was suffering from strategic incompetence.

There is a Gresham's Law of strategic planning. It states that routine and familiar operating activities tend to displace novel, episodic, strategic activities. Add to that law government's chronically short time horizon and its "debilitating preoccupation with survival", in the then Taoiseach's words, and you would be forced to the conclusion that there was only one position from which to analyse management in government: on your knees. However, if we were stayed by that affliction, we would not think at all.

Two propositions flow from systemic resistance:

◆ When immediate problems compete with strategic problems for a manager's attention, the immediate problems win.

◆ A manager's resistance to thinking about long-term issues will be directly proportional to his lack of practice and skill in doing so.

The solution was not to grab some operating managers by the scruff of the neck, free them from operating responsibilities and tell them to get on with it. Nor would it be wise to assume that, having reached Assistant Principal level, one knows everything. If strategic work were given to managers trained only to deal with day-to-day problems, their incompetence would compound the conflict of priorities and add to the overload.

New capacity was needed. That meant training in strategic decision-making, in implementation and in control. It meant providing new information and systems. It meant protecting the new capacity from incursions of the that-may-be-important-but-this-is-urgent type.

Systemic resistance came, therefore, from a conflict of priorities – the short-term always driving out the long-term; from strategic overload – taking on too many things, particularly trying to handle long- and short-term problems simultaneously; and strategic incompetence – a function of what I have just said, compounded by lack of training and systems.

It would be naïve to expect the strategic view from a bureaucratic system. In other words, and as experience has amply shown, the system is capable of managing only marginal, not radical, change.

I was not suggesting that we knew all. But we knew enough to be getting on with. The Irish path to progress was, and still is, littered with reports. My point was that, if we gave to the implementation of change as much energy as we gave to our reports, if, more important, we changed radically the way those reports and recommendations were arrived at – and that means also change in our governing system and in the knowledge, skills and attitudes of the people who make up those systems – then we might stand a chance of reversing trends. There was the possibility that the right use of *planning and of process in parallel* could lengthen woefully short political policy perspectives, and could guide political managers to systematic choices instead of the lunges that have passed for problem-solving.

Where to start? There was only one place: at the top. The stimuli might come from below or wherever. Without commitment at the top, nothing would happen.

It would no longer do to say that a politician "held office", as though it were fragile and would break if handled roughly. It was not meant to be held. It was meant to be hurled to heights where it could be seen and followed.

Government's first responsibility is to comprehend the potential of society and then to balance mixed coalitions of opinion, criticism and advocacy, and arrive at workable syntheses. Whether people equal to the job are given the chance to try will depend on how the party system performs in producing them, and on the perceptions of an electorate that will have little excuse for misjudging its politicians. The politicians, in turn, will not be checked in the use of their powers if they use them as they should. If they cannot sense the possible, they will exhaust themselves in attempting the impossible.

The ordeal of change is only in part a question of efficiency and managerial corrections. It is fundamentally a crisis of values and of perspectives on the goals and uses of power.

*

Now, 2006, how little we have learned. *Plus ça change.* We still squander millions on hare-brained schemes, on projects that cost substantially more than was "planned", and on consultants' reports that are never implemented.

It's cold comfort to know we may not be the worst. A recent study (2006) of the UK by David Craig and Richard Brooks is called

Plundering the Public Sector.[20] In 1997, New Labour attacked the last Tory government for spending £500 million a year on consultants. The Labour Government now spends four times that. In a review of the book, Andrew Wileman wrote:

> The public sector is 10 years behind the times in fad-surfing; it gets sucked into overblown budgets; it asks the wrong questions and it gets fixated on the *idée du jour*. It is risk-averse and spends much time and money on arse-covering. It uses consultants to advance political headlines and post-justifying political decisions, rather than to deliver cost-efficient action programmes.

And no one is held accountable.

My utterances on this subject attracted publicity. The book *Government and Enterprise in Ireland*[21] was the centrepiece of an entire two-hour and more *Late Late Show*, then Ireland's most popular television programme (and the longest running chat show in the world). It was on an icy February night when everybody was at home. A gentle critic on the show was Bertie Ahern. Another critic was the Labour deputy, Michael D. Higgins. He got lost in his circumlocutions, but had his revenge in an article he wrote for *Hot Press*, May 1986, entitled "Blessed Ivor and the Bean Baron's Ball". The show's host, Gay Byrne, asked me back to do a reprise of the programme. I declined. It was not so much my distrust of the medium, as a growing repugnance at the personal publicity and the fact that I was becoming trapped, labelled a lightning rod for the then New Right.

The Broadcasting Complaints Commission upheld a complaint about lack of balance in the Show. It stated that Gay Byrne "clearly aligned himself with the views of three members of the panel – Ivor Kenny, Des Peelo and Tom Murphy". The complaint was made by Brendan Ryan, an Independent member of the Senate.

I decided to take the advice of Sir Peter Medawar: to stop wringing my hands over the human condition and to try instead to

---

[20]   ISBN-13: 9781845293741.
[21]   ISBN: 0717113744.

help remedy those things that were wholly remediable, to return to what I knew best – managers and organisations.

The problems of organisations are never wholly remediable, but they are considerably more remediable than the problems of the political/bureaucratic system. Underlying my writing about that system was an enduring concern about freedom: antipathy to ordinary folk getting pushed around by, and becoming dependent on, powerful and ignorant forces.

This same concern was to inform my work with organisations. It was a turning point in my working life.

The *Late Late Show* had a powerful imprint. After it, people would salute me in the street as if they knew me. That summer, my first on the Shannon, I berthed at a marina in Athlone to get some diesel. The proprietor welcomed me back. I explained that this was my first time ever on the river. He would not believe me. Then it dawned: "Now I have you. Sure amn't I in the same line of business? I have a dance band".

22

THE PAPAL VISIT

It was a beautiful day with a clear blue sky.

Dermot Ryan, Professor of Eastern Languages in UCD, was a member of the committee of the Catholic Communications Institute, in which capacity I got to know him well. In February 1972, John Charles McQuaid retired from the archbishopric of Dublin. Dermot was appointed his successor. Donal McCartney says in his history of UCD that it was the end of an era.[22] That same year, Jeremiah Hogan retired as President of the College. The relationship between mitre and gown was becoming more relaxed. In the days of John Charles McQuaid, letters from the President of UCD ended "Your Grace's most obedient servant". Letters between President Tom Murphy (1972-1985) and Tomás Ó Fiaich, Archbishop of Armagh and Primate of Ireland, were, both ways, "Dear Tom".

On the evening news, I heard the Pope was coming to Ireland on September 29, 1979, two months away. The following morning, I called Dermot to offer what help the IMI could give. I said, "I think you might have a management problem". He said, "You have no idea. We have to have a Mass for one million people in the Phoenix Park. I'll send Tom Fehily up to you immediately".

Tom, now Monsignor Tom, arrived at Sandyford in an ancient Fiat. When I asked him, with a cup of coffee in his hand, what resources he had, he nearly spilled the coffee. He did not laugh when I said, "You need a chief of staff. You need transport and a telephone system". This was before mobile phones. "You need a superb headquarters staff".

---

22   *UCD – A National Idea*, ISBN: 0717123367.

I thought the only way to tackle this was to do it now. I first called Carl O'Sullivan, the Army Chief of Staff. I told him I needed to borrow his best commandant or colonel. He asked me to describe the job. He said, "If he was that good, he would not be in the army". But we got a senior officer who was a winner.

I next called Paddy McLoughlin, the Garda Commissioner. Paddy was a gentleman. I was sure he would deliver. I asked him for access to some Garda cars, drivers and radios. He said, "I heard the Taoiseach say on radio the Government would give whatever help they could. I suppose we could do that. I'll call you back". That was the end of it, a disappointment.

However, I was still on a high. There was nothing spiritual about it. This was going to be a huge international media event, at which we could look incompetent.

Michael McStay in Philips gave us a phone system and motor dealers gave us cars. I rang chief executives and asked for their secretaries for six weeks. When they got over the shock, they rallied and a team was built.

Here are some numbers to grasp the immensity of the task to be accomplished in two months: 40 potters to make 2,400 pottery ciboria, each to hold 350 hosts; 2,000 Eucharistic ministers; recruiting and training a 5,000-strong choir and 10,000 stewards. The architect was Ronnie Tallon. He and many others, in particular the Office of Public Works and Telefís Éireann, surpassed themselves. All under the benign direction of Tom Fehily. To say he rose to the occasion would be an understatement.

Those who remember the day will remember it well. There was no precedent. The million and more people were comfortably accommodated in corrals that prevented dangerous crowding. Each corral held 1,000 people, each person having six square feet, enough room for a seat. The Popemobile – the first of its kind – from Fords in Cork, brought the Pope through a network of roads so that everybody got a close-up.

It was a beautiful day with a clear blue sky. For many of us, the most emotional moment was when the great green Aer Lingus jumbo flew low over the Park with its acolytes of tiny Air Corps fighter planes. When later the Pope appeared on the elevated stage, there was a roar of welcome.

Once I had done what I could, there was no further need for me, so I did not think any more about the visit. I would probably watch it on television. A week or so beforehand, I had a late call from the reception desk in the IMI telling me that a fat envelope with a crest on it and marked "Urgent" had just been delivered. I drove to the Institute and got an invitation for Maureen and me "to receive communion at the hands of the Holy Father".

We had reserved parking, were brought to a fenced-off area with seating for 200 out of more than one million, just by the altar steps.

When it came time to receive communion, we were gently asked to line up. First were Paddy and Maeve Hillery. There were many steps up to the altar. Maureen went before me. I had two impressions of the Pope: his red shoes or slippers, his beautifully manicured nails as he put the Host on my tongue.

Then came an unforgettable sight. As we turned around at the top of the steps, we had a unique view of one million happy people. The day was not marred by a single unseemly incident. It was marked for me by a mixture of emotions, too jumbled to pray. One has stayed with me. I thought, when I die, there will be no special seating, no VIP treatment. You die alone. An unoriginal epiphany, but one that endured.

We drove home through deserted streets. Tom Cox from the IMI helped with media relations. There was a tent for 600 media people. Seán Mac Réamoinn of RTÉ was one of the first to arrive. He said, "You know, Tom, when I came out of my house early this morning, there was a line of buses, their engines throbbing, the conductors and drivers smiling. I remembered the immortal words of Patrick Sarsfield, 'Would that this were for Ireland'".

Shortly after the visit, I had a call from Bill Finlay, Governor of Bank of Ireland. Bill asked if I would help raise the considerable sum the Dublin diocese had expended. I was familiar with fundraising for the IMI building in Sandyford. Bill said, "We have a week to do this. The afterglow will fade". We spent a hectic week. We got most of the money.

23

INDUSTRIAL DEMOCRACY
– IN THEORY AND PRACTICE

"This is a political decision. If it causes problems for you,
your job is to manage them."

- Michael O'Leary TD, 1936-2006

The term "industrial democracy" is an oxymoron. Chambers defines democracy as "a form of Government in which the supreme power is vested in the people collectively". The "people", so far as business is concerned, are a multiplicity of stakeholders, not just "the workers", in itself an ambiguous phrase in an age of technology. However, we shall stick with the term for this chapter because it was common usage.

Industrial democracy, more accurately worker representation, originated in Germany. It was called *Mitbestimmung*, literally "having a voice in". It completely separated non-executive directors from management. In Germany, the *Aufsichstat*, supervisory board, had no common membership with the *Vorstand*, executive board. The supervisory board's role was to oversee the plans and performance of the management board, its primary power lying in the ability to hire and fire the chief executive.

A starting point for Ireland might be 1951. The Congress of Irish Unions passed a resolution calling for a "workers' share in industry". The CIU asked affiliated unions to give their views on "co-partnership, which means participation in the management of industry by the issue of shares to the employees on a profit-sharing basis". Seán Lemass, then Minister for Industry and Commerce, was interested. He asked the CIU to submit proposals for Development

Councils, through which worker representatives would participate in determining industrial policy. The employers were hostile. The discussion died for about a decade.

In 1967, the ICTU adopted a resolution supporting "the principle and practice of industrial democracy, providing for workers' participation in management". In 1968, they called on the Government to introduce industrial democracy in the State sector.

In 1969, the IMI planned to have industrial democracy as the theme of its national conference. It was suggested to us by the employer representative bodies that we would be seen to advocate industrial democracy at a sensitive time. We backed down. We accepted that the national conference was not based on objective Institute research (the right to the publication of which we would defend to the death), and that the competing views given at the conference might compound a confused situation. This was partly face-saving. *Real-politik* was nearer the truth. We did not want to take on the employer bodies over what was hardly a matter of principle: an understandable, if unheroic, posture.

However, we published, as a sort of *amende honorable*, a symposium on industrial democracy. It was written by a judicious mixture of trade unionists, politicians, personnel managers, academics and the directors general of the FUE, FII and IMI. The book made one point, borne out by subsequent events: that the question was complex and that it was not, therefore, going to be "solved by simple slogans that stir the blood". This was coolly agreed by all the contributors, despite the fact that the air was thick with slogans at that time.

More to the point was that it was agreed that the problem was not going to go away.

The Government view was that worker participation should begin at the lower levels of organisation and only then work up to workers' directors. The Minister for Labour, Paddy Hillery, put it: "I am sceptical of the evocation of workers joyfully flocking to their industrial democracy work-places and singing their way through a day of honest toil because some of their mates are helping to take decisions above in the board room".

By the beginning of the '70s, the subject was on the agenda of the Employer-Labour Conference. By 1971, the employers were considering a paper commissioned from Charles Mulvey of TCD. His "inescapable conclusion" was that "workers probably cannot participate effectively in the management of the enterprise". He advocated instead the "extension and deepening of the collective bargaining process through works councils". This conclusion may sound bleaker than it was. It was a change in the employers' stance.

Up to now, things were at a theoretical or polemical level. Two things gave the movement – if so it can be called – a harder edge: the proposed EEC statute on the European Company Law and the Worker Participation (State Enterprises) Act of 1977.

The EEC proposal, the Fifth Directive, was for a supervisory board, with one-third employee representation for companies with more than 500 employees. The supervisory board would appoint the board of management, the nearest thing to an Irish board of directors. The employers pointed to reservations about the idea throughout the EEC: reservations about "interference by unqualified people in the decision-making process". The proposal was rejected, particularly by Britain and by US companies with European associates.

In January 1974, an Employer-Labour Conference sub-committee on worker participation recommended that an agreement should be ratified providing for the establishment of works councils. There was to be no question of legislation. The councils were to be arranged by voluntary agreement and flexibly.

These were hardly revolutionary proposals. The employers' acceptance of them was, however, a further modification of earlier attitudes. Negotiation was now an integral part of a manager's job. Institutionalising it held few terrors.

The boardroom, however, remained inviolable, except for seven State companies at the initiative of the then Minister for Labour, Michael O'Leary, of the Labour Party. (Michael died suddenly, aged 70, in May 2006 while this book was being written. He had just retired as a District Court Judge.) The companies were Bord na Móna, CIE, ESB, Aer Lingus, B+I, Irish Sugar Company and NÉT, three of which no longer exist. A 1988 Act extended the list considerably and included Aer Rianta, which will be used as a case study later in this chapter.

While the Employer-Labour Conference report gathered dust – the sub-committee did not meet again – Michael O'Leary was preparing the ground for his Worker Participation Bill. The trade unions favoured a single board, on which they wanted 50% representation. The employers said that the idea that only trade unionists could stand for office was both "undemocratic and illiberal". The Minister's arguments were weak, they said. They would be unsound in practice. They were rigid and undemocratic. They would certainly not be acceptable to private sector employers.

Meanwhile, the EEC had adopted a more flexible approach.

In 1975, it produced a Green Paper on a revised Fifth Directive. The employers found the new approach sensible. But not so the Worker Participation Bill. A submission expressing concern was made to the Minister. It fell on deaf ears. The Bill, unmodified by the employers' representations, became law on April 4, 1977. Significantly, it met no substantial opposition on its way through parliament. It was implemented by a Fianna Fáil Minister, Gene Fitzgerald, following the election of July 1977.

Government thinking on worker participation – at least on State boards – had come a long way from 1959, when Seán Lemass, Minister for Industry and Commerce (then including labour affairs), said that "the arrangement which is sometimes urged, of having staff representation on the controlling boards, would, in my view, be highly undesirable both from the viewpoint of the organisation, of the public and of the staff".

The most significant developments in worker participation in Ireland have come from Government. The Worker Participation Bill was first announced by Michael O'Leary, while Minister for Labour, to a conference room full of managers in the IMI. He said, "This is a political decision. If it causes problems for you, your job is to manage them".

At least until he left the Labour Party, of which he was then leader, to join Fine Gael, he wore his ideology on his sleeve. He said, "The claims of industrial democracy rest on nothing less than the ending of the dehumanisation of work ... the State companies followed in every detail the *via dolorosa* of management practices of the private concerns".

Charlie Cuffe, director general of the FUE, for whom in his rhetorical flourishes the end was always nigh, said, "If the way to industrial democracy lies through industrial chaos, we certainly seem to be on the right road".

*

Ten years after Michael O'Leary's *démarche*, I ran into Dermot Desmond at an Institute of Public Administration conference in Dublin. He was then Chairman of Aer Rianta, the State-owned Irish airports authority. (He worked well with a strong and clear-headed chief executive, Derek Keogh, who resigned not long after Dermot left. When they both left, some years later, Dublin airport spiralled into the abyss.)

Dermot said, "I want you to do a study of the Aer Rianta Board".

I said, "I don't do boards".

He said, "You will", and I did. It was a productive study, that led to a Board Charter signed up to by all the directors, including the worker directors.

At the concluding conference of the study, I distinguished between a directive and a representative board:

♦ A *directive* board is usually small – nine maximum, seven is better. This helps understanding. It is decision-making. Its members are not appointed to represent constituencies, but to bring complementary skills and wisdom to the board.

♦ A *representative* board is designed to encourage consensus between different, and often competing, constituencies. This usually means large, because no constituency can be left out. The problem for governments is not so much who is appointed, as who is left out. Representative boards are no good at running things (more accurately, at seeing that things are done). Either management will be preoccupied with politicking or it will ignore the board and go its own sweet way. Either course will be ineffective.

There was no question in the minds of any of the Aer Rianta directors – worker directors included – about the nature of the Aer Rianta board. It was not a representative board. It was a directive board, whose job was to ensure that the company was run in the long-term interests of *all* stakeholders – State, workers, customers etc.

In the 1970s, there were pressures, predominantly in the United States, for boards to be representative, not only of shareholder interests, but of all stakeholders who could be affected by company actions. These so-called corporate democracy developments identified employees, customers, depositors, creditors and even local and national societies as constituent stakeholders.

There was also pressure on the boards of influential companies to have directors to represent the "rights" of minority and activist groups. In Ireland now, there is some concern to have women on boards. This trend has at times been criticised as tokenism, not least by women.

All board members should be able to contribute in full to board deliberations, not from a sectional perspective, but from broad business experience.

Nominee directors appointed to watch out for the interests of third parties – such as a substantial shareholder or a joint venture partner – would find conflicts of interests between their duty to act for the company as a whole and their perceived duty to their principal. This is a particular constraint for State companies, where there is always a number of arrantly political appointees, whose primary loyalty is to the minister who appointed them.

Stan Vance, a vice-chancellor in the Academy and author of several authoritative works, said:

> There is a pragmatic reason for not having representative directors – there is no demonstrable proof that adding representatives of constituencies improves sales, productivity, growth, morale, or even better relations with the constituents themselves.

Aer Rianta had three elected worker directors. The task was to clarify ground rules, through which they could make their best contribution to the board, while maintaining a good relationship with the people who elected them.

Worker directors were, in effect, *executive directors* – full-time employees of the company with definite jobs to do *and also* members of the board. As full-time employees, they had the same boss-subordinate relationships that any employee had; as directors, they assumed corporate responsibility for the long-term success of Aer Rianta as a complex entity with many stakeholders, a dual role.

The key to their effective contribution to the board (and to a level of personal fulfilment) was to maximise their contribution to corporate direction and to minimise any representative role.

The first would depend on what the board did. If the board concentrated on corporate direction, on long-term strategy, this would raise members' sights above day-to-day questions. Meetings would leave little time or tolerance for day-to-day matters. There would be occasions where long-term strategies would affect jobs and fair play – two primary concerns of the workers who elected the directors. In such instances, the worker directors' particular contribution at board level could be to ensure that business objectives were informed with humanity. It was the chairman's job to reach consensus without injuring the integrity of the decision. Where consensus was not possible, dissenting directors had the option of having that dissent recorded, or, in the ultimate, of resignation. What would make life difficult, if not impossible, would be for any director to subvert the board process by going outside it, behaviour that no chairman could tolerate.

Once a decision had been taken by a board, all members were bound by it, whether or not they agreed with it. It was then a board decision and no director was at liberty to disown it publicly. The internal workings of a board are matters for the board only.

It is a cliché to say that all directors are equal. In practice, it means that there should be no "squaring" of directors outside meetings. Lobbying of particular directors by the chairman or chief executive or by caucuses of directors could destroy trust and make board meetings political, unpleasant and unproductive. Alliances between directors would quickly become transparent and, in any event, would be unstable and temporary, clustered around a particular event, ready to break up when circumstances changed. The board would become politicised, arguments would be *ad hominem*, not *ad rem*, and strategy would go out the window. Any coalition of directors would have the effect of excluding others, leading to simmering alienation that was bound to find an outlet, usually a negative one.

On the other hand, frequent communication between the chief executive and individual directors to increase understanding was to be encouraged. It minimised speculation or folklore that would waste board time. It could be useful to the CEO, in that he could be made aware of pitfalls or opportunities he did not know about.

The point was made that worker directors, with their unique position in the organisation, had direct access to the chief executive on particular matters: this was a representative or intermediary function, outside the working of the board.

There was a suggestion that, in the event of disagreement between the chief executive and a worker director, the matter might be brought to the board or at least to the chairman. Either a matter was for the board (strategy/policy) or it was not (management/operational). If it was not, then it should never come to the board – management were paid to sort it out. Nor had a director the "right" to bring it to the board simply because he was a director – that would be self-indulgence. It was a matter ultimately for the chairman as head of the board to decide what was or was not a board matter.

And if the board or the chairman were to assume the role of arbitrating between (worker) directors and management, they or he would be diminishing their roles, alienating the losers, and inhibiting the good working of the board.

A board must firmly resist delegation upwards.

It's time to hear some of the unlaundered views of the elected Aer Rianta directors. You can see that they were a joy to work with. In contrast with another State company I worked in where, at the coffee breaks, the worker directors telephoned their mates, the Aer Rianta worker directors at the time were in an organisation that had the essential ingredient: trust.

> To be honest, that's what I want – that I can trust him and that he can trust me. I want to be treated as an equal. I may not be as well educated but I am here only to do the job to the best of my ability.

> I think unions are afraid of worker directors. The ICTU wants to control them. It should be sufficient to report back

to your own industrial council. No necessity for anything else.

We report back to the Industrial Democracy Council once a month. Each director gives a report without betraying anything confidential. No figures given/no money. We use our own judgment on what is confidential.

When I came on the board, I saw the company as a whole – a marvellous company. It was not just my section.

I enjoy the board meetings. I felt I was dealing with very professional people with whom I felt I could not compete. I now feel confident enough that I can make a contribution. They're very helpful – a good board to work with.

If a situation was definitely loss-making, I could not support it but I would be concerned that the business would be handled in a way that the jobs were protected so far as possible. You have to be realistic – I would, for example, support early retirement. I would not block, I would try to act responsibly.

24

THOUGHTS ON BOARDS
OF DIRECTORS

*The first necessary thing is that the board must be clear where it
wants the business to go.*

Once upon a time, this was what some eminent authorities said
about boards:

♦ Boards are often little more than high-powered, well-intentioned
  people engaged in low-level activities.

♦ Ornaments.

♦ Largely irrelevant.

♦ Ants on a log in turbulent waters who think they are steering the
  log.

♦ And my old friend Peter Drucker's condemnation: "Boards do not
  function".

The world has changed. We've had a litany of reports and legislation:
Cadbury (1992), Greenbury (1995), Hempell (1998), Higgs (2003),
Sarbanes-Oxley, The Combined Code, to name, as they say, but a
few.

When I served on my first board, there was little literature on
board practice. When, in 1991, I did my first board study my
bookshelf was beginning to fill up. Now, the air is thick with journals
and with seminars for considerable fees run by consultants and
academics. The weight of restrictive legislation and regulation bears
heavily and expensively on boards, much of it a bureaucratic over-
reaction to the misdeeds of a minority: never in the field of human

conflict was so much owed by so many to so few. Gone are the days of the grunt-a-month director waiting for the clink of ice-cubes in the lunch-time gin. Boards, their members, and their sub-committees, particularly the audit committee, are collectively and individually *accountable* in ways they never were before and no one can quarrel with that.

This does not apply to State company boards, which are creatures of their sponsoring departments and where there is unfathomable accountability – the buck never stops.

A properly-constructed board, with a strong proportion of genuinely independent non-executive directors, will add value by bringing to the table different perspectives and experiences. Any senior management team can become self-reinforcing, like bouncers inhibiting the entry of disturbing ideas. On the other hand, a board that does not add value will earn the carefully-concealed contempt of the CEO.

In practice, most boards spend their time on three things:

♦ How's business?

♦ Significant random events or crises.

♦ Strategy – usually meaning an accumulation of strategic decisions, for example, restructuring, new businesses, M&A, significant capex, divestments, trade union confrontation.

This may work quite well – for a time. In my limited experience, few boards have a clear agreed strategic framework against which strategic decisions are regularly tested and taken.

The first necessary thing is that the board must be clear where it wants the business to go. How can anyone – shareholders, analysts, directors or managers – evaluate a company's performance, if they cannot anticipate its future?

Strategy, then, should be a continuing creative tension between *present reality* and a clearly articulated and agreed *vision*.

Present reality is slippery, difficult to get hold of, because all organisations encourage dependency relationships that inhibit truth, reality. Boards can be particularly removed from the reality of a company, not really knowing what's going on.

Vision is an overblown word. It is simply a picture of the company that is measurably better – on several measures – than the company is at present. This requires teamwork, creativity, originality, inventiveness, intuition, imagination, courage and listening – none of them the subject of precise measurement. This is where a good chairman can demonstrate skill, so that management emerge from a meeting with their confidence enhanced.

There are several good points in Higgs. I part company with him when he says a non-executive director should normally serve two three-year terms. If a NED's contact with the company is, at most, 11 meetings a year, it will take two to three years fully to understand the company, its people and its markets so that contributions can be measured, can really add value. What you are looking for in a NED is, above all, experience – best someone who has been a CEO with international, not parochial, perspective. Better someone who has successfully coped with failure. "It's all common sense" or "It's not rocket science"? *No.* In choosing a NED, the inescapable measure is track record, not eloquence.

Boards are usually fed tons of numbers as facts. They are mostly about the past – steering the ship by the wake. They are interesting, but useful only if they identify trends or accurately foresee impending disaster. The death of strategy is to get it mixed up with budgets. Budgets kill the long view. They encourage micromanagement, even by enlightened boards. They hijack the time available to discuss the important issues. Budgets are coffins. What is needed, in broad brush-strokes, is the financial envelope within which the company must operate.

A good strategy is a *comprehensive* strategy. An incomplete strategy can lead to bad surprises. I have tried to outline the questions that need answering in the Strategic Cascade (following page).

Provided, of course, you're in the right business *ab initio*. "There's a gap in the market, but is there a market in the gap?"

The Strategic Cascade

ENTRY TO THE PROCESS IS INTERACTIVE / AT ANY POINT / NOT SEQUENTIAL.

→ **Environment**
Rapid and continuous change – social, political, technological, commercial, values.
Do we really know/understand what's going on?

→ **Vision**
What do we aspire to?
What inspires us?

→ **Mission**
What business are we in?
What is our unique legitimacy, our USP?
Where are we going?

→ **Strategy**
How do we get there?
What are the obstacles?
How do we overcome them?

→ **Structure**
What is the best way to organise/distribute power and work?
What kind of engine/structure do we need to overcome obstacles, get things done?

→ **People**
Do we know the kind of attitudes, skills, knowledge, energy and motivation we need?
Do we have them now?
Do we develop and reward people appropriately?

→ **Standards**
Against what criteria/benchmarks do we continually measure ourselves?

→ **Control**
How do we know when we're off course or need to change direction?
Do we have accurate and comprehensive information freely and continually communicated?

→ **Leadership**
What kind of leadership will make all this happen?
Do we have it?

Boards seldom ask questions about whether the organisation has the *capability* to achieve what it wants to achieve. All boards subscribe to the mantra that people are our most important asset, and often walk away with their fingers in their ears. Human capital is not what you own, but what you know. The primary resource has shifted from physical capital to human capital, to which standard accounting rules assign no value.

A company is valued essentially on present and future cash-flow but, critically, on the perception of the competence and vision of its board and management. What happens to the share price when an under-performing CEO is replaced or a respected CEO retires?

How many boards spend any time evaluating the human capability? How many boards come unstuck when their fine plans fail because they don't have the people skilled enough to implement them?

Once more with feeling, a board cannot manage anything. Only managers can.

The essence of the board's role is *to create tomorrow's company out of today's*. A board's role is, or should be, all about the future.

A director must avoid becoming *la mouche du coche*. Remember La Fontaine's fable? On a stifling day, a coach drawn by six sturdy horses got stuck on a sandy hill. The passengers got down. The horses struggled. A fly approached and stung the horses. They moved quickly to the top of the hill. The fly alighted on the nose of the coachman and surveyed his great victory. "Look what I have done. Now we can all rest", he thought.

So, as a director, the question of conscience is: *"Does my presence on this board add value?"*.

25

INTERLUDE: WATER MUSIC

Jolly boating weather,
And a hay harvest breeze,
Blade on the feather,
Shade of the trees,
Swing, swing together,
With your bodies between your knees.

Rugby may be more clever,
Harrow may make more row,
But we'll row for ever,
Steady from stroke to bow,
And nothing in life shall sever,
The chain that is round us now.

Others will fill our places,
Dressed in the old light blue,
We'll recollect our races,
We'll to the flag be true,
And youth will be still in our faces,
When we cheer for an Eton crew.

Twenty years hence this weather,
May tempt us from office stools,
We may be slow on the feather,
And seem to the boys old fools,
But we still swing together
And swear by the best of schools. [23]

---

[23]   *The Eton Boating Song*, first performed June 4, 1863.

"And what did you *do*?", she said. This was at a cocker's pee (cocktail party to the uninitiated) in London. She was clad in a black body stocking, leaving nothing to the imagination. She smoked a black gold-tipped Balkan Sobranie cigarette, in a yard-long ebony cigarette holder.

"I rowed". Her face lit up. "Ah", she said, "at the Dablin Hoss Show?". "No. In boats." She sighed, "Ah yes", and went to find more interesting company.

If there was a distinct beginning, it was at age 12, when I coxed a St. Ignatius College, the Jez, schoolboy four. We didn't do well, partly because my idea of aggressive coxing was to ram our ancient enemy, St. Joseph's, the Bish, a futile exercise when you're behind. In those days, it was easy to get out of sight of the umpire. In the very early days of Galway regatta, they started the races by firing a shotgun across the bows of the boats.

When I graduated from cox to oarsman, we brought a school IV to Trinity regatta on the Liffey at Islandbridge. Over a shortened schoolboy course, we were up against Methody from Belfast. We decided to put a hex on the black Protestants. Just before the start, while the crews were side-by-side, we solemnly blessed ourselves. The Belfast lads turned away, embarrassed. They beat the hell out of us.

UCG had an idyllic site for a boat club on a quiet canal leading to the Corrib. My first day in college in 1948, I headed straight there.

We had a huge stroke of luck. A tall, distinguished gentleman wandered into the club one evening. He was Dermot Gogarty, son of Oliver St. J. Gogarty, writer, poet and eye surgeon, to whom Dermot bore a strong resemblance. Dermot had set up an architect's practice in Galway. He was a Cambridge blue and had won the Grand at Henley Royal Regatta, the summit for an oarsman, for London Rowing Club. He had been coached by the greatest coach, Steve Fairbairn, who famously said, "If you can't do it easily, you can't do it at all". Coached by Gogarty, in a direct line from Fairbairn, UCGBC were close to the *fons et origo* of the emerging style of rowing, breaking free from the old Orthodox style.

Gogarty was an epic coach, standing in the prow of the coach's launch, megaphone in one hand, stop-watch in the other, blue and white London Rowing Club cap – or straw boater, if he'd had a gin in the County Club before he came down to the river – his Churchillian tones echoing across the Corrib. On a limpid evening, he startled the courting couples in row-boats in the rushes, when he said through the megaphone: "I want you to enjoy your rowing as you enjoy your fornication. Concentrate on the immediate. Forget about the consequences".

One Saturday, we were looking forward to a normal outing. We noticed a small crowd on the riverbank. Then we saw our arch-rivals, Galway Rowing Club, waiting for us. Gogarty stopped us beside them and called out, "Both crews will row a full regatta course. I shall ask you once if you are ready. On receiving no reply, I shall say go. Go!". Bloody hell, everybody in Galway knew about the race except us. Forgive me if I can't remember who won. I suppose if we had, I would remember, so we must have lost.

My most vivid memory of rowing on the Corrib was not of a race, but of a summer's evening. When you head up the straight to Menlo Castle, you are facing into the west. The colours of the approaching sunset were indescribable. Gogarty was silent. The crew were absolutely together. We felt we could row to the end of the world. Gogarty said quietly, "You are the kings of glory".

The captain was a well-built and handsome medical student. Everybody knew he was captain when he came down to the club in his maroon blazer and flannels. Girls were playing tennis. A ball flew over the net-wire and landed in the river. He said, "Righty-ho, girls, I'll get it for you". Then he did something no one ever should. He put one foot in one rowing boat (called a randan) and the other in an adjoining boat. What happened had a slow, film-like inevitability. The boats began to part until he was doing the splits. Then he fell in, maroon blazer and all. The girls in their tennis shorts waited on the bank, at first looking anxious and then trying hard to look sympathetic. He stood in water up to his waist and said, "Here's your effing ball".

Gogarty pointed me to another river, the Thames, on whose bosom I spent happy years rowing for London Rowing Club. We practised on the tideway at Putney, on a winter evening with a bicycle lamp on the bow, the oars making phosphorescent puddles. Usually, we would row up the Boat Race course, Putney to Mortlake. Occasionally, we'd go below Putney bridge past a big brewery –

Mann, Rogers and Greaves, a translation of *post coitum, homo tristis est.*

Only someone who has felt it can appreciate the precise shock of the icy wash from a Thames tug hitting you in the middle of the back. Spinechilling. Spring Sundays, we'd row 15 miles through the locks up to Molesey, near Hampton Court, lunch and row back. In summer, we'd compete at Marlowe regatta a week before Henley and then row the boats up to the Henley course.

My first sight of the course was from the start. You could see right up the straight, all one mile 550 yards of it. Even experienced Henley oarsmen fell silent as we rowed up the course to the boat tents.

Henley is not just a regatta. It's a British rite. There may be no more old, old Leander men who drink their port from pewter tankards, fall off the Leander Club balcony and have bits of gravel extracted from their purple wattles, but the Henley tradition and rituals are strong and a delight. The man who rowed in front of me in the LRC 2nd VIII, turned and asked: "Kenny, do we still have a garrison in Dublin?". He had been to Eton and Balliol.

Maureen and I go there every year and stay with the Emmanuel family in their elegant hotel on an inlet of the Thames, willow trees dipping into the water.

Maureen said to me, "I know why we come here. You want to recover your youth". A few years ago, I was standing idly by the river. The modulated tones of the announcer came over. "At two o'clock precisely, a flight of the Royal Air Force will fly over the course to commemorate the 50th anniversary of their victory in the Thames Cup". A few Brits scoffed, "I bet they'll be late". They were not. Two jets streaked up the course, wing-tip to wing-tip, and then broke off into the clouds. The date they were celebrating was some years after I first rowed at Henley ...

The announcements at the regatta are immaculate, including the pronunciation of Garda Síochána Boat Club.

My active Henley years had a revival in the '60s, when I coached the guards at Henley, on the Liffey and at Blessington. We had some great years, winning all before us. At Islandbridge, I would coach from a bicycle on the towpath. Once I hit a pot-hole and went arse over tip. The crew had the decency not to laugh out loud. I made some enduring friendships – John Mee, who was captain, and his wife Vera, and Peter Fitzgerald, whom I coached. Peter, who we met in **Chapter 10**, is now Deputy Commissioner, easily our most distinguished policeman, having been trouble-shooting in, amongst other places, Beirut, Namibia, Cambodia and El Salvador.

I took the gardaí to the London Head of the River Race, 200 crews taking off at 20-second intervals. It was the guards' first time, so they started way down at the back. They ploughed through the other crews and ended up in single figures. I borrowed a stray bicycle to follow them. 4¼ miles to the start over a gravelly tow-path, then 4¼ miles back with the race. God must have been watching – both tyres blew. When I got to the finish at Putney, the top of my head was ready to blow off. I saw John Mee on the balcony of National Westminster Boat Club. He was holding two tankards of beer.

Spring of this year, 2006, I had been at a meeting in Harvard, and walked along by the Charles River. There were many crews out. I watched them closely and "remembered the willowy sway of my own hands away".[24] To my surprise, there was a catch in my throat. It was just like yesterday.

> The willowy sway of the hands away
> And the water boiling aft,
> The elastic spring and the steely fling
> That drives the flying craft.
>
> The steely spring and the musical ring
> Of the blade with the biting grip,
> And the stretching draw of the bending oar
> That rounds the turn with a whip.
>
> And the lazy float that runs the boat,
> And makes the swing quite true,
> And gives that rest that the oarsman blest
> As he drives the blade right through.
>
> All through the swing he hears the boat sing
> As she glides on her flying track,
> And he gathers aft to strike the craft
> With a ringing bell-note crack.

---

[24]   Steve Fairbairn, 1862-1938.

From stretcher to oar with drive and draw,
He speeds the boat along,
All whalebone and steel and a willowy feel –
That is the oarsman's song.

*

It must have been in the '60s that I first hired a cruiser from the late, and sadly missed, Ted Barrett. He then had his fleet at the Twelfth Lock on the Grand Canal – before he settled at Lowtown, just below Robertstown. Ted taught me my first cruising lesson. We arrived, wife and family, with enough food and drink to take us to the Azores. All fuss and business, I asked Ted when we could plan to reach Tullamore, as we had invited some friends to meet us there. He said simply: "I won't hire you the boat". The shock showed. He relented. "Look. You're not *going anywhere.*"

In the event, the engine broke down near Sallins, and it was two days before we felt the need to telephone him to come and fix it. And it didn't matter at all that we never reached Tullamore.

Bitten by the canal-bug, I began to show symptoms, like driving down to Robertstown on a summer evening and staring at the clear waters of the Summit Level. Maureen said in her kindly way: "I suppose you want to buy a cruiser". A week later I had (a) been refused an overdraft in the National Bank, Westland Row, whence I got my first cheque book; (b) got an overdraft – and a lobster lunch in the Moira – from the legendary Ted O'Boyle of the Ulster Bank, College Green; and (c) bought the *Saidé R* from John Farrington of Naas.

The *Saidé R* was (and, I hope, still is) an old beauty, all brass and teak and two Volvo Penta diesels that would drive the *Queen Mary*. It was late summer when I bought her, so, until it was time to put her to bed for the winter, we just pottered up and down the canal, our farthest foray to the perfect little harbour at Edenderry, from which you look *down* at the passing cars. Ted Barrett lifted the *Saidé R* from the canal with a small mobile crane (none of your pukka Dun Laoghaire jobs) – an alarming experience for the owner, whose overdraft was accumulating interest. He did splendid things to her, inside and out, installing a Mark-inhibitor in the bow cabin – a device to prevent our youngest son falling from his bunk.

Spring of the following year, we set sail for the first time for the Shannon: one day Lowtown to Tullamore, one day Tullamore to Shannon Harbour.

The crew that year, and subsequent years, were two members of the Garda Boat Club and myself. There can be no better company than policemen. They have seen it all. We yarned into the night.

Having braved fertiliser bags, old bicycle wheels and a spring mattress, all of which the twin screws unerringly attracted, we would reach the haven of Shannon Harbour, having eschewed the fleshpots of Tullamore, where a single portion of chicken and ham in the Bridge House was enough to feed a family.

Shannon Harbour is one of the most peaceful spots in Ireland, the ruined hotel, the same as the restored ones at Robertstown and Portobello, recalling the Grand Canal's glory. A dog barking in Shannon Harbour is an event, a cruiser arriving, high drama.

So far, I had cruised the *Saidé R* only in the canal where, if you exceed the limit of four knots, you build up a wall of water and damage the boggy banks. The first minutes on Shannon's broad stream, having descended the final canal lock, gave a glorious freedom. No more narrow banks, fertiliser bags and eternal vigilance. I pushed the *Saidé R* up to her maximum speed of 11 knots. The Volvo engines had plenty left in them but, from 11 knots on, the boat sat up and begged.

On the opposite bank of the river from Shannon Harbour is the entrance to the old Grand Canal-Ballinasloe line, long closed but now [2006] restored and with a new marina at Ballinasloe. We turned left, downstream, past the marina at Banagher, past Shannon Grove and on to Meelick Lock. Our first Shannon lock after the canal, it seemed huge. No skylarking here, we treated the lock-keeper with respect, did what we were told and fended off German tourists who steamed into the lock at full speed. From Meelick Lock to Portumna Bridge is pleasant – and dull. Portumna Bridge opens only at set hours, so we explored the little canal that runs past one of Uncle Arthur's two splendid marinas (the other is at Carrick) into Portumna's tiny harbour, where the only thing to do is turn round again (this is where the *Saidé R's* twin engines could show off) and get back to the

Shannon. Through Portumna Bridge, where the hired cruisers behaved as courteously as passengers boarding an aircraft, and on to Lough Derg.

In later years, I explored nearly all of the Shannon, but, when the bridge swung at Portumna, my heart swung with it. Once you have the freedom of that great lake, I could find little reason to go back upstream.

I shall draw a veil over our first crossing of Lough Derg, heading for Killaloe. On the reach between Hare and Scilly Islands, when you are heading due west, we ran into a gale funnelling down from Scarriff Bay, causing a confused sea. It was frightening, particularly as I did not know the boat's capabilities. It taught an enduring lesson: treat the Shannon lakes, especially Ree and Derg, with great respect, no matter how salty a mariner you fancy yourself.

The *Saidé R* is long since sold. About every second year when the kids were young, I would hire one of Uncle Arthur's beautiful but expensive craft, expensive, that is, unless five others share the cost – and our family rule was that, for seven people, you need an eight-berth cruiser, with father paying. Anyway, to hell with poverty. If you haven't woken up in Mountshannon on a clear, summer morning and sat in your pyjamas on the warm stone of the quayside and gazed out over Bushy and Cribby Islands, Holy Island and Scarriff Bay on your right, Garrykennedy and far Dromineer on your left, and then been called back to your boat by the smell of coffee and bacon, you haven't lived. And you're not going anywhere.

26

LIFELONG LEARNING: THE REPORT OF THE COMMISSION ON ADULT EDUCATION

We adapt to change by learning.

I was in London in October 1981 to give the opening address to a British Institute of Management Conference. The telephone rang in my hotel bedroom. An Irish voice asked politely whether I would take a call from the Minister for Education. John Boland, of Fine Gael, came through and invited me to chair a Commission on Adult Education. These were my last days in the IMI. The Government grant was getting shaky. I could not refuse a Government minister. I said "Yes" and we continued to chat affably. John Boland asked where I was. I said "London". He said, "Where are you staying?". This may well have been mischievous because I'm sure he knew. I said in a small voice, "Claridges" and added quickly, "As guest of the British Institute of Management". The Minister said, with a sigh, "You guys live well", and hung up.

The Commission was to be "an advisory body to prepare a national development plan for adult and continuing education". Submissions were invited.

The Commission first met on November 16, 1981. It met in plenary session 14 times, frequently over a two-day period. Subgroups met on 30 occasions. The last meeting of the Commission was on May 23 and 24, 1983. The Commission met in the IMI, where an office was also provided for the Secretary, Liam O'Connell from the Department of Education. Halfway through the Commission's work,

I retired from the Institute. I felt uncomfortable returning there to finish the job.

At our first meeting, ground rules were agreed that were to influence considerably the style of the Commission's work. The Minister had given wide terms of reference, a large and potentially unwieldy Commission, 30 members, and a deadline of slightly less than a year.

We agreed that the best should not be the enemy of the good and that we would strive for the deadline. We missed it, but not by too wide a margin.

We decided that, however difficult the process, all members of the Commission would be involved in writing the Report. At the first meeting, we agreed on priorities. Members then self-selected into sub-groups dealing with the priorities to which they could make the best contribution. My IMI training proved useful. (A cynical IMI specialist might say, "When you're stuck, break 'em into groups". However, it worked.) The plenary sessions, meetings of the whole Commission, were used to get agreement on the reports of these sub-groups. This tested us. Groups, and, in several instances, individuals who had given voluntary hours to preparing a report, were subjected to tough criticism. They willingly tried again. In the event, the Report represented the genuine consensus of a Commission composed of people of varied backgrounds and responsibilities, but who shared an abiding concern, the education of adults.

In our *Introduction*, we said:

> We reported at a time of uncertainty. Basic institutions were increasingly unable to command allegiance and obedience. The family was not the disciplinary power it had been in the past. The churches, faced with the problem of communicating their message to a world whose thought processes were changing, found their methods and structures under strain. The carriers of human tradition, the schools and the universities, were caught in uncertainty about the nature of truth and the selection of what was to be taught. The gap between political rhetoric and economic reality was leading to a loss of confidence in our leaders, in our institutions, and in ourselves: all this made more painful by a recent, artificial prosperity.

We said we could adapt to this changing world by learning. When change is the most significant feature of the age, the first demand of those who live through it is for adaptation, for understanding, for grasping the significance of what is happening to them and around them. If our rate of learning exceeds our rate of change, we adapt. If it does not, we fail.

Of old, the apparent stability of the world made it possible to divide life into two distinct parts. In the first one, the formation period, we were taught the knowledge and experience of our predecessors considered as an accumulated legacy. We learned rules of action for future situations, since these could be relied on to resemble situations in the past. In the second part of our lives, we were to face up to reality by means of this knowledge and this wisdom, transmitted by the voice of authority, enriched by our own values and our experience.

The acceleration of history changed all that. For decades, we had seen both individuals and institutions, prepared to function in a stable world, in fact function in another world, where the kinds of problems had changed completely from those with which they were taught to cope. Perhaps, in the end, we would run the film backwards and stop it at the point where we found something to our liking. More probable was that tomorrow would be so different from yesterday that an updating, a complement to previous education, would no longer be sufficient. What was needed now was permanent education, constant renewal for a world in constant ferment.

Our Report was not about night classes. It was about lifelong learning. Whatever the Report's imperfections, we hoped the Commission's concern was clear: that is, that adults would have, through continuing education, the opportunity for fulfilment as individuals, as members of a community, and as citizens of a free and democratic state.

As we neared the end of our work, two thoughts crossed our minds.

The first was that the condition of the public finances was such that a cold eye was likely to be cast on any suggestion of additional funds. Our immediate financial proposals were modest. Of more importance was the fact that, unless the Government set up a system through which policies and plans could be developed and with the participation of those who had to carry them through, even existing resources would be wasted: a hidden, costly process.

The second thought was expressed by Ken Galbraith:

> Nothing or not much ever happens in response to a report. Something happens only when someone obsessed by belief fights the proposal through.

We finished the Report in June 1983. In the short span of 21 months, we had four Ministers for Education: John Boland, Charlie Haughey for a day or two, Ger Brady for a month or two and, finally, Gemma Hussey to whom we presented the Report. She gave us a lunch in a hotel in O'Connell Street.

And nothing happened.

27

THE SOCIETAL STRATEGY PROJECT

Business reacts to societal pressures only as they occur.

As I write this, I have in front of me a beautifully printed report called *Facing Realities*. The project had 39 participants, who formed two groups, the Legitimacy Group, which I chaired, and the Capability Group. It was conducted over a two-year period under the joint auspices of the European Foundation for Management Development and the European Institute for Advanced Studies in Management, both in Brussels. We had a multinational group of academics and business managers, with three Irish participants: Dermot Egan of AIB, Louden Ryan of Bank of Ireland and myself. The project was under the overall direction of Igor Ansoff, a good friend from whom I learned much. He wrote the seminal *Implanting Strategic Management.*[25]

The origins of the study [1981] were a conviction that social and political pressures were reducing the time needed to concentrate on profit-making, consistent with much that has gone before and more that will come after in this book. The project set out to be a policy analysis rather than academic research. The work, it was claimed, was by its nature a reasoned judgment.

It concluded that, increasingly, business was an arena for the conflicts of economic, social and political influences and demands. And then, portentously, that only firms which recognised and behaved responsibly towards these competing demands would

---

[25]   ISBN: 013451808X.

survive and prosper; aloofness from, or the ignoring of, this were patterns of behaviour leading to the demise of profits.

I had spent much of the first half of my working life failing to get senior and successful businessmen to take a more active role in "societal strategy". As a result, I wonder if this elegant report had any influence at all, except on its authors.

There is no doubt that societal pressures are mounting. However, my experience is that business reacts to societal pressures as they occur. They don't develop an anticipatory strategy for, for example, the costly Sarbanes-Oxley. What follows is a table showing the 11 roles of the firm. Where would you place your organisation?

The Eleven Roles of the Firm

Type	Economic	Social	Political
Profit maximiser	Profit dominates	Regarded as an impediment to profit	Actively avoids involvement with political system
Profit satisfier	Growth dominates	Reacts against societal and social pressures as incursions	Avoids interaction with political system
Defender of free enterprise	The business of business is business	Reacts against social component as being not within firm's proper scope.	Stands up for "free enterprise"
Lone wolf	Prime emphasis on profit	Voluntarily, but unilaterally, assumes responsibility	Avoids involvement unless cornered
Societally engaged	Prime emphasis on profit	Interactively engaged	Engaged only in negotiation of the rules of the game
Societally progressive	Prime emphasis on profit	Interactively engaged	Positively involved in formulation of national industrial policies

Type	Economic	Social	Political
Global actor	Prime emphasis on profit	Interactively engaged	Assumes a responsibility to foster a balance between national and international economic policies
Developer of society	Financial self-sufficiency	Produces changes in the lives of mankind through innovation	Positively involved with emphasis on planned development of social infrastructures
Social servant	Secondary to societal obligations	Provides essential but non-economic goods and services	Positively involved in formation of national industrial policies, with emphasis on social matters
Employment provider	Subsidised operation	Provides jobs	Subsidised and supported by government
Impotent	Forced to be unprofitable because of stultifying rules of the game		

28

DEPARTURE AND ARRIVAL

I looked around. The street was empty. I let out a loud "Yahoo!"

The last two years in the IMI were the unhappiest in my working life. I had decided to retire at 50, which would have been April 1980.

We advertised the position widely and in advance, in a relatively austere ad. We got only 11 replies. Staff had been told that, if they applied, they would be automatically short-listed.

We set up a search committee. Mark Hely Hutchinson was then Chairman of the IMI and chief executive of Guinness. Ian Morrison was chief executive of Bank of Ireland and had been Chairman of the Institute in difficult times. We had Louden Ryan of Trinity and of Bank of Ireland to measure intellect, and myself.

We met in the beautiful old Guinness house, 98 James's Street, opposite the brewery. We would interview in the afternoon, then adjourn for dinner where we were joined by Dr. Pat Elliott, our adviser. He would already have given comprehensive psychological tests to the candidates but did not reveal the results to us lest they influence us before the interviews. Pat's invaluable advice saved us from some mistakes.

Since the ad did not produce anything and since – to my shame – none of my IMI colleagues was considered suitable, we decided to hire British search consultants. Highly recommended, they may have been good in London. For us, they were useless and expensive.

The search committee were depressed. I told them I would stay on until a successor was appointed. Then Tom Cox mentioned a cousin of his, Detta Ó Catháin (later Baroness Ó Catháin). She worked with the Milk Marketing Board in the UK and was close to Peter Walker, the Agriculture Secretary under Thatcher. She frequently appeared on British television. Notwithstanding the Irish version of her name, she spoke with a flawless upper-class English accent. She had started her working life in Aer Lingus, and married a pilot, Bill Bishop. Her father was Caoimhín Ó Catháin, a senior inspector with the Revenue Commissioners.

She agreed to go forward for the job. She was put through every hoop known to man (a) because she was a woman and (b) because she talked posh. She came through unscathed. She was intelligent, articulate, and determined.

The only time I could get the search committee together for her final interview was during the IMI National Conference in Killarney.

Heathrow closed. My secretary, Margaret Fulcher, was fully engaged in Killarney. I rang Mark Hely Hutchinson's secretary, Ann Dardis, in Dublin. Ann was a person for whom nothing was impossible. She it was who christened the head of the Guinness Group, Ernest Saunders, "Deadly Ernest". I asked her to get Detta to Killarney. She had one question, "Budget?". I said, "Just get her here". She came back to say Detta would arrive in Farranfore airport that afternoon. We had a car waiting. She arrived at the Great Southern Hotel unflustered. I asked her how the flight was. She said, "Interesting. The pilot looked down and asked whether I thought that was Farranfore".

She got the job. The sense of relief – of freedom – to me was immense. It was hard not to tell anybody until the contract was signed. Though, when I came out of the meeting, I ran into Sylvia Meehan, first Chairwoman of the Employment Equality Agency. She was the widow of Denis Meehan, one of my bosses in Radio Éireann and a valued mentor. I could not resist hugging her and telling her the next head of the IMI was going to be a woman.

Detta came over to sign the contract a week or so later. It was a Saturday evening. She and Bill were to have dinner with Maureen and myself. First, we looked at some houses. She was attracted by one at the corner of Herbert Park/Morehampton Road. Then we met for a drink with David and Una Kennedy. David, of Aer Lingus, had succeeded Mark as Chairman. In the Kennedy's living room, I turned to Detta and said, "But, Detta, you have not said 'Yes'". She said, "Oh yes" and David went to the kitchen to get a bottle of champagne.

The following day, Sunday, she was to come to my house at 3.00 pm to sign the contract. At 11.00 am, she rang me to say she had decided reluctantly not to accept the job. It was a short conversation. I commiserated, more with myself than with Detta.

With hindsight, she was right. The cultural break with the UK would be difficult enough. Coming back at chief executive level to a culture she had left as a junior would be even more difficult.

Around that time, I met Charles Handy casually at Dublin Airport. His sister, Ruth, was a psychologist on the IMI specialist staff. Charles, whose father was Dean of Kildare, said, "I heard you're leaving the IMI". I asked him if he'd do the job, even for a short time. He hesitated for a beat or two and then, almost reluctantly, shook his head. Would that he had said "Yes".

The search committee reconvened. It was like a wake, punctuated by empty silences. I turned to Mark: "Someone said to me you had a man named Patterson working with you".

I shall not forget the look of pain that crossed Mark's face. He looked down at the table and said in a low voice, "He could do it". Brian Patterson, working with Paddy Galvin, had succeeded in reducing the Guinness workforce by 1,000, where jobs were from cradle to grave. The exact moment when Brian got the job was when Mark said, "He could do it".

Brian went through due process and came to my home to agree terms. He was tough, had a quick intelligence and was a skilled negotiator. He got a good deal and a long contract. I was pleased with the difference between him and me. He would have seen himself as a mud-on-the-boots manager – a phrase he used – while I believe he would have seen me as academic. The Institute was in need of renewal and a fresh approach. My foot was not on the pedal those last two years.

I was sorry when Brian left after a five-year stint. Paddy Hayes had moved from Ford in Cork, which was closing, to be both chairman and chief executive of Waterford Glass. (Brian had met Paddy Hayes while he was Chairman of the IMI.) Paddy McGrath, the major shareholder, and Noel Griffin, the CEO, in the past had virtually abdicated to the powerful craft unions, leaving a difficult legacy. When the unions asked, the management added a dollar or two to the price of crystal in New York. Paddy Hayes needed help to sort out a situation that was out of control. Brian was ideal. He went initially to Waterford Wedgwood. He was joined by his old boss in Guinness, Paddy Galvin, who was appointed chief executive of Waterford Crystal. Brian was made managing director of Wedgwood in the UK, whence he returned to Ireland to become chairman of the board of *The Irish Times* and of the Financial Regulatory Authority, in which capacity he is also a director of the Central Bank. It does me good to see old IMIees do well when they leave the Institute.

Brian's successor in the IMI, Maurice O'Grady, was appointed with Feargal Quinn as chairman. Brian did not participate in the recruitment process.

There are arguments for and against this. *Against* is that the outgoing chief executive may be looking for an alter ego or, God forbid, someone who would not outshine him.

For, in the circumstances of the IMI, which had an honorary board that changed frequently, it would be unreasonable to exclude the advice of a chief executive of five years' standing.

Brian overlapped with me. I still occupied my tycoon-type office at the top of the building with a view of Howth. Brian occupied a more modest corner office on the ground floor. Three incumbents later, it's still the chief executive's office.

Dermot Ryan told me that, when he took over the archdiocese of Dublin in February 1972 from John Charles McQuaid, he had a half-hour handover.

I had planned a reasonably long hand-over to allow Brian to read himself in and to talk to every member of staff. I was wrong. Brian was keen to take the reins – and I was glad to give them to him.

On my last day, March 31, 1983, the staff gathered outside my office. Margaret brought me a final few letters to sign. I felt nothing. When I went out to meet the gathering, Brian made a graceful speech and presented me with silver – not before someone noticed the price-tag and quickly scratched it off. I said, "I'll miss you all", and departed.

Leaving behind the Council and members was a little more formal. The members had contributed to a parchment and a portrait by Edward McGuire. At the presentation, I was elected a Life Fellow of the Institute, an honour given sparingly. I cherish it.

Edward McGuire's studio was in a little house on Burdett Avenue, in Sandycove. He was one of our best portrait painters. I had seen his superb paintings of Paddy Molony of the Chieftains and of Willie Whitelaw. He would absent himself from the sitting for brief interludes and, I assumed, a Guinness. On his return, he would gently belch some fragrant fumes. On one occasion, he bent forward and the canvas fell on his nose, leaving a pink spot. He said it did not matter.

He was a most likeable fellow himself but he did not like Charlie Haughey at all. Charlie had commissioned some portraits, including equestrian ones, sideways on. He told Edward a particular portrait was fine but "Don't you think my leg is a little short?". "I have painted your leg exactly as it is, Mr. Haughey. I shall lengthen it. It will cost you a hundred pounds."

April 1, 1983, the day after I departed the IMI, I was walking down to the bank in Dundrum. That afternoon I was to be conferred with an honorary LlD by the National University of Ireland. The following day, I was to pick up a new Mercedes. I was to start a new life in UCD. I looked around. The street was empty. I let out a loud "Yahoo!"

*

At the end of the National Management Conferences, the most relaxed moment was lunch with the speakers. It was held in a private room in the Great Southern Hotel, Killarney. The hotel would have got its stock of Waterford crystal for the tourists and used it (just once) for our table. The lunch was always attended by the Taoiseach.

I was sitting beside Louden Ryan. I told him I was becoming engaged in this business representation thing, would like to get my thoughts clear and the best way to do that would be to write a book about it.

He said, "Why don't you come to Trinity and we'll make you a Research Fellow?".

I thought that would be good. I needed outside discipline.

We had another glass of wine and Louden said, "No. With your status, we'll make you a Senior Research Fellow".

By the time we reached the cheese, Louden looked across at Don Carroll and said, "We'll make you a Research Professor and get Don to fund the work".

That was April 30, 1977. On June 23, less than two months later, the Provost, Lee Lyons, announced the appointment and funding of £20,000 from Carrolls. The announcement attracted publicity. The appointment was to be concurrent with my job in the IMI. There was a picture in *The Irish Press* entitled "Coming and Going". I was to share an office with Martin O'Donohue, Professor of Economics. He had thoughtfully got himself elected to the Dáil, was appointed Minister for Economic Planning and Development, and left his office in the new Arts block all to myself.

Trinity was kind to me, even though the appointment was only part-time, contemporaneous with my IMI job. There were still many of the old values. It was nice to ramble across the cobbles to the Common Room and have coffee and a chat. I made friends.

*

September, 1980, I made a proposal to Bank of Ireland for a three-year study of the role of private enterprise in Ireland. It was based on four premises:

♦ That free enterprise was the most effective way to create wealth;

♦ That the future environment for free enterprise in Ireland would not be the same as the past;

♦ That free enterprise could be helped develop its freedom by a clearer view of its own role and of its relationship with other forces in society, particularly government;

♦ That firms would need new capabilities to deal with these forces.

Based on these foundations, it was proposed:

♦ To mount an objective study of the relationship between business and government in Ireland;

♦ To identify the points of conflict and of misunderstanding between business, government and other significant interest groups such as the trade unions and the media;

♦ To develop strategies for the private enterprise firm, consistent with its essential role of wealth creation and with its wider responsibilities;

♦ To identify and develop the capabilities required by the firm to implement these strategies;

♦ To identify activities now undertaken by the public sector that could be provided better by free enterprise.

While written studies would form the intellectual underpinning of the project, to have any practical effect it would require a continuing series of workshops for senior managers, both on their own and with other constituencies, such as politicians and trade unionists. It would require a continuing discreet relationship with bodies representing business and management. It would require access to individual firms to develop practical strategies, capabilities and case studies.

The project would begin on May 1, 1982, at a cost of £100,000 over three years.

On March 11, 1982, the Bank confirmed its agreement to fund the research.

On February 25 and March 11, two inspired articles appeared in *Business and Finance*. I enjoyed taking no telephone calls from the magazine, thus depriving them of the oxygen of facts. The result was the articles were a mixture of fact and fiction:

> Ivor Kenny has been nominated for a Senior Research Fellowship in Trinity. Not everyone welcomes the proposal. There are reports of strong dissension within the College. The nomination has been discussed at both faculty and council levels and in each case has resulted in a failure to reach a conclusion.
>
> The College will provide Kenny with two free offices in the new Arts Block. (The supply of offices seems to increase or decrease with the power of the applicant. The most recent occupants of new offices found themselves in a prefab in an uncongenial part of the College known as "the wilderness".)

John Bristow, the Dean, wrote to the Faculty:

> Having failed to convince us through the well-established
> procedures of open debate within College, an opponent of
> the appointment has now taken to the public press,
> presumably in the hope that Mr. Kenny, the Bank of Ireland
> or the College will withdraw through embarrassment at the
> publicity. As academics, we like to pride ourselves on
> subscription to the principle of conclusion through reasoned
> discussion. The informant for this article has publicly shown
> contempt for that principle and has brought disgrace on us
> all, most notably in the eyes of the rest of College.

The opposition came from Douglas Shingle McLernon, a lecturer in
economics.

Lee Lyons, a gentle historian, was Provost when I was originally
appointed. He was succeeded by Bill Watts, a robust botanist who
would have little sympathy with flower-power.

Meanwhile, I'd had a phone call from Tom Murphy, President of
UCD. He said, "Would you not like to be with your own?".

There was an echo of the time when, if you went to Trinity as a
Catholic, you would emerge with a cloven hoof. I recognised Michael
MacCormac's hand in the phone call. I asked Tom, "What about Bill
Watts?".

"Oh, I've been talking with him."

The welcome was warm, the Trinity affair unpleasant, the choice
was made.

I called Bill Watts, who was not surprised. He asked me not to
make any announcement until the Board had decided on the matter.
He told me the affair had consequences beyond my appointment. On
March 5, 1982, he wrote to me, unknown of course to *Business and
Finance*. He enclosed a minute of the Board's decision "without a
division". By then, the decision was irrelevant to me – but important
for Trinity, so as to maintain the Board's authority.

> I hope that you will now be in a position to accept the
> Board's offer and we look forward to hearing from you in
> due course. I regret that the matter has been to some extent
> controversial and particularly that controversy has to some

extent spread to outside the College. I think you understand that the officers of the College have at all times acted with goodwill and that we wish you a successful period of research over the next three years.

Basil Chubb, a distinguished Fellow of the College and Professor of Political Science, wrote to me:

I was astonished and saddened to learn that you had been harassed into choosing UCD in preference to us. I am so sorry. Nothing but ill can come of the whole episode.

There seems to have been little enough news in those days. The story made the front page of *The Irish Times* on St. Patrick's Day, 1982, supported by a factual article by Eoin McVey. I must have broken, at least to him, my vow of silence.

Tom Murphy asked what they would call me, Research Professor as in Trinity? I said, "I'm not going to go poncing around UCD with an honorary doctorate, no earned doctorate yet to my name, and be called 'Professor'. In any event, it would be a barrier between me and the business people I'll be dealing with – 'Professor Kenny is here to see you'".

We settled for Senior Research Fellow, a title that could do no harm to anyone.

Tom Murphy, a medical doctor, told outrageous stories at formal dinners in mixed company. He once met defeat. He was the tail-end Charlie at a Bankers' Dinner. His job was the dreary one of responding to the toast of the guests. He stood up to speak at 12 midnight. The dining room was steaming. Tom fought the buzz of inebriated conversation. But, in a dying fall, he said, "As the man sick of the palsy said to Christ, 'Christ, I'm sick of the palsy'".

Joe McHale was the Secretary and Bursar of UCD. Joe ran the College. If you misbehaved, an interview with Joe struck terror. I met from him kindness and concern, as I have met from Eamonn Ceannt, the present Bursar. On one occasion, my research fund was running low. I told Joe I would raise a personal overdraft. He said, "You will not. College will carry it".

Equally kindly was Pat O'Beirne, the Buildings Officer. Space (and car-parking) are at a premium in universities the world over.

What part of the nest they would put the cuckoo in caused concern. Pat tried to put me in Richview with the architects. They welcomed me, until they heard I was from the Commerce Faculty and then said not an inch.

Pat brought me to The Hut. The Hut is a temporary building, temporary since pre-history. It was full of delightful pre- and post-doc students in medical science. They laughed a lot. Pat showed me what was to me a huge room, a dirty old lab. He was embarrassed. All I could see was space beyond my dreams. Pat said, "We'll put a carpet in it for you".

It's where I've lived happily ever after.

Coda

However, before I left the IMI, I was concerned that the Institute in difficult times might go into survival mode. In fact, some years later, a virtue was made of necessity. The Government grant was shrinking anyway but the rhetoric was about sturdy independence. The State grant enabled the Institute to grow. But it had another important effect. It kept the Institute central, rather than peripheral, in the economy. Evidence for that was, for example, the amount of consultation with Government figures, from the Taoiseach down, in the proposal for the failed Confederation of Irish Business.

With difficulty, I persuaded Mark Hely Hutchinson to head up a fund to be used for R&D. With difficulty, because Mark kept sending back to me drafts of a case statement for the fund. He was right, because at last, when he was persuaded, we could venture forth with enthusiasm and with some success.

I have been fundraising all my working life. At Trinity, the case statement had in it Uncle Tom Cobbley and all. Academics will do anything for money. They contributed their ideas variously and enthusiastically to the case statement. A case statement is the answer to the question, "What do you want the money for?". Trinity's was a mess. I suggested no one would give money for it, but they would for *Trinity* undiluted. It was agreed and it worked.

The same principle of fund-raising applied to Maynooth. Michael Olden, the President, came to see me in Sandyford. He told me he had got half the funding for a new library. He now wanted to raise the other half. I suggested half a library was not an attractive proposition but he could well raise the funds for *Maynooth*, pure and simple. They were changing times and Maynooth stood for something solid. I told him he also needed professional fundraisers, to which the bishops had some aversion. The professionals would work with a committee, the members of which had to be substantial donors.

We were fortunate to get Niall Crowley, Chairman of AIB, to head the committee. He never took "No" for an answer. Meeting in the splendid boardroom in AIB gave us confidence.

29

THE NORTHERN IRELAND MANAGEMENT INSTITUTE

*The distinction is not between the public and the private sectors. The
distinction is between what different people actually do.*

Every now and then in my time with the IMI, somebody would get a
rush of blood to the head and advocate the amalgamation, merger or
takeover of the Institute. I had that same rush of blood to my own
head in the proposal for the Confederation of Irish Business (**Chapter
9**). It failed, as other such proposals did.

The first proposal was for the IMI to merge with the embryo
Institute of Public Administration. As I mentioned earlier, the IMI
Council threw it out, just before I joined in 1959. On another
occasion, Richie Ryan, as Minister for Finance, thought a merging of
facilities would bring economies to two institutions getting
Government funding, the IMI and the IPA. Neither I nor Tom
Barrington, Director of the IPA, wanted that and nothing came of it. I
spent a lot of time fending off more subtle encroachments on our
territory (see also **Chapter 30**).

The Institute's shield and buckler in these forays was its
membership. It was owned and controlled by those it served, and
answerable to them.

I confided once to Tom Barrington that I did not know why we
held an annual conference. Tom said, "It's a show of strength". I had
no more doubts.

However, shields and bucklers are not much use if what goes on
behind them does not anticipate and meet needs that no one else
meets, or meets as well, or meets in the same way.

These were the thoughts when I agreed in 1983 to advise the Northern Ireland Economic Council on the setting up of a Northern Ireland Management Institute. The British Institute of Management presence in the North was vestigial. Business studies in the universities had not developed.

I worked with Sir Charles Carter, Chairman of the Council, Leslie McClements, the director, and Gerry Loughran, Assistant Secretary in the Department of Economic Development, from whom the initiative came. (Now Sir Gerry, he eventually headed the Northern Ireland Civil Service.)

The commitment of Government to the development of managers gave us some optimism. It provided an opportunity, which might not readily recur, to develop a focal leadership centre that could make a contribution to Northern Ireland's economic and social development.

There was a consensus among both users and providers of management education that a centre was needed. There were different views about what kind of centre that might be, influenced by whether the views came from the providers or the users.

A new centre would not be worth considering if, as was suggested by some, its purpose were merely to add to existing institutions or to "co-ordinate" their activities, the latter an impossibility without powerful muscle. There was agreement that there was a need for a leadership initiative.

I defined leadership as an institution that could encourage, facilitate and accelerate the development of managers.

It required the creation, through a membership function, of an identifiable community of Northern Irish managers, committed to the continuous improvement of their work.

It required the provision of management development services of a quality that met the complexities of the problem and the seriousness of the need.

I was concerned that these pure objectives could get buried, as they did in Canada, under special interest job protection. (See also **Chapter 20**.)

What distinguishes organisations, one from the other, is not mission statements, or branding, or speeches from the chief executive, it is what they do. If organisations really believed that, they would avoid the pitfall of believing their own propaganda.

When I set out on the study, there was a suggestion that one institution could help solve the problems of both business management and public administration.

That's worth knocking on the head once and for all – until it surfaces again, which it does. (See also **Chapter 30**.)

For the purposes of management development, the distinction is not between the public and the private sectors. The distinction again is between what different people actually do: on the one hand, central and local government officials at administrative level, whose primary duty is policy analysis and advising elected representatives, and, on the other, managers primarily in the market sector. (The market sector is that in which sellers obtain revenue as a result of voluntary decisions by buyers about how they will spend the money at their disposal. It is not necessarily synonymous with the private sector.)

The arguments advanced for having a single institution are:

♦ First, there are many market sector techniques that could be used to advantage in public administration.

♦ Second, there is a gulf of misunderstanding between public officials and market sector managers. This leads to conflict and waste. A single institution, in which both could discuss common problems, away from negotiating or supplicant circumstances, could increase mutual understanding and avoid waste.

♦ Third, Northern Ireland in particular was too small to support two centres with the necessary critical mass of staff. Putting the market sector and public administration together would give a population sufficient to support that critical mass (and an institution of a size sufficient to attract a chief executive of calibre).

First, a management centre is an institution of adult learning. Adults do not learn much from what they are told. They learn a lot from what they do. Unlike the more traditional institutions of learning, where, to an extent, knowledge is imparted with the voice of authority to pre-experience students, a post-experience (or experience-based) centre draws out, builds on, and synthesises the experiences of seasoned practitioners. Its teaching/learning effort must be relevant to those experiences. This limits the opportunity for training together market sector managers and public officials. While they share some areas of mutual interest, their experiences are different. They serve different masters and purposes under different constraints. They operate in different organisation cultures. They need different kinds of knowledge. They have differing degrees of personal accountability.

The skills they share are important: for example, human relations skills or project appraisal techniques. But the differences outweigh the similarities. The similarities are not, of themselves, sufficient on which to build a management development institution.

The second argument is that both sectors could benefit from events in which they could come together and share views. That is not a sufficient basis either on which to build a management centre. It is not its main function. (It might be an attractive idea if there were unlimited resources: both sectors could come together, in, say, an institute for strategic studies, to discuss broad issues. That was not the subject of the study.)

Third, the "critical mass" argument does not hold. A "critical mass" means a professional staff sufficient to cover the requisite range of homogeneous skills and disciplines across the (market sector) management spectrum. While a very large business population – for example, that served by the London or Manchester Business Schools or by Ashridge College – would require a large professional staff, even a very small population, like Northern Ireland, still required an essential minimum. That business population is not extended by adding to it public officials who require specialised skills and knowledge.

Finally, mixing public administration and the market sector would give the new institution a blurred image and make unnecessarily difficult the key task of creating a supportive, identifiable community of Northern Ireland managers.

If the Northern Ireland Management Institute was deliberately designed and organised to serve both public administration and the market sector, it would do neither well.

We got agreement on the characteristics and capabilities of a leadership institution:

♦ A clear, unambiguous, attractive and attainable objective.

♦ A unique focus and competence – the market sector.

♦ The capacity to command the respect and commitment of managers – from its membership base and from the quality and relevance of its work.

♦ A development capability – otherwise, it would simply reinforce current practice.

♦ Linkages with Government and other providers.

♦ Linkages with the rest of the world, through, for example, membership of the European Foundation for Management Development.

♦ A capacity to evaluate its own performance.

♦ A size and lifestyle reflecting the reality of resources in Northern Ireland, so that it was not accused of empire-building and alienating its constituencies.

These characteristics and capabilities are as relevant today as they were in a different world in 1983.

Following extensive consultation, the detailed recommendations on structure, governance, staff and funding were accepted both by the Council and by the Department of Economic Development.

A Board was appointed under the chairmanship of Charles Carter. I was glad to be invited to join and to meet there an old friend, Ron McCulloch, a Scot and head of C&C in Belfast.

Our first job was to appoint a chief executive. We were not knocked down in the rush. I was out of the country for the final interviews. Charles called me to say they had a candidate of whom he was not certain. I reminded him of the unbreakable rule in selection: if in doubt, do nowt. Charles was impatient. He may have wanted to return to his university in England. An appointment was made. The Board met a few times. The Northern Ireland Management Institute never really got started. Other interests sensed the weakness and gathered strength.

For an institution to succeed, the time must be ripe, the conditions must be right, and you need a strong, focused and politically-witful chief executive – "if you know the enemy and know yourself, you need not fear the result of a hundred battles" (Sun Tsu). For the

Northern Ireland Management Centre, the first condition was there. The second and third were not.

30

THE ADVISORY COMMITTEE ON MANAGEMENT TRAINING

The IMI had lost its centrality.

The surest sign that the IMI had lost its centrality was the setting up by the Minister for Labour, Bertie Ahern, July 1987, of the Advisory Committee on Management Training. The Minister said, "The challenge for the Committee was to identify whether we can fashion a coherent system for the development of Irish managers that would be respectable [sic] and far-reaching, providing for the achievement of standards equivalent to those which we rightly expect from those engaged in the well-established professions". Which ones – medicine, law?

The Committee was to examine the cost-effectiveness of existing management training; to identify deficiencies; to advise on co-ordination and rationalisation; and, ominously, "to have regard to the need to minimise State expenditure", a *non sequitur* in the light of its qualitative, comparability, task.

The Committee of 17 consisted of four civil servants, including the secretary, two State company managers, two academics, the head of the CII, one trade union official, three private consultants – two of whom were accountants, and four private sector practising managers. The IMI was represented by its (part-time) Chairman, Howard Kilroy, then President of the Jefferson Smurfit Group. Three members of the Committee had worked in the IMI. They included Brian Patterson, who had been Director General two years previously, and Liam Connellan, Director General of the CII.

There were several submissions by other bodies but I can find no record of one from the IMI.

The Committee were well-served in their Chairman, Paddy Galvin, then Operations Director, Guinness Ireland, before joining Waterford Crystal. Paddy was also a former President of the Federated Union of Employers.

The first recommendation the Committee made was:

♦ That the need to increase the level of commitment to management development be adopted as an urgent national priority and that Government and business aim to improve the situation significantly within three years. This should be achieved through effective, high-profile promotion, spearheaded by an Action Group for Management Development. The Action Group's over-riding objective should be the promotion of management development to decision-makers in both the private sector and the public service. This Group should be conceived deliberately as a short-life entity, with a definite time-span for completing its task.

This ran into the sand, as did the following two recommendations. They recommended:

♦ That a set of Guidelines for Management Development drawn up by the Committee be endorsed and promoted to Irish management as a code of good practice;

♦ That providers of business education should offer a broadly common curriculum.

More pointedly, they recommended:

♦ That State funding in the public service and the private sector be redirected from the present support of provision of management training, to the support of users and activities that will ensure the more efficient realisation of national objectives. That all direct funding by the State to providers for the provision of post-experience management training should be phased out over a period of three years.

This gave legitimacy to the phasing out of direct State support for the IMI (but not for its customers).

The Committee also recommended:

◆ That the management training activities of the IMI and the IPA should be integrated.

◆ Areas of common ground between the IMI and the IPA should be identified.

◆ A practical proposal to integrate these common activities be implemented within three years.

In the chapter on the Northern Ireland Management Institute (**Chapter 29**), I said that business management and public sector management are two different *markets*. For a Report that wanted market- rather than supplier-driven management development, these last recommendations were a classic *non sequitur*. It reinforces a suspicion that a prime motivation in setting up the Committee was "rationalisation" and its consequence, reduced government expenditure. Anyway, nothing happened as a result of the recommendations. It is a mystery why members of the Committee who knew the IMI well and, indeed, the IMI representative, acquiesced in this moth-eaten proposal.

However, there are good things in the Report, though it would be hard now to pick up a copy.

There is a graceful tribute to Charles Handy of the London Business School and to myself of UCD, "who provided a valuable input, particularly in regard to future scenarios for managers". I cannot for the life of me remember anything I said about future scenarios. I remember well, however, that I enjoyed the meeting, that I said they would enjoy the work, that they would learn from one another and that nothing would happen.

Paddy Galvin gave me a lovely Wedgwood bowl.

31

INTERLUDE: INDIA

January 12, 1972, Maureen and I arrived in Delhi on an Air India flight. Cabin crew in saris, easily the most beautiful woman's attire – especially on beautiful women. Met at the airport by our old friend, Paul Dole. We were to stay with him and Paddy, his wife, from the Canadian embassy. (Paddy, in time, held a number of ambassadorial posts.) Paul drove us in his Volkswagen to their home in a diplomatic neighbourhood near the Red Fort. The Volkswagen had an automatic horn. When you turned left, it sounded loudly.

I had come at the invitation of the All-India Management Institute and the Indian Social Institute to consult with them and to give a number of lectures.

We had just about time to shower after the long flight when we went to the Irish embassy for lunch with the Ambassador, Val Iremonger, a distinguished poet and author.

The embassy was a splendid building with a splendid garden. Lunch was served on the lawn. The *pièce de résistance* was a whole salmon carried on a tray on his shoulder by an embassy steward. A huge black kite flew down, claws extended, to snatch the salmon. The steward waved it away nonchalantly.

Before lunch, Val had closeted me in a small dark room with a stunning Indian journalist from *The Statesman*. She asked me all sorts of questions, including whether I had ever written poetry (I had). I would have told her anything.

Her column in the paper the following day began: "The President of India and Mr. Ivor Kenny have one thing in common: the two of them went to University College, Dublin. While the President was thrown out for political activities, Mr. Kenny wasn't".

Val brought us to meet the President, V.V. Giri. A wonderful drive up the Raj (King's) Path to the magnificent Presidential Palace, designed by Edwin Lutyens. Val sat in the ambassadorial car "behind the flag". We were greeted at the Palace by a Sikh officer in red and blue dress uniform. Giri received us in a large room. We sat on a sofa. He sat in an armchair. He talked at some length about his student days in Dublin at the time of the Troubles.

My attention wandered. In a corner of the room, which was heavily carpeted, a family of mice were playing happily.

Giri gave me a small paperback of his writings. When I sensed we were coming to the end of our visit, I produced a copy of Breffni Tomlin's book on the management of Irish industry. It was calf-bound in a silk slip-case. I said, "Your Excellency, this is the first study ever of the standard of management in a country. The Irish Management Institute would be privileged if you would accept it". He looked at the presentation, took the book out of the slip-case and said, "This is for me?". He picked up the phone and said, "Bring me in the other book, the good one", and presented me with a silk-bound copy of his thoughts.

I worked with the All-India Management Association. I gave my first talk to the Delhi Management Association the day after my arrival. Val Iremonger was kind enough to join the platform party. Jet-lag had kicked in. I'm sure I wandered a bit. My Indian colleagues were far too polite to pass remarks.

The next stop was way down south in Madras in Tamil Nadu, where I walked on a deserted golden beach. I talked to the Madras Management Association about small business management development, pioneered in Europe by the IMI's Chris Park. Proprietors of small businesses don't need courses, they need hand-holding, especially approaching the bank manager.

Next was a lunch meeting with the Public Relations Society of India – a huge poster outside the hotel door with my name on it. Madras had a staff college. I was sitting beside the commander of the college, a full general. The Indian Army had just defeated the Pakistan Army. I said, "General, I don't quite know what to say to a general who's won a war. Congratulations or well done ...?". He answered in perfect Sandhurst English, "Mr. Kenny, it wasn't that we were any good. They were just bloody awful."

Some of the Indian states were dry. Val Iremonger provided me with a brown paper bag of liquor before I set out. As we said goodbye, he asked if I knew anyone in Foreign Affairs. I said I knew the Secretary, Hugh McCann (I was to succeed him on the board of Independent Newspapers) and his American wife, Virginia. Val said, "Would you ask them, please, to respond to some of my letters?".

My guide on the tour was Joe Britto of the Indian Social Institute. I said to him that everywhere I went I was shown the good side of things. I would like to see one of the poorer places. Joe gave me an old-fashioned look and said, "Are you sure?".

We drove some kilometres out of Madras to what I would call a shanty town, but it was more than that. The hovels stretched literally as far as the eye could see. Out of them would come sari-clad women looking, to me anyway, immaculate. The impact was gut-wrenching but more than the sight was the stench. I understood for the first time that you have to smell poverty. Joe looked at me closely. I could not say anything. We came back to the hotel. Joe asked me if I'd like some of Val's whisky. I sat on the side of the bed and burst into tears. The image hit me again, when on our return, we drove from Dublin Airport through O'Connell Street. It was a damp night. I thought how sleek the place looked. With time, that feeling faded.

I'm not sure how I ended up in Bangalore in Mysore on my way back to Bombay (Mumbai). I visited a convent of nuns, many of them Irish. They were so attentive. I could have gone on forever telling them about home.

During a break in Bombay, I walked along the seafront, the gateway to India. I had never seen a snake-charmer. I paid my rupee and the snake-charmer began to play his flute or whatever at a basket in which I could see a black snake. The snake did not budge. The snake-charmer gave the basket a kick. The snake still did not budge.

When Indians are agreeing with you, they waggle their heads where we nod. On my very last workshop in Bombay, I was in a small hot room with green distempered walls on which geckos darted. A very rich Indian gentleman who had a large family business had brought with him his son to listen to the Irish guru. As I was talking, he was waggling his head sympathetically. I said, "You are agreeing with me, Mr. Patel?". "Oh yes, Mr. Kenny, I am agreeing with you." I asked, gently, I hope, "What are you agreeing with, Mr.

Patel?". "What we need is more human relations." "What would you mean by human relations, Mr. Patel?". "Nobody will do what I tell them".

In India, the workers had an effective ultimate sanction, a *gherao*. They would surround the factory and not let the bosses out until they capitulated: a lock-in rather than a lock-out.

At a party, I sat beside a tall handsome Sikh (they were all tall and handsome). I asked him to explain to me the Hindu religion. He was telling me some of the rules and shook his tall Scotch and soda glass while he said, "We don't drink."

Back to Delhi to rejoin Paul and Paddy Dole and Maureen for a few days' leisure. Paul insisted that I get a silk jacket tailored overnight. The raw silk and the silk lining and the tailoring cost at most 15 rupees. I also got some hand-made shoes. Neither the shoes nor the jacket fitted but sure you couldn't be cross with them. However, I got for Maureen some beautiful sari silk that made a smashing skirt. Paul brought us to a small jeweller's shop. The jeweller strew diamonds on a velvet cushion. He told us his last customer was Jackie Kennedy, which Paul told us was true. When we discussed price and he mentioned astronomical sums, he saw we were not in the same league as Mrs. Kennedy.

I bought Maureen a lovely amethyst and silver necklace. Years later, she had hardly worn it and decided to have it broken up to give the amethysts to our offspring. We found they were purple glass.

Nothing could sour our memories of India. On my desk is a book *Discovering Dainik Jagran's India. Dainik Jagran* is a newspaper published in eight Indian states. Independent News and Media have just taken a substantial stake.

On the book's cover, the President of India, A.P.J. Abdul Kalam is quoted: "It's a nation that is one of the best places to live in on this earth and that brings smiles on a billion faces".

32

THE END OF IDEOLOGY?
CAPITALISM AND
STATE SOCIALISM

The most unreported fact of our era is the death of socialism.

\- Daniel Bell, 1919-

An ideology is a total system of thought: political, social, cultural, economic, religious, personal. It effects to move not only the minds but also the hearts of men. It is all-embracing. Its most stirring example was the *Communist Manifesto* (1848).

The dominant political ideology in Ireland is a woolly sort of socialism. Solzhenitsyn described socialism as:

> A vague, rosy notion of something noble and good, of equality, communal ownership, and justice: the advent of these things will bring instant euphoria and a social order beyond reproach.

Variants of socialism are the oldest and most common way of organising society: the majority of states in the history of mankind have been socialist. It has been studied by legions of thinkers and propagandists. Books on it are numbered in thousands.

On the other hand, democratic capitalism which, basically, seeks to allocate resources and distribute output through the economic process, that is, markets, has attracted few philosophers and humanists. Most of those who treat of it have been economists. It means a triple system of liberty: economic liberty, political liberty and liberty of spirit. Only a handful of nations in history have found their way to a three-fold system – an *economic* system, a *political* system and a *moral* system – that institutionalises such liberties.

Socialists usually talk about an ideal society. In this way, socialism exerts its powerful attraction. By contrast, the inadequate statement of the ideal of democratic capitalism, neglected by philosophers and humanists, leaves a vacuum.

My answer is that, at all times, but particularly in changing times, our first obligation is to think clearly.

There are advantages in concentrating on immediate, practical tasks, in being concrete, in compromising, in working with a certain flexibility. But deliberately to neglect the entire battlefield of ideas and appeals to the human spirit (and to leave them only to the partisans of State Socialism) is deliberately to make clear thinking impossible.

Unless we take account of, and make explicit, the ideologies that underlie the conduct of our affairs, we cannot understand the choices made.

We need to ask ourselves the question: with which economic system is democracy compatible?

In traditional and non-democratic social societies, the social order is unitary. One authority is granted powers over political, economic and moral matters. In fully differentiated societies, these three systems are kept distinct, autonomous, inter-dependent but separate. Capitalism ranks high among "the despised and abject" things of this world (Isaiah 53). There are many reasons for this.

First, capitalism, like all rival systems, has many faults, distortions and ill effects. Second, it lacks a theory, in particular a moral theory.

In the third place, the intellectual history of capitalism suffers from internal flaws and sources of distortion. The theory of capitalism was first developed in the Anglo-Saxon intellectual context of individualism and utilitarianism. In some ways, this context favoured economists. But it led to serious misunderstandings among humanists.

The distinctive social organism produced by capitalism is not individualistic at all. It is a corporate organism, the business firm. In addition, the inherent end of capitalism is not the well-being of the individual. It is the means of the well-being of all persons.

Capitalism has been transformed beyond the bounds of individualism, utilitarianism and social Darwinism. It is now a practice in urgent need of a theory. It is a primary responsibility of businessmen, who are the activists of capitalism, to help develop that theory, so that reformers might lead the system to a fulfilment of the original dream of liberty, equality and justice. If the activists do not develop that theory, it seems unlikely that anyone else will. The ensuing vacuum is filled, *faute de mieux*, by the State and the ideology of State Socialism.

If it is a typical mistake to think of capitalism as an economic system only, it is, analogously, a typical mistake to think of an economic system apart from its political and moral dimension. In real life, each one of us is an economic agent. But each is also a citizen. Each of us seeks a God, follows conscience and the pursuit of truth and understanding. Human beings are simultaneously economic animals, political animals, moral animals. It is useful to distinguish in order to unite.

A healthy democracy depends on a balance of powers and their separation: executive, legislative, judicial. So does a healthy social order depend on a separation of systems: political, economic and moral. As it happens, different personalities are commonly attracted to each of these different systems. Each type develops an interest in checking the other two. Poets, priests and philosophers cherish no excess of admiration for businessmen or politicians, and the reverse.

There is no such thing as "economic man". No economic system lives in a vacuum apart from a political and moral system.

Throughout history, most economic systems were relatively stagnant. Few showed sustained growth. All experienced cycles of prosperity and famine. The very concept of sustained economic development was lacking.

In order for it to become possible, individuals had to believe they could improve their own economic position. They needed liberty, they needed law and stability, they needed patterns of social co-operation, they needed systems of long-term accounting, they needed new institutions in which risks could be shared. They needed to be willing to defer present gratification, to invest and to work for future rewards. They needed to be able to concentrate on small savings and small gains, cumulatively recorded.

I believe the deepest problem capitalism faces is its estrangement from moral values. Wealth is created (or is not created) in accord with, and through, the expression of a particular set of values. The divorce of capitalism from the moral order results in the kind of demoralisation that faces businessmen today. The essence of the problem with Irish private enterprise is that it has no clear view of itself, no vision of the future, no articulated ideology.

Faced with hostile ideologies (of which the archetype is State Socialism), it has to fall back on a purely circumstantial defence.

Businessmen are particularly apt at neglecting this truth. Ideas do have legs. Businessmen cannot dismiss ideological debate as academic froth or idle intellectualising, remote from the real and serious business of making money. In a world of instantaneous mass communication, the balance of power has shifted. Ideas, always a part of reality, have today acquired power greater than that of reality. In previous generations, taking its moral inheritance for granted, democratic capitalism felt no acute need for a moral theory about itself. The age of such innocence has passed.

The glaring inadequacies of actual socialist societies do not seem to discourage new-born socialists. Entire nations, in Africa and Latin America, cast themselves over the precipice like Gadarene herds.

Socialists are eloquent about visions of the future. Yet they seem nostalgic and wistful about political and economic institutions. They are hostile to capitalism, but vague about future economic growth. Their strength lies in the moral system, their weakness in political and especially economic analysis. This weakness no longer seems to be innocent.

State Socialism now seems to me incoherent. It is consistent with democracy only where large components of democratic capitalism remain. The issue of planning, for example, no longer divides socialists from democratic capitalists. But what the content of planning should be still divides them. The debate is, first, about the nature of the state (the limits of politics) and, second, about the degree of independence best left to economic agents.

Capitalism is far more social in character than its enemies – or its friends – have yet grasped. The growth of trade unions, of collective management, of profit-sharing and pension schemes has been implicit in the ethos of capitalism from the beginning. They may have been won through struggle, but they were won in relative peacefulness, because they were inherent in capitalism's inner logic.

For example, when a wage contract is a voluntary exchange, both parties to it are entitled to renegotiate it constantly. The original historical weakness of the position of labour was bound, over time, to become a position of strength, at least where there was "full" employment. The idea of contract remains intact, even as the contract becomes more favourable to labour.

Democratic capitalism is neither the Kingdom of Heaven nor without sin. Yet all other known systems of political economy are worse. Such hope as we have for economic growth, for alleviating poverty and for standing against an oppressive state lies in this much despised system.

A never-ending stream of immigrants and refugees seeks it out. The majority, who stay behind, in fear and frustration, find the socialist message of Utopia-tomorrow attractive, if only because they hear no other message.

Businessmen, who could be the activists, the champions, of capitalism, fall back on "pragmatism", on "knowing how things work". Their pragmatism, divorced from any moral basis, fails to move hearts and minds other than their own. They end up talking to themselves or, even less heroic, keeping their heads down.

There is a palpable moral vacuum in Ireland today. I am not suggesting that it should be filled with capitalist slogans. But what businessmen are guilty of is of marketing a good product – democratic capitalism – poorly. The sound from their trumpet is not only uncertain, it can hardly be heard.

A decade ago, Francis Fukuyama wrote *The End of History*.[26] By that, he meant that liberal western ideology had triumphed, and ideological disputes were therefore at an end. In his latest book, 2006, *After the Neocons*,[27] the US is embroiled in Iraq, faces hostile régimes in Iran and Palestine, has no clear strategy for North Korea and has lost in its own back yard with country after country in Latin America swinging to a socialist philosophy. History did not die.

*

---

[26] ISBN: 0743284550.
[27] ISBN: 1861979223.

In the *Sunday Independent,* May 11, 1986, I wrote:

> A recent leader in *The Economist* said that governments, stock markets and motorists were right to celebrate the new era of cheap energy. "But", it continued, "the revellers need also to remember an old saw: that the time to repair the roof is when the sun is shining."
>
> No serious person now questions the fact that the roof is leaking. The level of taxation pushes inexorably upwards, well past the margin of tolerance, and is accompanied inevitably by a rising level of unemployment.
>
> Until we get off that particular push, there is little hope that we shall have the energy to do anything as structural as fixing the roof, however bright the sun may shine.
>
> Despite growing cynicism about the purposes and performance of government, people go on demanding that it do more and more. Government departments do not normally sell their services to people at market prices. They provide them free or at less than cost. They compel people to pay for them indirectly, through taxation. There is no certainty that they provide the amount of service – health, education, security or roads – that people would wish to pay for, if they could express their preferences through personal choice rather than through taxation.
>
> Elections, in the form of a ballot paper marked once every three to five years, are a blunt and ineffectual instrument.
>
> Our system of proportional representation using the single transferable vote is, perhaps, the best that has been devised. It still does not enable voters to express continuous personal preferences for more of one government service and less of another.
>
> If it did, it is doubtful if we would, albeit involuntarily, have allowed government expenditure to rise to two-thirds of our national output. Even that avalanche was not enough to choke the rise. In 1985, government spending was a third higher than government income.

One result is that the total of the pounds painfully extracted from us in PAYE is not sufficient to pay even the interest on our national debt. In other words, those pounds are dead. They were spent long ago. They are not available for investment, for growth, for jobs. They are merely keeping the bailiff from the door. And the sharp fall in energy prices will not change that.

It may seem churlish in this month of May, and when we do have some good news for a change, to remind ourselves of these bleak facts, but we have a great capacity for self-delusion. For at least 10 years, from the early '70s, we lived in Disneyland.

We lived beyond our means, borrowed abroad to pay for public and private consumption and juggled public spending plans to meet the demands of political expediency. It was like bailing water into a sinking ship. Oil price increases, combined with militant wage demands and surging interest rates on top of a fragile international trading position, created the kind of recession with which government could not cope and has not yet coped.

With each passing budget, we are taxed, directly or indirectly, more heavily: a 12% increase in income tax alone for 1986 compared with 1985. But things do not seem to be getting any better as a result of our involuntary sacrifices. It is hardly remarkable, therefore, that there is disenchantment with the political process. More significant is the fact that we may at last be catching up with the new conservative trend in most Western countries, a turning away from government intervention.

What has been clear for some time in those countries is that, when we assign to government an ever-greater proportion of our income, we are on a road that leads to an economy that is no longer consistent with democratic government.

We are too ready to suppose that democratic government is secure.

Democracy is not inevitable. We live in a small minority of states where it is the rule. It rests on an economic foundation. It may be strengthened or destroyed through the choice of economic policy. The policies we are choosing are tending in the wrong direction away from democracy, from a system of plural choice, and towards state socialism.

"Men can always be blind to a thing so long as it is big enough", says Chesterton. One of the things most of us are blind to is the politicisation of man. This does not strike the State socialist as particularly sinister. If he notices it at all, he thinks it is a good thing: the radicalisation of the masses. After all, he is a thoroughly politicised man, and isn't all of life essentially political anyway? Isn't it up to us to decide what sort of society we are going to build, what sort of laws and morals and distribution of wealth we are going to have? He is too busy making war on poverty to think of making his peace with prosperity: if the real economy does not spread wealth as quickly and evenly as he would like, he blames it and tries to remake it, taking no responsibility, however, for the adverse results of his efforts.

A distinguished Irish economist, Louden Ryan, has written: "They who make the ground barren blame the grass for not growing".

The economy, they think, has failed, private enterprise has failed, the family has failed, the church has failed, the whole world has failed. But their visions have never failed, no matter what their costs.

As Burke said of the French revolutionaries: "In the manifest failure of their abilities, they take credit for their intentions".

The ideologue puts himself in the position of privileged accuser, always judging, never judged. The structure of his rhetoric is: heads I win, tails you lose.

This sort of thinking, if that is quite the word we want, is really the detritus of ideology, a few tricky habits picked up from the rhetoric of Marx, a slippery way of commuting from the specific to the general, the voicing of the question *cui bono* to wrongfoot the conservative capitalist.

State socialists have succeeded brilliantly in controlling the perspective from which public discussion is conducted. They occupy in Ireland the high ground. They speak piously of Left and Right, only for the tactical purpose of consigning their critics to the Right. This weary image of Left and Right conveys very little and indirectly expresses the perspective of the Left itself. We speak of right and left wings because it serves the purposes of the Left that we should do so.

There is a naïve and excusable form of State socialism.

Its best motive is a disillusionment with the world as it is, a world of contention in which there is both surplus and need. The naïve mind sees capitalism as anarchy, unbridled competition, in which desire distorts the pattern of distribution. It reasons that the earth is abundant enough to provide for everyone, but that the price system prevents the equal satisfaction of universally-felt needs. Supply follows demand. Control demand, and supply will reach its proper recipients.

What this view overlooks is that a price system itself is a way of taming desire. A price is the point of agreement between buyer and seller. The naïve socialist imagines an abstract humanity in which all desires are more or less identical, and people produce more or less steadily, without such various motives as status, revenge, worship, lust, envy – all the things that make the world so messy. The socialist is obsessed with only one motive, greed. He fails to see that more random motives are here to stay.

Those who seek power have a natural interest in creating dependency on themselves. It was written of that wiliest of statesmen, Bismarck:

In seeming tender to the welfare of individuals, State socialism works above all for the State. The great political realist knew what he was about. He saw that the State, by accustoming the citizen to turn to it to beg of it a law, binds himself to it in bonds of dependence and subjection.

He saw clearly that the State, as State, strengthens its hold by what looks like concessions.

State socialism works by incremental measures: progressive taxation, redistributive measures of a piecemeal sort, regulations in the use of private property, inheritance taxes.

Its *modus operandi* is to anaesthetise its victims. It does not seize property: it prefers to intercept wealth at the transmission points, so that the owner's loss is regularised and made painless.

It makes good use of inflation, which drives the mass of the employed population into higher tax bands without the necessity for tax increases: and since inflation makes it hard for people to save for retirement, the elderly are made more and more dependent on State welfare, which is adjusted upwards to keep pace with inflation by the inflaters themselves.

Anyone rash enough to challenge the dependency programmes can be put back in his place by a spate of fearful demagogy. He will be accused of lacking compassion. He will be accused of representing greed and favouring the rich.

He will be transfixed with the dread epithet "monetarist" (a policy so far from what any Irish government has ever adopted as to make its attribution in this country a bad joke).

Conservatives have adopted various strategies for coping with redistributionism. One has been in the supply-side approach, which argues that the way to maximise revenues is to reduce tax rates to a certain optimum level. High tax rates can be self-defeating for the tax collector. But the supply-siders made the mistake of thinking they were dealing with economists rather than with ideologues. They were arguing that the goose, given a little more latitude, would lay more golden eggs. But the State socialists did not want the golden eggs, they wanted the goose.

Consider the implications of the word "compassion". As used by State socialists, it implies that we owe a duty of sympathy, payable in cash through the State, to total strangers, a duty, in other words, to be discharged through redistribution. The simplest reply is that the world does not work that way.

Even kindhearted people take no satisfaction in beholding that portion of their pay slips that has been taken in taxes, regardless of whether they can infer that some of their money has gone to help the poor or, more likely, the members of public sector trade unions or other powerful pressure groups. So far as they are concerned, the money is simply gone, period.

There are natural limits to our sympathies, limits socialism can only condemn, never respect. And there is no reason to credit it with idealism. A robin that took worms to every nest would not be an ideal robin; it would only be an odd bird. And socialists are odd birds. Politicians are not Mother Teresa of Calcutta. Yet we are expected to trust them to act more compassionately than we ourselves would.

People will not exert themselves for the socialist State, and not because they are selfish, but because they are rational. To act is to be purposeful. When a man does not even know what purpose his action has served, he can hardly be said to have acted at all.

It would be inadequate to say that redistribution reduces profits. It deprives human action of the tangible results that make profit even intelligible. Working for money that will be spent by strangers on other strangers means that the worker literally does not know what he is doing.

And State socialism is not solving problems. It has been shown that most major "schemes" – education, housing, health – have been socially regressive.

Money honestly earned is a person's property: it is proper to him. Property rights are hard to justify or even to explain to those who begin with a utopian disposition, because property is always concrete, here and now, irregular and unequal. Every human being needs to possess something to have a little area of sovereignty over the material world.

Socialist rhetoric has done wonders to obscure the value of property rights. It implies that these rights, because they are unequal in their effect, are mere expressions of raw power. But, in fact, they are safeguards against such power. They protect the weak against the strong. They proclaim that what a man owns cannot be taken from him without his consent.

It is not the property of the rich and powerful that needs protecting, but the property of the poor, and the right of the poor to acquire property.

In maintaining property rights, the State is not "doing nothing". It is doing all it can for liberty and prosperity alike.

There are limits to property rights. But what State socialism really means, as its practice testifies, is that there are no limits to the violation of property rights. There is always some excuse for a new or an increased spending programme, a new regulation. We have ceased regarding departures from the norm as abnormal because we have forgotten what the norm is.

An example is the annual regularity with which commentators in the news media hail as a soft budget one where the increase in taxation is less than they expected.

Redistribution – brought to its present excess – can only consume wealth and dry up its springs. We have been long enough at it now to know this is true.

There is no reason to idealise the market, but there is every reason to appreciate it. The order of the market, with all its irregularity and unpredictability, is better than any order the State socialist can think of. He denounces the profit motive, while he thinks of his own power motive as an innocent, and even noble, thing.

In order to prosper as a capitalist, you have to please people. In order to prosper as a socialist, you have to threaten them.

The socialist vision of a social order in which all share with all, driven by what Heilbroner calls "new motives of co-operation and confraternity", is sheer sentimentalism. But the State socialists' conception of the alternative – a society of greed and selfishness – is sheer cynicism. It is perfectly normal for people to share, to take satisfaction in generosity, but they do not do so impersonally, anonymously, through the medium of the State.

A man may give money to the St. Vincent de Paul Society or the Simon Community, but he will not leave a pound note in the street as a gesture of benevolence to the next person who comes along.

We are a small, vulnerable economy. A healthy economy is a prerequisite to a healthy democracy. The oppressive State apparat is squeezing the life out of the economy. The ever-increasing level of taxation and of public debt are simply gross manifestations of a system getting beyond our control.

Underlying the countless incremental decisions that got us into this mess is a partly-conceded State socialist ideology, an ideology where every problem is a problem to be solved by government: a negation of democracy.

There is a bit of hope. The pendulum, having swung so far to the left, may begin to swing back again, as it is doing in other countries. Having failed to solve the problems it purported to solve, the State may begin to withdraw. But, in the insidious process of creating dependency, the State has encouraged an awesome array of special interest groups designed to unleash disruption and intimidation as soon as they get a whiff of a threat to their privileged positions.

So the process of withdrawal, now just possibly inevitable, will be painful, turbulent and will take a long time. In the course of it, we should be ready for torrents of abuse from the State socialists.

The alternative, and that, too, is possible, is that we shall have a State where the government purports to protect us from the workings of the market. The result will be a stagnant society. The entrepreneurs who succeed will do so despite, and not because of, the system. Others will simply get the hell out of the country. Both those trends are now evident.

The hope is in the swing of the pendulum.

*

One of Ireland's leading businessmen, Gary McGann, chief executive of the Smurfit Kappa Group, in an upbeat speech as he ended his term of office as President of IBEC, June 22, 2006, found it necessary to say:

> It is absolutely fundamental to recognise that unless we create wealth, we cannot share it. Therefore, any moves towards an exclusively socialist model where everybody would move at the same pace and the "passengers" share the same benefits as the drivers and risk-takers in the economy would be deeply flawed. It would not work and would undermine all that has been achieved.

Now that Sinn Féin has chosen the political path and eschewed terrorism, intimidation and crime, their website is sweetness and light. Preparing for the next election, 2007, they don't want to frighten the horses. Chameleon-like, they choose their message to suit the audience. But when they address the faithful, they revert to their clear goal, a 32-county socialist republic. Even in their website, they say, "We are the only party bringing a distinctly republican and socialist analysis to Irish politics".

They ignore the legacy of hatred in our six sundered counties:

> Out of Ireland have I come.
> Great hatred, little room
> Maimed me from the start.
> I carry from my mother's womb
> A fanatic heart.

Sinn Féin is bedevilled by the past. They invoke not only the dead in support of their stubborn positions, they invoke dead or dying ideas, an ideological necrophilia.

If it was the error of 20th-century State socialism to ascribe to governments a wisdom denied to any human institutions, it was the error of the Right to suppose that market forces, if only they were left alone, would achieve a sort of natural co-ordination, which only government intervention disrupted.

Rightists are neither angels nor devils. The Right has its vice, and that vice is selfishness. New Rightists mutter, "Let me rest; I lie in possession". State socialism has its vice, and that vice is envy. State socialists growl, as in *Dr. Faustus*, "Why shouldst thou sit, and I stand?".

What we are faced with, instead of these counterpoised ideologies, is the desperately humble task of endless improvisation, where one good is compromised for the sake of others, where a price has to be paid for everything, where a balance is sought among the necessary evils of human life and disaster is staved off for another day.

In the *Sunday Independent*, November 11, 1984, as a response to a policy document of the Irish Congress of Trade Unions, entitled *Confronting the Jobs Crisis*, I wrote:

> Despite the injunction in the *Book of Common Prayer*, "O put not your trust in princes", we cling to our faith in the State. The State is expected to be a comforter of the afflicted, a refuge of sinners, a shelter from every blast. When it fails to meet our expectations, we redouble our prayers and repeat, at more frequent intervals, "The Government must do something."

> The Irish Congress of Trade Unions in an important policy statement [1984] posed a stark choice: "... between government control or private control".

> This either/or is nostalgic. You would go a long way nowadays to get a reputable economic or social commentator to waste breath debating the relative merits of two highly artificial concepts: "the free market" or, according to the Irish Congress of Trade Unions, "the economic Darwinism" of the rich and powerful and the "planned economy" that Congress espouses.

> As Lord Roll has pointed out, Western democracies have had nothing but mixed economies for about 200 years.

Perhaps Congress's introductory ideology was meant only as a rhetorical flourish, a grace before meat. (A distinguished Irish economist called it a "culchified English Fabianism, spiced with envy".) But then, as that excellent study, *Irish Values and Attitudes*[28] showed, the Irish hard left are "somewhat mixed up in their social, economic and political views".

The danger is that, in troublesome times, we listen to the rhetoric and we turn to the State as a sort of living umbrella. For two centuries, European society has been seeking stability. What it has found has been a cumbersome State authority.

When the ICTU takes its "progressive view of the ability of society to create (through the more active intervention of the State) more favourable conditions for economic development", they are in a stream of thought that has been flowing for quite some time. To paraphrase Keynes (see **Chapter 39**), none of us is immune from the ideas of defunct economists – or political philosophers. The State socialism of the Irish left was not invented in 1913 as a response to William Martin Murphy. It is, however, as we often are in Ireland, a bit late. It misses the point that, as Daniel Bell said, "The most unreported fact of our era is the death of socialism".

Leszek Kolakowski, until 1968 the Professor of History and Philosophy at the University of Warsaw and Eastern Europe's most distinguished Marxist theoretician, has written that State socialism has been the greatest fantasy of our century: a repertoire of slogans serving to organise various interests.

Yet State socialism continues to grow around the world, particularly in Africa and Latin America. It is not easy today to know what socialists stand for. The difficulty arises less from the fact that socialists are divided in their views, which

---

[28]   ISBN: 0907271359.

they are, than from the fact that they are embarrassed by the historic totalitarianism of socialist states.

"Socialism" appears to designate, in the West at least, two vague and shifting sets of attitudes: first, idealism about equality; secondly, hostility towards capitalism – the "selfishness and profit-making of private enterprise", in the ICTU's words.

Socialism was once presented, negatively, as a way of analysing the deficiencies of democratic capitalism. Positively, socialism once meant the abolition of private property: State ownership of the means of production through the nationalisation of industries; State control over all aspects of the economy; the abolition of "bourgeois democracy" through the creation of a classless society. Socialism meant the banishing of the profit motive, which was judged to be the root cause of the exploitation of labour. It also meant the abolition of imperialism, a word familiar in Provo propaganda, since capital and the profit motive were judged to be the root of Empire. Socialism promised a social structure that would end competition between person and person and give to each according to need, while taking from each according to ability, a social structure that would thus effect a change in what earlier generations had erroneously regarded as "human nature". It was confidently predicted that socialism would bring about a new type of human being, "socialist man". Such a human being would act from motives of human solidarity, community, cooperation and comradeliness.

Socialism is, therefore, quite high-minded. Socialists sound like much nicer people than capitalists.

But, apart from the fact that the socialist dream has sometimes resulted in a nightmare of oppression, totalitarian control and ruthless imperialism, specific elements in socialist doctrine have been shown to be deficient in practice.

Take our own State industries. Are industrial relations in them any better than in the private sector? State ownership of industry does not, of itself, improve working conditions, or, if it does, it does so by workers appropriating part of the "monopoly rents" at the expense of other workers in the private sector and of the community at large. It does not raise levels of efficiency, does not diminish environmental damage. Again, administered prices and wages have been shown to be far less intelligent, efficient and rational than the market mechanism, as has been emphasised to me again and again in the Soviet Union and other socialist states. In the economic sphere, therefore, nearly every central Socialist doctrine has been shown to be in need of critical transformation.

In the political sphere, the central administrative state has proved to be a thorough instrument of oppression and exploitation. In the moral sphere, no fully Socialist state has yet shown that it can tolerate a broad range of dissent, human liberties, and human rights.

Dogmatism and sectarianism bedevil Socialist and Irish cultures, perhaps because they claim to represent science rather than opinion. Socialism is not a science. It does not offer a scientific method of predicting the future. It is not an explanatory theory. Its purported predictive capacities are fantasy. The romantic ideal of social unity comes from the idealised image of the small Greek city. This romance fed a common appetite for illusion. Abolish capitalists, and presto!, human beings will become more co-operative. Forbid private ownership, and presto!, human beings will cease to be selfish.

Human needs exceed the limits of reality as far as do romantic dreams. Since to fulfil all of these needs is patently silly, Socialists promise to ensure the satisfaction of "true" or "genuine" needs, not whims and fancies, scorning the "waste" and "vulgarity" of the desires fulfilled through the free market. This, however, gives rise to a problem that no one answered clearly: who is to decide what needs are "genuine" and by what criteria? When the State undertakes to make such decisions for individuals, "the greatest emancipation in history consists in a system of universal rationing" (Kolakowski). Capitalism tries to give people what they want. Socialism would give them what others believe they ought to have.

Wherever there is resentment, wherever there is injustice, wherever there is inequality, wherever there are expectations met too slowly, the ideas of State Socialism channel frustration and aggression. As businessmen are the activists of economies, socialists are the activists of politics. Their trade is grievances. This trade has its own graveyard. Its energies spring from hate, envy and a thirst for power. It announces that all dissatisfactions are against the natural order of things, and that history itself intends immediate and full relief.

It directs frustration and aggression against malevolent enemies, whose identity may change at a moment's notice.

It asserts that only such enemies stand between the aggrieved victims and the historical satisfaction of their dreams. The fault lies never in the victims. Too late does the victim realise that those who think of themselves as victims decline responsibility for their own condition and surrender their liberty to the absolute State.

You may say, "Hold on a minute. We have not gone that far yet. We have our property rights. We have *habeas corpus*. We have free elections, free media". My answer is that, with the State disposing of two-thirds of GNP [1984], we are farther down the road along which the ICTU wishes to push us than we seem to realise and that the historical conditions are now ripe to push us farther. You may well say, "But Congress, or other Irish socialists, do not really mean full-blooded socialism and, anyway, if they were serious about 'altering the nature of our society', as they say, they would soon meet the essential conservatism of the Irish".

You may be right, and indeed, one might wonder at times if any Irish political activists seriously mean what they say. But consider also that you may be wrong.

It was, at least, heartening to see a former Labour Minister, Dr. Conor Cruise O'Brien, write recently: "I used to believe, with the belief general among Democratic Socialists, that a strong State with virtually unlimited powers to define and circumscribe the rights of private property, was entirely compatible with a high degree of individual freedom. The longer I live, the more I think; and the more I think for myself. And the more I think, the less probable that Democratic Socialist assumption seems".

So, State control instead of private control? With Dr. Cruise O'Brien, I would say, "No thank you".

Congress would have it that "to leave things to market forces is an expression of conservative fatalism", as if the market were some evil influence imposed mystically upon us to discomfort our daily lives. The market is no more than the decentralised outcome of the decisions of millions of ordinary men and women buying and selling, saving and spending, adopting new tastes, taking holidays in Spain when they can afford them.

The market is a massive signalling system, pulling all these decisions together to ensure that consumer demands are satisfied at minimum cost. The price mechanism transmits vital information backwards between producers and consumers, indicating the true economic cost of their decisions and the relative scarcity of different resources and products. Present profits tell entrepreneurs where investment in existing lines of activity is most needed, while prospective profits encourage them to innovate to provide new goods and services that will appeal to the consumer. And competition ensures a constant search for low-cost methods of production.

The idea that we, an open economy, could ignore or control market forces is a delusion. In an indirect way, we have tried our hand at it for the past decade or so, by borrowing to pay ourselves prices we had not earned. One of the more depressing characteristics of left wing thought in Ireland is that, when something has been proven not to work, their answer is to try harder.

Anyway, as I said earlier, the choice is no longer between a "market" and a "planned" economy. What we have is a mixed economy. It has always been a difficult economy to manage. Of late, we have not been very good at it.

Our task is not made easier by spurious claims from any group – employers, farmers or trade unionists – that they have the whole truth, and that, "if only" we do such-and-such, Utopia is around the corner. When Congress proposes the issue as an "either/or" one, they subtract from the sum of human knowledge.

It is not a question of either/or. It is a question of boundaries between the State and the market sectors. The Irish State, partly in response to the demands of us, the people, partly from its own internal momentum, has pushed its boundaries past dangerous limits – ask the taxpayer.

John Quincey Adams said that the essence of free government consists in an effectual control of rivalries. It is a question of balance. Politicians are elected to hold that balance.

33

"TURNING THE ECONOMY AROUND"[29]

There is an invisible hand in politics that operates in the opposite direction to the invisible hand in the market. In politics, individuals who seek to promote only the public good are led by an invisible hand to promote special interests that it was no part of their intention to promote.

- Milton Friedman, 1912-

Last Sunday [December 16, 1984], on this page, the Taoiseach, Garret FitzGerald, put a brave face on things. He was replying to Joseph O'Malley's strictures of the previous Sunday. O'Malley judged the Coalition Government's results to be poor, the outlook ominous. He was accompanied by Professor Brendan Walsh, who pointed out that any turnabout in the economy in the past two years was simply in line with the European trend and that, so far as unemployment was concerned, we had done notably worse than Europe. This did not deter the Taoiseach from claiming that, in the two years since his Government was elected, it had turned the economy around.

The facts are that the Government has not "turned the economy around", if words are to retain their meaning. Turning around means going in the opposite direction. It means reducing government expenditure rather than increasing it. We have not done that. We have reduced the rate of increase in public expenditure. We have not halted

---

29   *Sunday Independent*, December 23, 1984.

and reversed the trend. So long as public expenditure increases, however fractionally, direct and/or indirect taxes will increase and/or borrowing, which simply means taxes deferred. The Government will paint itself still further into a corner where it has no room left to manoeuvre and that is where things can become very unstable indeed. Room to manoeuvre to a politician is to us lesser mortals as the air we breathe.

In their more fatherly moods, Ministers for Finance will tell us that the management of the public finances is basically the same as the management of our household finances: you cannot for long spend more than you earn.

So, when the money runs out, you do without. The last people to live by this rule are the politicians. Governments have an insatiable appetite for money. They get that money by increasing taxes or by borrowing on the collateral of higher taxes in the future. But then they lose favour, at least with those who pay. So when they win, they simultaneously lose. On the expenditure side, when they launch a new programme or increase resources for a current programme, they gain favour with that segment of society that benefits, but they commit or increase a continuing drain on resources. So to win, they lose.

Let us compare running a government with running a business, if only to put a nail in the coffin of the dotty concept of "Ireland Inc.". As a particular government programme becomes established, government has to provide increasing amounts of cash. In business, a product with similar growth would be well worth getting into. You would spend more money to make more money, but stop spending money when the product declined. Not so with government. As the programme gets taken for granted, its political attractiveness declines, but not its cost. Government, unlike business, finds it difficult to get out. Its strategic choice is not so straightforward. Government responses to new needs create greater chaos in government finances. Yet responsiveness is the lifeblood of politics. But getting additional finance by additional taxation leads to a decline in political popularity.

Thus, government has to cope with the first paradox of political economics: increases in taxation, to get the finance necessary to introduce new programmes or to fund old ones, ultimately cause discredit.

This dilemma means that government must strategically manage its finances so that revenues grow faster than the cost of continuing present programmes. As the late Dr. Jim Ryan told us, a budget debate is seldom about the untouched hull of public expenditure, which goes sailing massively on. It is always about the discretionary bit, the bit that is being added to the visible superstructure. It is the nature of governments always to try to increase that discretionary bit, otherwise they have no room to manoeuvre to win approval through the introduction of new programmes or the enhancement of old ones.

The second paradox of political economics is the other edge of the Keynesian sword: when money is short and gives minimum room to manoeuvre, the need for that room to manoeuvre in order to maintain political popularity is greatest.

Governments want the public to like them and want to act in the public interest. With no room to manoeuvre, they cannot achieve either. This leads to frustration, which can, in turn, lead to irrational actions by government and irrational reactions by voters. More serious is the inability of government, impaled on its several dilemmas, to change strategic direction, to break away from creeping incrementalism, to, in the Taoiseach's words, "turn around the economy". The result is unsustainable budget deficits, a weakening of our balance of payments, the destruction of employment in the exposed sectors, and inflation.

Governments are encircled with restraints. The resultant conflicts deny them the power and energy to do difficult and unpopular things. The concentration of constitutional power in the government does not produce political power.

Pressure groups, whether they be public sector unions or farmers, come up the backstairs and try to take command. This does not lead to venal government. Irish government is rarely venal. It is usually well-meaning. If not always in tune with the popular mood, it is seldom more than a semi-tone out of tune with it. But it is not far-sighted. "Things are in the saddle and ride mankind", wrote Emerson. No doubt that is true in all democracies, but governments in some countries are better poised than others to stay in the saddle or to swing into it. The Irish State may be a well-meaning horse. But the Irish Government is seldom a jockey, with the result that we are never quite sure where we are going.

Our confusion is made worse by the main opposition party who, obsessed with regaining power (just as the Government is obsessed with retaining it), keep chipping away at efforts to contain public expenditure. Faced with government proposals to cut back public costs, Fianna Fáil unsheathe the ancient weapon of whataboutery. Whataboutery is, for example, when somebody is patiently explaining the dull, and perhaps painful, facts of economic life and from the back of the hall there is the shout, "What about the working man?". Reason flies out the window. Michael O'Kennedy, when he was Minister for Finance, provided £100m for increases in total public sector pay. The nurses alone walked off with the bulk of that. "Ah, but the nurses", you may say, "angels of mercy". Angels of mercy they are, but that is not the present issue. The issue is the amount we can raise in taxes to pay them and all other worthy public servants. When the cool hand on the fevered brow is brought into the argument, the ground is shifted and rationality made impossible.

Fianna Fáil, who have been longer at it than anyone else, know that we love soft ould governments, someone to take care of us. Well, we may pray for the Rainmaker of whatever party. The evidence suggests that we shall get no rain.

To bring some semblance of certainty into our affairs, some sense of direction, governments occasionally publish plans. The best one we had was the *First Programme for Economic Expansion*, which covered the period 1959 to 1963. A Fianna Fáil Government published *The Way Forward* to cover the period 1983 to 1987. It recognised that the real problem was the gap between government expenditure and revenue and that the gap had to be reduced. The trouble was that reducing the current budget deficit would be deflationary at a time when unemployment was high and rising. The planners solved the problem by assuming that Irish costs of production would be more competitive. The policies set out in the plan were neither specific nor strong enough to make that assumption come true.

The Taoiseach, in his article last Sunday, spoke of the new mood of realism, of a transformation in public attitudes. I believe we can detect an increment of realism, but hardly a transformation in public attitudes. The present Government's plan, *Building on Reality*, has, as a major ingredient, the assumption (or, more accurately, the hope, para. 7.22) that public sector employees will accept an effective pay freeze up to 1987. There is little sign that public sector employees have suffered the transformation in attitude which will cause them to do that.

There is an interesting test ahead both of the Government's determination and of its power. If the public sector arbitrator were to recommend rather more than the Government in *Building on Reality* said it intended to pay, the Government would be faced with bleak choices. It could go back to the Dáil, where it might not secure a majority. Then what? Or it could (further) increase taxes *pari passu* with the increase in pay, a clear sign that it was presiding, not deciding, and becoming merely a conduit through which the demands of muscular interest groups were passed on to all the citizens. Or it could borrow to meet current expenditure, further mortgaging the future, further decreasing its room to manoeuvre, breaking its own canons and lessening its credibility (both inside and outside Ireland) and its authority. Or it could fudge – and nobody would believe it. Meanwhile, the opposition would be waiting in the wings, ready to come centre stage and save Ireland to a chorus of the *Soldiers of the Legion of the Rearguard*.

Edmund Burke said that "a state without the means of some change is without the means of its conservation". The Irish State – the political and bureaucratic system – has shown little inclination to change. But then people have never really changed until faced with a choice clearly more pleasing than their present condition, or perhaps, more forcefully, no choice at all – until, in the latter instance, they are up against it. "It" in affairs is, however, seldom clear-cut. It recedes like the horizon. And the forces of inertia are strong. The difference between now and Edmund Burke's time is that the future, the horizon is rushing towards us. Change that caught us unawares could be painful. Perhaps, without putting too apocalyptic a tooth in it, what we face is an ordeal of change. It would be serious enough for a country confident of its goals and values. It will be doubly painful for us, because we are being wrenched from a period when things went well. Government could muddle through. The rising tide lifted most boats. Now our sense of purpose has been replaced by a sense of anxiety.

There is, however, one trigger that will influence change in governance. It is the trigger of failures. To the extent that government is tardy in recognising realities and anticipating contingencies, or clumsy in addressing its internal deficiencies, correction will be forced on it. Overspending, based on past economic legends – or, more likely, on expediency – has now found its limitations. The failure of the party system to produce better than mediocre men will open up new options for the electorate and advocacy groups. The failure of the cities – or at least of Dublin – may force an urban growth policy. Evidence of the erosion of the national character may at last force changes in the educational system, away from conformism and dependence.

But failure is not always disastrous, since much of human history, not excluding our own, is a record of better performance built on a rejection of failing systems, it means only that man and society can learn something from experience. If this is to be one of the routes to the ordeal of change, we can bear with it.

What we can least afford is drift, the political laziness of closing our eyes to the problems of choice that are certainly coming. These choices, in large part, are value-laden and, therefore, critical. The ordeal of change is only in part a question of efficiency and economic corrections. It is fundamentally a crisis of values and perspectives on the goals and uses of power.

As we face into 1985, we badly need some lights to see our way forward. A trade unionist I spoke to recently asked: "Who dares to govern?". Who indeed?

It is not as if we don't know what needs to be done. The National Planning Board, in its *Proposal for Plan 1984-1987*, told us, unambiguously and in detail. We had known at least since the National Economic and Social Council's *Report on Public Expenditure of 1976* where profligacy would take us.

*

Those words seem sepulchral now [2006] when Government coffers are awash with cash, when we've never had it so good, when we're the richest nation in the universe – for all of which the Government takes credit, particularly with an election less than a year away. In words attributed to Milton Friedman, "Thank heavens we do not get all of the government that we are made to pay for".

Plato, among others, regarded democracy as a chaotic and unruly form of government. We are a democracy, with our share of chaos and unruliness, because we believe in our right to govern ourselves. We share a belief in the essential equality of all men. In it is a strong concept of individual freedom and rights. It is a system that works when there is a balance of power. A state of euphoria may not be the best state in which to expect balance. With inflation looming, the excessive money supply will be like trying to stop water coming out of a leaky hose without turning off the tap. With an election looming and a slow-down in the economy forecast for 2008, we can be sure

Government will inevitably pursue a pro-cyclical policy, the opposite of responsible husbandry. Charlie McCreevy, when he was Minister for Finance, said, "When I have money, I spend it and, when I don't, I don't". This is at the same level of economics as a primitive tribe who kill a buffalo and gorge on it immediately, thinking nothing of the morrow, as I'm sure Charlie McCreevy well knows.

34
SUMMING UP: THE CORRIGAN MEMORIAL LECTURE

Let lights be brought.

This is an extract from a lecture I gave in my home town, Galway, November 28, 1983.

It was a summing up of what I had been advocating with increasing conviction in the IMI, which I had just left. I have two feelings about it: how time-bound the illustrations were; and yet, how enduring the underlying principles are, regardless of the changes that surround us.

This is what I said in 1983.

> It is nothing new to rail against the State, particularly when it puts its hand into our pockets. We have been doing it since Adam Smith and before. What is new is the dismaying realisation that the State is increasingly incompetent. The State has taken on more than it can handle. It is doing badly things it should be doing well and doing badly things it should not be doing at all.
>
> Difficult times produce thought-substitutes. Thought-substitutes are declarations of the kind public figures make on occasions when they are desperately hard up for things to say. Private enterprise in Ireland has been the recipient of some of them. The finger of scorn is pointed. We are told that private enterprise has failed, that Irish private enterprise is neither private nor enterprising.

The outstanding characteristic of the successful private enterprise firm has been its ability to adapt to new circumstances rapidly and economically. Since its emergence as the dominant form of doing business in the 18th century (as the joint stock company), it has flourished in many cultures and conditions. Within the last century, it has coped with unprecedented changes in technology, basic changes in wealth distribution and consumption patterns, and a redefinition of its relationship with trade unions and employees. Competitive enterprise has a dynamism and ability to innovate that bureaucracies divorced from markets can never possess. Despite its faults, the profit-seeking enterprise provides the best mechanism we have for spurring efficiency in resource allocation, for encouraging innovation and for applying resources in entirely new ways.

I do not want to get involved in the debate over the relative merits of two artificial concepts: the "free market" and the "planned economy". The real problem of the Irish economy is how to adapt ourselves to meet international competition. If we are to do that, government must be actively involved with business.

The attitude of private enterprise to government is ambivalent. It is sometimes suggested that government should refrain from interfering with the market. It may even be acknowledged that the market itself is a product of public institutions that establish property rights and liability rules and determine how contracts are to be enforced. But these are seen as neutral rules of the game that do not selectively affect specific industries or businesses. The array of State aids, incentives and bail-outs, the subsidies for inefficiency, are somehow thought to be isolated exceptions to what should be government's normal role of benign neglect.

That mythic assumption does not fit our economic reality. Every industry in Ireland is deeply involved with, and dependent on, government. The competitive position of every Irish firm is affected by government policy. The economic effects of public policies and business decisions are intertwined.

The rhetorical gaps between business ideology and reality conceal that truth. Neither government nor business like to admit to the intimacy of their relationship. It has the whiff of an illicit affair.

The problem (the problem, that is, for proponents of private enterprise) is not a simple one. It cannot be solved by simple solutions – or, indeed, by looking elsewhere. We may look wistfully at Japan, or Germany, or Switzerland, and ask, like Professor Higgins, "Why can't we be like them?". The answer is that we are not Japanese, or Germans, or Swiss.

The enemy is us.

The problem of the relationship between the State and enterprise is as complex as Irish society itself, with its tangled expectations, allegiances and constituencies.

Faced with complexity, there is sometimes a primitive urge to look for a simple solution. This may be particularly true of the business culture, which is an impatient one. Yet every businessman knows what has been well said, that, for every complex problem, there is a simple solution – that does not work. He comes up against the Law of Requisite Variety: a complex organism cannot survive in a simple environment and a simple organism cannot survive in a complex environment.

Private enterprise has two choices: to do nothing or to do something.

There are various ways of doing nothing. You can say that "the business of business is business" and that politics are best left to politicians. This posture is at variance with the public attitudes of business leaders Or you can hanker after the old days, when William Martin Murphy was able to say to the Dublin Chamber of Commerce on September 1, 1913: "The employer all the time managed to get his three meals a day, but the unfortunate workman and his family had no resources whatsoever except submission". This is a sentiment hardly ever expressed, except in moments of inebriation, but nonetheless somewhere in the subconscious. Another way is to lay blame – on the quality of our political leaders, on the obduracy of the bureaucracy, on the irrationality and selfishness of other pressure groups, particularly trade unions. But the laying of blame has the disadvantage that it does not change the people blamed. Finally, there might be acceptance of the inevitability of rape. Such supine surrender would be so far from the ethos of enterprise as not to be worth considering seriously.

The serious option is to engage with the world as it is.

The first two necessary steps in that process are: (1) to understand that real world, and (2) to be clear about what you are advocating. To do both these things, Irish private enterprise needs an intellectual buttressing that it does not now have in sufficient measure.

Irish private enterprise is a segment of Irish society as a whole. Behavioural scientists see that society as authoritarian. The person of authoritarian values is a strange mixture. On the one hand, he believes that the ideal person is strong and tough but does what he is told by those who are stronger and tougher. He believes that wild and dangerous things are going on in the world and that power is needed to sort them out. On the other hand, he distrusts himself and everybody else; he is reluctant to accept personal responsibility; he prefers to blame other people for his own misfortunes; he is pessimistic and anti-intellectual.

This latter characteristic – anti-intellectualism – is near the heart of the matter. There is among businessmen a suspicion of the intellectual process and of the value of ideas. When I worked in the IMI, I found that *obiter dicta* from the world of practice – hard-nosed-manager-tells-all – would get a more receptive audience than someone who put forward a conceptual framework.

One cannot but have sympathy with the business manager who shows impatience at the world of ideas, of generalities. Many managers are under fierce day-to-day pressures merely to survive. And yet, I believe, as Keynes said, that ideas do rule the world and that practical men are their prisoners – if only in the sense that the environment in which practical businessmen operate is largely shaped by political action which partly gets its direction from a prevailing ideology or set of ideas.

We need to be clear about what business is advocating. When Lord Devlin looked at how British business interacted with governments, he said: "The emphatic declamation of a written statement, prepared in committee and delivered in the presence of a rock-like deputation, can be used as a blunt instrument to stun civil servants into silence, but it is no way of entry into Government thinking and it is not much of an invitation to the Government to enter into industrial thinking. Nor is a solution to the problem of business advocacy to be found in public relations campaigns or the hiring of clever people to keep the media at bay while the real managers get on with the serious business of making money, undisturbed".

The problem is too deep and too serious to be trivialised. Niall Crowley, Chairman of AIB, said recently: "Let's not put our heads down and withdraw from the political fray in 1983. We can no more keep out of politics than we can keep out of being alive!".

What, then, needs to be done?

The minimum need is for sustained financial support for first-class research to make clear the essential role of enterprise in society. Throughout this century, the case for enterprise has been smothered by hostile ideologies and folklore memories of 1913. Now that most of those ideologies have proven bankrupt, a well-argued, objective case for enterprise will fall on open ears.

But here, let me tell a cautionary tale.

Following the 1913 lockout, the employers were concerned about what would now be called their image. At a meeting of the Employers' Executive Committee on March 25, 1914, at William

Martin Murphy's initiative, a Mr. Arnold Wright was commissioned to write "a history of the strike".

The book, *Disturbed Dublin*, hardly achieved its purpose: to make widely known the righteousness of the employers' cause. By January 1915, it was agreed to distribute the book free to police officers and others. The story ends on June 7, 1918, when Longmans told the employers that they had 471 unbound copies in stock. The Committee "directed that the firm be asked the value of same as waste paper".

James Connolly thought that Wright "faithfully, if clumsily, tried to earn his money". Connolly's main criticism was that Wright, who had been brought over from England, did not really understand what had happened in 1913:

> A stranger, without any knowledge of Dublin people ... without any grasp of the blended squalor and heroism, pride and abasement that environment has woven into the Dublin character, and absolutely blind and deaf to all knowledge of the countless cross-currents, interests and traditions that played their part in moulding and shaping that historic struggle – it is only such a fatuously ignorant stranger that the employers of Dublin could count upon to describe the struggle as they wanted it described.

Wright's book may have provided some comfort for the employers. It did not change the views of others. 1913 has brought forth a wealth of literature from the labour side and from neutral scholars. *Disturbed Dublin* was the only contemporary account told from the employers' point of view.

The moral of the tale is that very little "from the employers' point of view" has been written since. The vacuum thus created has been well filled, and not with views sympathetic to enterprise.

Earlier in this book, we talked about a "societal strategy" for the private enterprise firm.

Three points about this. It should be *clear, practical and solid*.

First: whatever the content of a societal strategy, it should in no way inhibit the economic capacity of the firm. Any demand, such as employment maintenance or resistance to technological innovation, which is incompatible with sound economic performance, should be contested in good time and in a way that does not encourage conflict. Fundamental choices must be made by business leaders between acceptable and unacceptable societal strategies. They are not soft choices.

Second: a large diversified firm will assume several social roles, just as it assumes several economic roles, according to the life cycles of its products. It will manage a portfolio of societal strategies, as it manages a portfolio of investments.

Third: which needs continual emphasis, the firm's economic performance will remain its principal contribution to the good of society. The alternative to profit is loss, a naïve point, but one either ignored or lost sight of by those who do not favour private enterprise.

The extent to which our deliberate actions can affect the future is, in any event, limited. Continuity of cultural change, institutional inertia, unexpected events, and subliminal social forces conspire to shape the course of history and to thwart attempts to design the future.

However, we can choose either to understand and to move with the tides of history, whatever they may be, or to attempt to resist them.

I will not guess at which course we choose. I see some evidence among businessmen of a growing concern about social and political issues. It is often accompanied by some puzzlement about what should actually be done. But I see also some recidivism, declamations of the "we-must-get-back-to" kind.

To summarise.

The State is becoming increasingly incompetent. Many people are near the limits of their patience with government's costly disabilities. They cannot fathom its objectives, take its word, depend on its effectiveness or see where it is taking them.

The private enterprise firm is the best way we know to innovate and to create wealth. The ideology of enterprise needs an intellectual underpinning. Without it, private enterprise is naked in the face of hostile ideologies. They are many and clever.

It is not a question of going backwards to the sturdy independence of 19th century liberal capitalism. The world is changing and complex. The roles of the State and of enterprise are inextricably intertwined.

To manage its way in this complex world, the private enterprise firm – the large and visible one – needs a wider view of its *raison d'être*, one that does not lessen its need to make profit, but which takes genuine account of, and does not merely pay lip service to, the firm's social responsiveness.

At this penultimate point, there is pressure to end with a flourish. That flourish would frequently begin: "I am, however optimistic ...", a statement that has the effect of undermining all that went before.

Geoffrey Vickers, in a memorial lecture in the University of Pennsylvania on *The Demands of a Mixed Economy*, said the situation was:

> Beyond Optimism and Pessimism ... Nothing less than this, as I believe, describes the demands which are made on us, both as doers and as done-by in the politico-economic systems which history has bequeathed to us. We may be biologically incapable of meeting these demands; or, if theoretically capable, we may yet be unable to make the cultural change required in the time available. The prospect could not be more uncertain. But to such situations neither optimism nor pessimism is appropriate. The situation is beyond both – as all serious situations are – and our proper response to it was well defined two centuries ago by an American whose utterance will never be bettered. In 1780, while the House of Representatives of the State of Connecticut was in session, the noonday sky was so strangely darkened that some members, anticipating the approach of Judgment Day, called on the Speaker to adjourn the session so that they might prepare to meet their God. The Speaker ruled: "Gentlemen, either this is the end of the world or it is not. If it is not, our business should proceed. If it is, I prefer to be found doing my duty. Let lights be brought".

35
INTERLUDE: AUSTRALIA[30]

The best way to be an expert is to be a long way from home.

Friday, February 16, 1979

The Qantas flight number tells you something about the relationship between Australia and the UK. Qantas Flight One is Sydney to London. Qantas Flight Two is London to Sydney. Flights to lesser parts of the world are in anonymous numbers. The flight leaves Heathrow at 8.45 pm Friday and gets into Sydney the following Sunday morning, 7.35 am: 26 hours flying time plus 11 hours' time change.

Since I was working with Qantas, Maureen and I travelled first class. It was splendid. The cabin crew were efficient, attentive and cheerful.

Saturday, February 17, 1979

Bahrain airport. First bit of sun we've felt since last summer. Very smart, unarmed militia, with glistening toe-caps. Bahrain airport is hardly exciting. It is peopled by recumbent Arabs and passengers shuffling from one pointless duty-free shop to the next. It is a relief to get back to the air-conditioned womb of the 747. The steward announces cheerfully that, if joining passengers think they are on QF1 London-bound, they are going in the wrong direction.

---

[30] First published in *The Irish Times*, March 15/16, 1979.

Singapore at night. Wonderful approach giving us a long view of the city and its islands. Sorry I had not the time to accept an invitation to do a workshop there, and see the place. Airport hot, steamy and crowded. World-renowned duty-free turns out, to us anyway, a total frost. However, a glass of excellent, cold Singapore beer with the change in miniscule Singapore cents. Both of us totally unconscious that we have moved from one civilisation to another on tournedos Rossini.

As we take off on the last leg, the captain says ominously that there may be turbulence. There is. We wake up over what we are subsequently told is the Molucca Sea. We are being thrown around a bit, which is not so bad. Then we have one of those endless, sickening drops, which is. It is accompanied by a noise like giant hailstones. When it's over, the captain comes on and admits frankly that he did not expect that one.

Sunday, February 18, 1979

Sydney. Lovely sunny Sunday morning. Uncrowded, cool airport. Friendly immigration, customs and porters. Met by old friends, Paul Dole, who had arranged the trip, and his wife, Paddy, then Canadian Consul in Sydney. One of the great pleasures in life is being met at an airport.

This was our longest trip ever. We had been warned about the awesome effects of jet lag. Though we were a bit light-headed, our friends insisted that we stay up and awake until early Australian bed-time. They made it easy for us with libations of Australian Kaiser Stuhl "champagne" which, they told us, Her Majesty had much admired on her last visit. We slept round the clock and woke with the journey far behind.

Australians are great at knocking themselves, just as we are. Ronald Conway, a psychologist, is one of their sharper commentators. The titles of his books are *The Great Australian Stupor* and *Land of the Lost Weekend*. One was dedicated "to all the friends and acquaintances I may lose for writing this book". Managers were to be my constituency. Of Australian managers in the '60s, he wrote:

> The merchant-industrial establishment of the cities carried over from the pre-war years a gawky amateurishness which came from too much forelock-tugging to overseas financial principals, chiefly in Britain. As a managerial class, its top men were simply not sufficiently broadly experienced or efficient to cope with the huge influx of capital and the suave combination of seductive funding and arm-twisting provided by the new multinational corporations. Not surprisingly they were often outclassed and outmanoeuvred.

Maybe so. The 200 managers I was to meet had either matured very quickly in the '70s or Conway was indulging in over-kill.

Sydney is clean, prosperous, expensive and windy. The wind is welcome in the, to us, hot Australian autumn. Cars are immaculate. They are very expensive, essential and driven (on the left) with aggression.

Tuesday, February 20, 1979

Tuesday, I was to be interviewed for the Qantas in-flight magazine. My hosts had the good idea of doing this over lunch at Peter Doyle's. Peter Doyle has two restaurants on Sydney harbour, one on a jetty, one on a beach. We ate overlooking a collection of yachts and cruisers that would make the Irish boat show seem like Carraroe currach races. The waitress told us that Mr. Doyle had chosen the menu. So we ate, in succession, oysters (served all the year round), huge prawns, mud crab and fried John Dory. If you have not experienced Australian mud crab, it would nearly be worth the detour. The flesh is finer, more succulent and there is more of it than the sweetest lobster.

After lunch, a black-mustachioed figure in white shorts and T-shirt waved to us from the jetty. It was Peter Doyle

himself, third-generation Irish fisherman and restaurateur
with the face of a genial pirate and a generous heart. We
were off to explore Sydney harbour in his glistening 40-foot
cruiser. I asked diffidently whether I might handle her.
When he was satisfied that I was not going to sink us, he let
me away with her. We explored one of the most beautiful
harbours in the world. Peter gave us an account of the
interesting mores of the wealthy inhabitants of the houses at
the water's edge. The wheel of a cruiser in one hand and a
can of Toohey's beer in the other is not a bad way to be
interviewed for an in-flight magazine. A luxurious interlude
before the hectic days to follow.

The workshop I have developed here and in Canada
lasts a little more than half-a-day. It has a simple thesis, but
one that is difficult enough to get across. It is that the
barriers to change lie principally within ourselves, and not
in mindless social, economic or systemic forces. The
teaching theory, which is at the basis of all the IMI's work, is
that adults learn little from what they are told and a lot
from what they do. It is, therefore, highly participative. The
participants themselves (albeit with a little steering from
me) analyse the forces for change in their environment:
social, political, cultural, economic, technological values. We
end with a shared conviction that we are living at a time of
deep change or turbulence, particularly social turbulence,
and with organisations out of phase with present reality.
My thesis is that the individual's first need in this
uncertainty is for understanding, for knowing what's going
on. And, since change is continuous, his understanding or
learning must be continuous.

We turn this on its head and the participants, in small
groups, identify the symptoms by which you would
recognise an individual who is not learning and is,
therefore, not coping. The best way to learn is from what
you do, from your job. A job is not an objective thing. I
don't have much faith in organisation charts or job
descriptions. A job is a relationship between a particular
individual and a particular series of tasks. Many managerial

jobs inhibit learning because they are almost totally goal-oriented. The manager lives a lot of his life in a non-existent future and lives it in some discomfort, if not desperation. The answer is in a *balance* between goals (goals *are* necessary) and process, that is being turned on by the now-ness of the job, the present and actual task.

Well, anyway, 45 senior managers turned up at 10.00 am at the Wentworth Hotel. The workshop was formally opened by the Hon Neville Wran, MP, Premier of New South Wales. A suave and pin-striped QC, Wran exuded style and confidence. As well he might, having been chosen as Australian of the Year by *The Australian* newspaper. Asked by that newspaper if he thought there was a "vacancy of leadership" in Australia, he said there was no doubt about it: "I think it's a bloody tragedy that there is no will in Australia to get out of the mire and get on top of the situation". While, he said, Australians liked to cut big-headed people down to size, "it doesn't mean that, because you've got aims for your country, you need to have a swollen head about it".

His introduction to the workshop was spot on:

Under the Protestant ethic, work provided intrinsic satisfaction. But in an increasingly secular society, the Protestant ethic no longer has value as a means of legitimising the relationship between man and work. We cannot expect therefore that the process of transition will be an easy one. A great deal of fear of the new technology arises from a lack of understanding of it. When people see what the new technology can do, and what it can't do, there will be less irrational fear of it.

In the first break in the workshop I was interviewed by Miss Catherine Harper of the *Sydney Morning Herald*. She asked me a question that was to recur with (thankfully) diminishing frequency: did I think that "Irish management was self-contradictory?". I asked her whether she had read the *Financial Review* (the Australian equivalent of the *Financial Times*) of the previous day. She had not. In it was an article entitled "The Best Irish Joke of Them All". It pointed to our growth in GNP and in exports and described us as a small-scale economic miracle. In the event, she wrote a perceptive piece (which means she agreed with me).

On the workshop, there is a simple test. It is designed to find out people's tendency to internal or self-control of their lives, or to a belief that their lives are largely subject to external forces over which they have little control. A score of less than five means a self-controlled person. A score of more than 10 means a fatalistic person. The Irish norm is 7.5. At this first Sydney workshop, I was to meet a phenomenon that was consistent in all the groups I had. Their norm varied only one or two decimal points from 5.5. That means that a sample of 200 Australian managers is a significant two points from us up the scale to desirable determinism.

Thursday, February 22, 1979

The first Qantas-Australian Airways seminar. It was for their senior staff, and to use the Australian word, for some invited heavies. It was organised by an ex-paratrooper, Clive Abbott, marketing manager for Qantas in Australia. Acquaintance with him was to improve with time, like good wine. More anon.

Occasionally on a workshop, one meets a "hero", someone who talks to show off. As soon as I heard the word "paradigm", I knew I had one. The trouble with them is that, if you react, you alienate the group and you are lost. This is not for any love the group might have for the hero. It is a simple matter of group dynamics. If someone outside the group attacks it, it closes ranks. The outsider – the lecturer – can never get back in. But *mo dhuine* went too far. I let fly. Thankfully, he *had* gone too far and I did not lose the group. Then he and I kissed and made up at the coffee break. But he did not come back after it.

Friday, February 23, 1979

Friday was a free day. In my dear friend Paul Dole's terminology, this meant two radio interviews and a television appearance. The most pleasant of these was on a live midday chat show on QCB with a skilful and charming man, Bill Dousatt. It lasted, to my astonishment, for half an hour, with two records and some commercials thrown in. I spent five years as an all-purpose announcer on Radio Éireann, so I'm used to the trappings of a broadcasting studio. But having watched Dousatt handle commercials, records, endless cigarettes and me, I ended from a relaxed start, with transferred nervousness. He earned whatever they paid him.

Delighted to read in *The Australian* that the Smurfit Group had taken over for $15.7m a stationery and packaging group based in Sydney, SC Penfold Holdings Ltd.

Sunday, February 25, 1979

To Thredbo in the Snowy Mountains for a workshop with the Hublein Corporation. Fokker Friendship to Cooma *via* Merimbula. Flying into the tiny, dusty airfield at Merimbula – it could not be called an airport, but was – I got a view of some of Australia's endless golden beaches. It was easy to understand why the beach culture is so much part of the Australian lotus-eating way of life.

At Cooma, the friendly Avis girl – matron really – pointed out that my international driving licence was years out of date, said "what the hell" and gave me a brand new Ford Falcon to drive to Thredbo. Narrow roads with wooden telegraph poles like Ireland. A few black cattle and rather grey sheep grazing off the brown grass. Then out of the flat lands into a wooded mountain national park. The road sign indicated kangaroos for the next 17 kilometres. I didn't see any. Thredbo is a winter ski resort, with a Swiss chalet hotel. In summer, they are developing it as a conference centre. I was given a warm welcome by John McKee, Director of Human Resources, and Vivienne Read, a distinguished consultant, whom I had met previously in Sydney.

Totally professional and committed, they were responsible for the three-day programme, the first day of which I was taking.

After a pleasant buffet with the participants and one final judicious beer, I went to bed at 10.30 pm. At midnight, I was awakened by shrieks from the swimming pool under my window. My sturdy students had thrown one of the secretaries into the pool and dived gallantly to rescue her. Women's lib had not yet got a grip in Australia. The pub culture, with the little wife waiting at home, was strong.

Monday, February 26, 1979

The Hublein participants came from all over Australia and from New Zealand. New Zealand has net emigration, almost entirely to its fabulously rich neighbour. A New Zealander just ups and moves to Australia. It is extremely sticky for anyone from any other country to get a permanent job there.

The Hublein participants were a delight to work with. The ambiance of Thredbo, the journey to it and the symbolic temporary leaving of problems behind, helped us start with cheerfulness and openness. It takes some time to get the concentration of participants who have come straight from the office.

Tuesday, February 27, 1979

Melbourne. Noticeably cooler than Sydney. My first job was to take a session with the management development course at the Administrative Staff College at Mount Eliza, an hour's drive from Melbourne. The college driver who met me at the airport was a Berliner, who had spent several years in a British prisoner of war camp. The mixture of German accent and Strine was fascinating.

I was given a little cottage to myself with sittingroom, kitchen, bathroom – and a snack and drinks thoughtfully laid on.

Awakened at 7.00 am by the plop of tennis balls. On the four week course, the participants try to keep their *mens sana* in a *corpore sano*. It gave me a useful analogy for my goal-orientation/process-orientation bit. People play tennis for two reasons: to win, to score, but more important, to enjoy the game. Playing tennis is not a meaningless infinite series of scores. Some management jobs are.

In the morning, I shared the problems of pedagogy with the faculty of the college, a tolerant, kindly and wise bunch with a wise and kindly principal, Ted Kelsall. The 25 acres of lawn and flowers and the view of the blue sea encouraged a relaxed approach. But we had the same concerns: the abiding one of ensuring the application in practice of what is taught and the deeper, underlying one of the continual development of faculty so that their work not only meets the real and present needs of managers but anticipates them.

The session with the students was as lively as one could wish for. Sixty managers: 48 from private enterprise, two from the armed forces and 10 from government. Average age 33. I enjoyed myself so much, I completely forgot to give them at the end the results of their psychological tests, until gently reminded by Leo Parker, the course leader.

Back to Melbourne, driving by mile upon mile of beach.

Melbourne considers itself more sophisticated than brash Sydney. It has trams, the lovely Catholic cathedral (the cross on top of the spire was presented to Archbishop Mannix by Dev), women who wear stockings in the heat, and the Windsor Hotel. The hotel is almost a national monument, half-owned by the State of Victoria. The lifts alone are worth a visit, with metal grills that can take the finger off you and brass levers to go up and down. We had a suite, called Flat 3, once used by Sir Robert Menzies: an enormous sitting room with dining area, three bedrooms and one bathroom.

We needed the three bedrooms because I was now joined by Paul Dole, my guide and mentor, and Clive Abbott of Qantas.

A talk with a faculty and a long session with 60 lively young managers can take a bit out of you. When I arrived in Flat 3, my guide and mentor had it full of media people. I made a hasty retreat to the shower to regain composure.

Having promised press, radio and newspaper in-depth (God save the mark) interviews, I took Paul aside and persuaded him to do the unforgivable. We stole guiltily away, leaving the media people happily talking to one another, and had a quiet dinner in a restaurant that was an exact replica of Jammets, of happy memory. The guilt wore off.

Thursday, March 1, 1979

My second Australian Institute of Management seminar was at their pleasant centre in St. Kilda's, a Melbourne suburb.

The seminar was opened by Sir Lenox Hewitt, chairman of Qantas. If Neville Wran, Premier of New South Wales, who opened my Sydney workshop, was a smooth man, Lenox Hewitt was a hairy one. A formidable person, he took the slings and arrows of running a national airline not just with equanimity but with fierce retaliation.

He said:

Australians are renowned for their do-it-yourself style. This is not just popular mythology of the pioneers who cleared the outback. This same resourcefulness in business in Australia today is a quality to nurture. I recall a similar individualism as characteristic of a country Professor Kenny knows rather well and to which not a few Australians can trace their ancestry. I am sure he finds here in Australia an instinctive and instant response to his approach. I am not the most ardent fan of management literature. All the nostrums and hand-me-down solutions are no substitute. This may be a more extreme view than Professor Kenny would put, but I think it is in line with his approach.

Extreme, it was not. In line, it was. We were off to a good start. But it was an edgy and tough seminar that left me drained. Most European participants will either be polite or stony to your face, and then mutter into their coffee cups. Australians give it to you instantly and straight from the shoulder. In fact, this makes teaching/learning easier, but you dare not let your concentration go for a second.

Back to Flat 3, and more newspaper men. One of them said, "You must meet Peter Janson". To describe adequately what follows would take more skill than I possess.

Janson, trim, bearded, elegant and eccentric, occupies the whole of the roof of the Windsor Hotel, the old servants' quarters. He has 38 telephones and nearly as many rooms, furnished with both treasures and rubbish from the four corners of the world, but mostly from India. He is a director of Air India and visits regularly with the Maharajah of Baroda in Kashmir. He drives racing cars, plays the organ and rides to hounds in New Zealand and Ireland. He is surrounded by pictures of himself with sundry notables, including the Duke of Beaufort and Bernard Levin. He received us with frantic courtesy and insisted that I return the next day so that he could take pictures of me (which he did, with his Australian Alpine dingo, a very rare and expensive dog, draped around my neck). My fondest memory of this faintly lunatic interlude was a brass plaque inscribed with the undoubtedly accurate aphorism: "If you have them by the balls, their hearts and minds will follow".

That night I was interviewed by John Tidey of the respected *Melbourne Age*. I was delighted to read subsequently of the "prestigious Irish Management Institute". We had moved in a short time a long way from the Irish joke.

I was surprised (and, of course, equally delighted) to see myself described as "one of a small handful of European management gurus". There is no doubt that the best way to be an expert is to be a long way from home.

Friday, March 2, 1979

Twenty-nine top civil servants in one room concentrates the mind. I got up at 5.30 am to gather my thoughts. Mandarins remind me of the Thurber cartoon of the puzzled swain on his knees beside the lady on the *chaise longue*. He is asking plaintively, "But what are you being inscrutable *for*, Marcia?". In the event, no one could be more scrutable than the men I met. We shared prejudices with enthusiasm. Interestingly, when I asked them what their priorities were, they responded not in statements of high policy but with deep concern about the development of their colleagues. It was a hopeful sign for the Victoria Public Service Board, the equivalent of our Department of the Public Service.

Thence to the last lap with a Qantas workshop. I started it by saying that it was the final one of my trip and that I was damn well going to enjoy it. Maybe this set the tone. Or maybe I was that much more in tune with Australian participants. It went like a breeze.

Not so breezy was our departure from Melbourne. I had to get the Sydney-London flight next day to get to an IMI policy committee meeting on Monday. I had not reckoned with an air strike. Melbourne airport was sticky from lack of air-conditioning and I was anxious. I had not reckoned either with the redoubtable Clive Abbott. He donned his identity tag, plunged into the bowels of airport and airline administration and came up with seats for us. Meanwhile, with his left hand, he sorted out the problems caused by the fact that Neil Armstrong, the astronaut, and family, were *en route* for Australia *sans* visas. You can walk on the moon without a visa but not on Australian soil.

Saturday-Sunday, March 3-4, 1979

A comfortable and uneventful flight home, after the hurried purchase at Melbourne duty-free of a furry koala bear and kangaroo. Shannon duty-free is still the daddy of them all.

Packed tight into the Aer Lingus flight, but nice to know the old firm is doing a thriving business, I am reminded of Basil Goulding's story. When he discovered that his ample neighbour was sitting on one end of his seat belt, he said, "Madame, I believe you are sitting on the end of my tether". For my own comfort and safe-etty, I remained seated until the aircraft had come to a complete stop.

36
CONSULTANCY REVISITED: THE STUDIES

The ability of managers to learn about their own behaviour, or about how their organisation as a whole is working, is limited.

The paper reproduced below was first given to the Fellows of the International Academy of Management at a meeting in New York on October 7, 1985.[31] It explains how the studies reported in *Freedom and Order*[32] worked in practice.

The idea for the kind of intervention outlined probably began when I worked with Professor Reg Revans, the father of Action Learning. He said there was nothing more frightening than ignorance in motion. Then with Professor Igor Ansoff, who described strategy as "trying to ride a bicycle while you're inventing it". Finally with Professor Gianfranco Piantoni, Bocconi University, Milan, whose motto should be: "O wad some Pow'r the giftie gie us To see oursels as others see us!".

> Contrary to the Peter Principle, you do not have to be promoted to reach the level of your incompetence. Managers who have satisfactorily performed assigned functions may suddenly find themselves unable to cope with growing complexity. Though they remain in the same job, the demands made on that job may change. Though they may have been competent in that job until then, they find

---

[31] The paper was subsequently published in the *Irish Marketing Review*, Vol. 1, Spring 1986.

[32] ISBN: 1860761208.

themselves incompetent from then on. Preoccupied with day-to-day problems, they do not anticipate quickly enough when their total system may have got out of balance: out of balance with its market or in its product-mix; out of balance with its technology or its financial structure; or, more subtly, out of balance in its sense of direction or in its capacity to get there. In some instances, it is then too late to save the enterprise.

The ability of managers to learn about their own behaviour or about how their organisation as a whole is working is limited. Organisations create dependency relationships that inhibit learning. Managers withhold from one another what they think and feel about what really goes on in an organisation. They are never completely frank with one another about the direction the organisation is going in, about the pressures from competing enterprises, about the way decisions are made or the style of leadership, about the way resources are allocated or who are the favourite sons. This is where they need outside help.

The management of an enterprise can appeal to an outside management consultant. In many instances, however, the outcome of such an exercise is merely a glossy report that subsequently suffers death in the drawer. There are two reasons for this.

The first is that conventional consultants know much less about an organisation than the managers in it do. The experience and knowledge the consultants acquire in one organisation are often irrelevant, even obstructive, to their ability to help an organisation with which they are not familiar. Conventional consultants can become slaves to their training and repeat themselves from case to case. There is more than a little truth in the joke about the Harvard graduate: "I have two solutions. Now tell me your problems".

The second reason is that conventional consultants, being outsiders and not a part of management, take no responsibility for their recommendations when they are put into practice. If they end in disaster, the blame is laid on the client, "who did not understand". It is not unusual for a client who professes an understanding of, and agreement with, a conventional consultant's recommendations to be nowhere near the same wavelength as the consultant. This is because the recommendations are drawn from training and experience of which the client is not a part and through a consultancy process in which he did not genuinely participate.

There is, of course, the occasional chief executive who will use a consultant to try to get his own way with an organisation, who will try to bolster his flagging authority by adducing an "authoritative" outside view. "Consultants are hired so that CEOs are not fired." Any reputable consultant will shun such an undertaking.

We should not confuse conventional management consultancy with consultants who bring a particular expertise to a company. A good example of the latter was the appointment in 1985 of Zeus management consultants, by the shareholder, the Minister, to manage the B+I Line, a State-owned Irish shipping company that was in financial crisis [and which went out of business].

There is another form of consultancy, which, though popular in many countries, has not taken root in the astringent Irish culture. Sensitivity training consists of a group of people who are encouraged to open up in front of one another, candidly analysing one another's behaviour. This is done under the guidance of a "trainer", who should be a psychologist.

The aftermath of thorough self-revelation is often the deep embarrassment of those who have disclosed their innermost feelings. Such a traumatic experience, when it involves members of the same organisation, may end in the inability of people to continue working with one another.

Sensitivity training is based on a belief that, in organisations, "we're all in this together". If not an outright fallacy, this is, at the least, naïve. Participative management, desirable and necessary in many types of organisation, is not conducive to entrepreneurial management, the kind in which new organisations are created. Participative management is not a sole mode. It is not consistent with the concept of the organisation as a contingency system, where there are no desirable or undesirable modes of management but where there is the freedom to choose the mode that best fits particular conditions.

If, as I have suggested, neither conventional management consultancy nor sensitivity training have been effective in helping management, who does the chief executive turn to when he wants general counsel and guidance (as distinct from specific expertise)? When the chief executive feels in his bones that there is something wrong in his enterprise, and cannot put his finger on it, then his organisation may be suffering from the no-disclosure disease – and the only way he can tackle it is by using outside help.

Managers worry that things threatening them may come to the notice of those who have power over their positions in the organisation. They worry about what their superior thinks of them. They worry about their peers, with whom they compete for the favour of a common superior. They worry about their subordinates, younger and more recently educated, whose acquired knowledge of the organisation may soon rival their own.

Consequently, they do not fully open up when communicating with those around them. Part of their inner truth they communicate, part they conceal, and part of what they communicate is contrary to their own thoughts and feelings. No organisation is free from the no-disclosure disease. Most managers, when they hear of it, are surprised at its universality – they think it affects only them. It is the major contributor to organisations not knowing where they stand. It causes defensiveness and dependencies that are barriers to the truth about the organisation, both internally and certainly in its external relationships, be those relationships with friends or enemies. The result is unremitting pressure on the chief executive.

Before sketching briefly the kind of action research the adviser will use to help the chief executive, let us look at some circumstances in which advice will not work.

It will not work where there is a low level of trust. It will not work where management, including the chief executive, are incompetent. It will not work where the "culture" of an organisation – its sedimented attitudes and behaviour – are deeply resistant to change. It will not work where a company is terminally ill anyway, from, say, product obsolescence. It will not work where management has degenerated into running errands for other groups, for example, the trade unions, or, in the case of State-sponsored bodies, the politicians. It will not work where people have time to sit around all day and plot.

It will work where there is a strong, but not domineering, chief executive. It will work where, despite no-disclosure, there is a good minimum level of trust. It will work where there is a future for the company. It will work where people are sufficiently stretched that they have little time for politicking.

The first ingredient in the adviser's successful intervention is that he himself is trusted. This will come from a variety of things: perceived track-record; personal qualities of wisdom and wit; skill dealing with all sorts of people; humility (humility of the search-for-truth, not Uriah Heep, variety); and, finally, from the prime and only purpose being to help the company, not to get a foot in the door for further assignments. This last point is key. The good adviser must know when to disengage so that management itself takes over the task for which he was called in. He is there to help the company get a clearer view of itself and of where it stands. He is not there as the chief executive's eternal auxiliary. His main strength is his independence, which he must jealously guard.

He begins work by having the chief executive define for him the population of managers with whom he has to deal. They will be the chief executive himself, those who report to him, and, likely, those who report to them. The criterion is managers whose actions influence the direction of the organisation.

He gets from the chief executive his view of where the company should be in three years' time (five years is asking too much). He gets the chief executive's view of what the barriers to progress are.

He then has lengthy (not less than three hours) interviews on a one-to-one basis with each manager in his given population. It is emphasised at the beginning and end of the interviews that they are totally confidential. What is disclosed is reported back in a general report, with no possibility of individual views being identified, no matter how pungently expressed. The one-to-one nature of the interviews is critical. One-to-one there is the possibility of real communication. With a third person in the room, you have a meeting.

These interviews, which are largely unstructured, produce a volume of data out of which comes a picture of the organisation that the organisation itself has drawn. It is as near a true picture as it is possible to get. That is not to say that the adviser is intellectual fly-paper. It is to say that he is not at liberty to massage the data to suit any preconceptions he may have. But he will have used his native wit on the (very rare) occasions when people are having him on, or are trying to make an impression at the expense of accuracy.

While the primary purpose of this first phase of the adviser's work is to help the organisation in general and the chief executive in particular know where they stand, it has a beneficial secondary effect. It helps free up the system and encourages participation by providing a partial catharsis, in that people have an opportunity to express freely to a trusted counsellor their thoughts and feelings about the organisation.

The second phase consists also of long, one-to-one interviews, but this time with a different agenda. The agenda comes from a comprehensive report circulated to all the participants, giving their unlaundered views collated in different chapters such as strategy, structure, style, capability etc. The manager now knows the adviser is reporting on what the organisation told him, not what may have been going on inside his own head. Secondly, the adviser now has a coherent shopping list of the "damp spots" in the organisation, the issues that need attention. Taking the manager through these is inevitably leading him into thinking about what should be done about them. We are edging slowly towards the solution/recommendation – but the recommendations are coming from the organisation itself, not from an all-seeing, all-knowing consultant. The recommendations are beginning to come: (a) from those who have the knowledge and (b) from those who will subsequently have to carry them out and be responsible for their success or failure.

At the end of this second phase, which is focused in a longer and more hard-nosed report, the organisation should know not only where it stands but have strong hints about what needs doing.

The third and final phase, Action, is the climax of the work. The participants have reflected upon a mass of authentic data – they know where they stand. There is now a concern to have done with diagnosis and to move on to action. The issues are out on the table for all to see. In a two-day conference, meticulously planned, the participants come together for the first time and discuss with the chief executive what they believe should be done. The quality of the output of these conferences is high, partly because of the release of motivation, partly because the participants are so well-informed. The conferences are recorded: there is an agreed agenda for future action. The chief executive, who chairs the conference, has three options: We'll do that; I'd like to think about that but will come back to you by x date; or we can't do that, and gives reasons with which the participants may not be familiar. The work is usually revisited six months or a year afterwards to see what was or was not done and why.

The results of this kind of intervention are as follows:

+ There is a clearer, shared view of what the organisation is about and where it is going. This frees up the system, strengthens managers' ability to delegate, enabling them to give time to the important as well as the urgent and to help their subordinates grow. It unleashes the motivating effect of a shared strategy – everybody singing from the same hymn-book.

+ There is less pressure on the chief executive. He is freed from many of the jobs that inevitably congregate around his office. He can (a) concentrate on strategy and (b) move more freely around the organisation, so that he can know what is really going on without treading on people's toes.

+ It increases the organisation's self-confidence and encourages it to be more open to the world around it, the real world.

+ It encourages a learning organisation.

Times change, and we change with them. The best organisations with time will develop institutional arteriosclerosis, what has been called a hardening of the categories. That is when it needs another check-up, another bit of action research: possibly every five to seven years. When is a question of balance. You don't want ivy to choke' your organisation; you don't want either to pull the plants up every year to see whether the roots are growing.

*

There are detailed (though anonymous) accounts of the studies up to 1999 in *Freedom and Order*. Below is a comprehensive list:

1985	Kerry Co-Op
1986	NÉT (later IFI)
1987	Gilbeys of Ireland
1988/89	Kerry Group
1989	Smurfit Paribas Bank
1990	Campbell Bewleys
1990/91	Bord na Móna

1991   C&C

1991   The Aer Rianta Board*

1992   The Avonmore Board*

1992/93   Aer Rianta

1993   National Gallery of Ireland

1994   Czech Management Institute

1995/96   Royal College of Surgeons in Ireland

1996/97   Smurfit Continental Europe

1997/98   Smurfit Ireland and UK

1999   IONA Technologies

2000   Kerry Group

- ❏ Kerry Ingredients America
- ❏ Kerry Ingredients Europe
- ❏ Kerry Foods
- ❏ Kerry Corporate and Agribusiness

2001/02   Smurfit Europe

2003   Dairygold Co-Operative Society Board*

2005   Higher Education Authority

*   Boardroom studies

Blaise Pascal (1623-1662) said:

> People are generally better persuaded by the reasons they have themselves discovered than by those which have come into the mind of others.

That is the beginning of wisdom.

I used the term "study", rather than, say, consultancy assignment or intervention, because I work from a university and the word study is more appropriate (and genteel) and because they are *research* studies. From the organisation's point of view, they are about helping it get a clearer picture of where it is and where it's going. From my point of view, they stem from an enduring curiosity about organisations and how they work, from an abiding belief that the more organisations make people unfree, the worse they function.

To sum up: the studies rest on five simple premises.

First, all organisations create dependency relationships that inhibit truth, the understanding of reality. All successful organisations tend to reinforce their own basic beliefs, to believe their own propaganda.

Second, the people who work in an organisation know more about it than any outsider: they know it in their bones. There is a crucial difference between the prescriptive style adopted by accountants or lawyers and the style adopted in the studies.

Third, the only way organisations can be helped to uncover that knowledge is to use a trusted outsider who brings a different, objective perspective. Organisations cannot do it by themselves, from inside. That is why internal group planning exercises or strengths-and-weaknesses analyses leave a sense of incompleteness.

Fourth, the most effective way to explore the organisation is to identify how it is experienced by individuals. Pope put it succinctly: "The proper study of mankind is man".

Finally, the only people who carry out recommendations with any energy are the people who make them. That is so why many finger-wagging consultants' reports suffer death in the drawer.

The chief executive is the key to the success of a study. He commissions it. He accepts responsibility for ensuring that what comes out of it is done. On a small number of occasions, when it looked as if I were to be commissioned to do a study, things went dead. It took me some time to realise that the reason was the chief executive's reluctance to "expose" himself to the organisation – a pity because he misses a unique opportunity to learn, not only about the organisation, but about himself. A pity also because his colleagues know infinitely more about him than they let on, particularly if, as is likely, he tends to autocracy.

In one study, a participant noted that I was writing quickly while he unburdened himself of some fruity opinions of his CEO. He said, "You're not writing that down?".

I said, "I am".

"You're not going to give him all that?"

I said, "I am".

"He'll go berserk."

He did not go berserk. A chief executive who did not want to know what his troops thought of him would not be worth his salt (and would not have commissioned a study in the first place). A personality change would be too much to hope for as a result of what he learns, but I have noticed a bit more listening, a bit more appreciation of subordinates, a modification of ballistic behaviour.

What happens following a study depends absolutely on the chief executive. If he has not really heard and absorbed what the organisation is saying to him, then nothing or not much will happen. Thankfully, it was never like that.

The chief executive is locked into a study from day one until its completion, but he is not a prisoner of the recommendations of his colleagues. First, only a chief executive who has confidence in his organisation (and his colleagues) will commission a study. Secondly, his personal authority will not derive from his having to win every argument. Finally, the recommendations are drawn from the deep pool of common sense in all organisations that possess the characteristics for an effective study. There will be criticism and maybe some blame-laying and cynicism. These are a necessary part of the catharsis. They disappear as the study focuses increasingly on what needs to be done. I never met with daft or destructive ideas.

The studies were hugely enjoyable. The day one starts is a sunny day, full of hope. And, in a way, they are never-ending. You cannot sit down for six hours with a manager who unburdens him or herself without making friends. When I meet participants, there's always a smile.

37

CONCLUSION

Success is the ability to go from one failure to another with no loss of enthusiasm.

- Winston Churchill, 1874-1965

Some people always tend to clamour for a final solution, as if in life there could ever be a final solution other than death. For constructive work, the principal task is always the restoration of some kind of balance.

- E.F. Schumacher, 1911-1977

I have been lucky – in my work, and in the people I have worked with. Many of them were brighter than me, so that I had a life of continuous learning. It's been a happy life. The bedrock of happiness has been a great wife and family. One of the advantages of having four sons is that you add to their affections and those of a beloved daughter, the hugs of four daughters-in-law. Now, we have the joy of grandchildren.

My educational philosophy for them was uncomplicated. I said, "Provided you get the entry marks, you are going to university. You have no choice in that. I've seen too many people who did not get to university and who resented it for the rest of their lives. However, in what you do at university, you have total freedom of choice". They all went to college. Some studied hard. Some, following in their father's footsteps in UCG, winged it and got by. They all have happy memories – as I have – of college years.

Following the IMI, my first two years in UCD were preoccupied with writing *Government and Enterprise in Ireland*. It was well received – but in a vacuum of like-minded publications. There was, for example, damn all coming from the business schools. There is still in the business world a paucity of fundamental thinking.

Gilles Trousseau was the first chief executive of the Smurfit Paribas Bank, where I was chairman. He said, "Ivor, you are too theorical".

I defend my right to be "theorical" or, indeed, academic in the pejorative sense. I am no scholar but I have an interest in searching for the causes of things. There's always a reason – and then there's the real reason. Because business managers are, by definition, busy, they may skitter across the surface of things like insects on a pond. They may not have the time (or the inclination) to think things through.

On the other hand, in writing the *Leadership* series of five books,[33] I was privileged to get inside the heads of 80 Irish business leaders. The success of those books came from trust. The participants knew I was not a journalist out to get them and to make a name for myself. And also the simple guarantee that nothing would be published without their consent.

Writing the books gave me an enhanced respect for the unique job of chief executive and optimism for the future from the foresight of those Irishmen and women. They had a breadth of vision, coupled with the ability to get to the heart of the matter.

I said that, at all times, but particularly in troublesome times, our first obligation is to think clearly and that, unless we take account of and make explicit the ideologies which underlie the conduct of our affairs, we cannot understand the choices made.

The plain blunt manager might say, "What ideologies? My job is simply to get on with it in the teeth of increasing competition. If others have the time to worry about ideologies, good luck to them".

I confided to a wise friend that I wondered whether I had spent 20 years of my life talking to myself. He said, "Remember the famous Keynes passage that you quoted in *Government and Enterprise*, 1984:"

> The ideas of economists and political philosophers, both when they are right and when they are wrong, are more powerful than is commonly understood; indeed, the world is ruled by little else. Practical men, who believe themselves

---

[33]   *In Good Company, Out on Their Own, Talking to Ourselves, Leaders, Achievers.*

to be quite exempt from any intellectual influences, are usually the slaves of some defunct economist. Madmen in authority, who hear voices in the air, are distilling their frenzy from some academic scribbler of a few years back. I am sure that the power of vested interests is vastly exaggerated, compared with the gradual encroachment of ideas. Not, indeed, immediately, but after a certain interval; for in the field of economic and political philosophy, there are not many who are influenced by new theories after they are 25 or 30 years of age, so that the ideas which civil servants and politicians and even agitators apply to current events are not likely to be the newest. But, sooner or later, it is ideas, not vested interests, which are dangerous for good or evil.

Once more with feeling. Ideologies have consequences that affect productive activity, however circuitous the route may sometimes seem. They influence the thinking of public policy-makers and of opinion-formers who are directly instrumental in moulding social attitudes towards private enterprise, profit, investment, taxation and management's ability to manage.

I was cheered somewhat by papers read to the Institute of Public Administration Conference, June 8, 2006, especially one by Dermot McCarthy, secretary general to the Government and to the Department of the Taoiseach. He chairs the Implementation Group of the programme *Delivering Better Government*:

It has been observed that restructuring organisations, making strategic plans, introducing quality improvement initiatives, measuring, auditing and evaluating the performance of others, are the components of a form of meta management, the practitioners of which are themselves able to avoid the hurly-burly of operations. They set the targets and others have to achieve them. They redesign the organisations and then others have to go and manage them. Hopefully, we avoid that degree of dualism in the Irish approach.

However, in practice, we have had a very slow pace of change. We have had a culture of suspicion of management proposals for change, and the resistance in certain circumstances where the only loss was to the public good. We have had defensive practices, and on occasion individuals who have supported under-performance, when we know public servants expressed exasperation at the underperformance, which has been allowed to go unchallenged around them.

We need to recognise that management of change, sustained implementation of change, in fact the permanent implementation of change, requires investment and attention. We have, I think, attempted modernisation "on the cheap" and that is not because of any parsimony on the part of the government. I think it is because, as a system, we have not recognised just how challenging it is to point the direction of change to those who are charged with leading it.

However, despite disappointments, I am still sufficiently "theorical" to believe that what is needed is radical change. The change can come only from outside, whether it is in the bureaucracy, the police, or the church. We have sufficient evidence that the physician cannot heal himself.

The word radical is often used to mean egalitarian aims, or political extremism, or the pursuit of change for its own sake. I want to use it in its correct sense of getting to the root of things.

In business, radicalism is the norm. Managers are not radical by choice, but by necessity. They are judged by results, not by appearances. Radicalism requires absolute candour, a refusal to change the subject when the conversation gets uncomfortable. I remember a report on *ICI in the Year 2000*. It opened with a sentence, "On present policies, there will be no ICI in the year 2000". Radicalism means realism rather than false optimism. Alfred Sloane, the founder of General Motors, said, "Don't bring me the good news. It weakens me".

Above all, radicalism requires intense effort to establish objectives: in particular, the distinction between "want" objectives (it would be nice if we can achieve them) and "must" objectives (it will be nasty if we can't). It calls for analytical staying power, the readiness to keep asking why as the network of cause and effect proliferates.

Radicalism is the opposite of naïveté or wishful thinking. It is the art of the necessary.

Radicalism in this sense is dismissed by experienced politicians as too theoretical. The idea that certain problems which have long been regarded as insoluble *must* nevertheless be solved, if greater evils are to be avoided, makes them uneasy. They will quote examples of how the unexpected upsets the best laid plans. Like managers in the '60s, resisting the encroachment of professionalism, politicians insist that their business is different.

Radical thinking in government is essential. But a determination to get to the heart of the matter will be useless unless there is a change in the *system*. The divorce of planning from action is disastrous. It has been a constant theme in this book. God knows we have enough examples of the waste of money on reports written by expensive consultants or the waste of time and motivation on reports of well-meaning commissions that are never followed up or are, at best, cherry-picked.

Why do we keep doing it? The word "strategy" is not understood as a step-by-step removal of constraints (administrative, political, economic), so as to make an insoluble problem soluble. There is confusion about winning today's battles, which is one thing, and making tomorrow's battles winnable, which is quite another. The first question asked, for example, on public spending, is, "How are we going to solve this problem?", when it should be, "Why is this problem at present *insoluble*?". It is like hamsters on a treadmill, going round in a strategic box too small to contain any solutions. A senior public servant said to me, when confronted with a problem, the answer always is, "Take down the file", piling Ossa on Pelion.[34] The process can degenerate into the trading of departmental views, stockpiled from previous years.

The limits of political possibility are dynamic, not static. There has always been, as in physics, a sort of uncertainty principle, where events are constantly displacing the targets (peoples' perceptions) to which they are directed. Governments, therefore, must display to the public their long-term vision, not just in terms of values, but in terms

---

[34] "Three times they endeavoured to pile Ossa on Pelion ... three times our father broke up the towering mountains with a thunderbolt" (Virgil, *Georgics*).

of strategic change. We now know that trying harder with what we've got is not going to do the trick. If this means big problems must be publicly debated, let the uncertainties and complexities speak for themselves. Keeping it simple is an insult to people's intelligence. They know the world is a complicated place. The media are skilled at teasing out the substance – provided there is substance.

The reason why reform at the centre remains out of reach is that we assume politicians and civil servants are the best judges of these things. After all, do they not, for practical purposes, own the processes of government? And don't the present processes appear to suit the owners? That is precisely the point. The owners of the system – insofar as a "system" is identifiable – are part of the problem, not the solution. They are not the arbiters of what is thinkable or unthinkable.

Somebody has to offer fresh thinking about reform. My years working with senior managers have convinced me that the way businessmen think and act is more relevant than the way most – but not all – of the politicians, civil servants, academics and commentators who have concerned themselves with Ireland's problems thus far.

It is past time business took an interest. I am suggesting that reform of governance is the place to start. I have no romantic notions about the wisdom of businessmen. Nor am I suggesting that we replace politics with management science. I simply look around for people who are not frightened of change.

Employers should spend less time in marginal lobbying for special treatment. Measured against the problem of government, that is an irrelevance. Instead, they should ask as disenfranchised shareholders that government equips itself with whatever political arrangements and technical competence to stop the dreary litany of expensive mistakes. Businessmen should offer help in developing that competence.

This book is littered with some of the failures, or partial failures, in which I have participated: Gaeltarra, NIBO, the Conroy Commission, the Confederation of Irish Business, the Atlantic Management Study, Adult Education, Societal Strategy, the Northern Ireland Management Institute, the Committee on Management

Training, all of them sharing a single characteristic: the chasm between thought and action.

That is why I have been pounding away at the only method of closing that gap, that is that *planning and implementation, thought and action, must go hand in hand, simultaneously, and with the deep involvement of those affected by the change*. Otherwise planning is the froth on the beer, a *jeu d'esprit*.

Herman Kahn said to me, "If at first you don't succeed, give up". However, I remain optimistic. I can do no better than quote David Landes from his great book, *The Wealth and Poverty of Nations*:[35]

> In this world, the optimists have it, not because they are always right, but because they are positive. Even when wrong, they are positive, and that is the way of achievement, correction, improvement, and success. Educated, eyes-open optimism pays; pessimism can only offer the empty consolation of being right. The one lesson that emerges is the need to keep trying. No miracles. No perfection. No millennium. No apocalypse. We must cultivate a sceptical faith, avoid dogma, listen and watch well, try to clarify and define ends, the better to choose means.

---

[35]   ISBN: 0393318885.

38

THE LAST WORD?

The Scene:	John B. Keane's pub in Listowel, in a break from one of the Kerry Group studies.
Dramatis personae:	Me and a Kerryman.
Me:	Have you lived all your life in Listowel?
Kerryman:	Not yet.

BIOGRAPHY

Born: Galway, April 15, 1930.

Father: T.J.W. (Tom) Kenny, founder, managing
director and editor *Connacht Tribune*
newspapers. Died 1940.
Tom Kenny had six children by his first
marriage, of whom one was Des.

Mother: Lou McGuinness, married Tom in 1925. Died
1946.
Ivor was the only child.
When Lou died, he was "adopted" by Des and
Maureen Kenny, joint founders of Kenny's
Bookshop and Art Gallery, still thriving, as is
Maureen Kenny at 88.

Education: Scoil Fhursa, national school.
Coláiste Iognáid, a Jesuit all-Irish school.
UCG.
Immediate post-graduate studies at the
London School of Economics and the *Institut
d'Etudes Politiques*, Paris.
Post-experience, Harvard Business School, as
a Fulbright Scholar.

Married: In 1956, Maureen MacMahon, RGN, only
daughter of Joe MacMahon, a Garda Síochána
and Annie MacMahon, a school teacher.

Children: Dermot, married to Geraldine McCarthy.
                           Conor, married to Judith Hayward.
                           Ivor, married to Karen Weavers.
                           Helen, engaged to Rob Lane.
                           Mark, married to Nathalie Desbiens.

Grandchildren: Maeve, Grace, Dermot, Alex, Christopher.

Jobs: 1955, Staff announcer, Radio Éireann.
                           1959, Information Officer and Editor, Irish
                           Management Institute.
                           1960, Head, Management Development Unit,
                           IMI.
                           1963, Director General, IMI. Retired 1983.
                           1983, Senior Research Fellow, UCD, to date.

En Route   1977-1980, Research Professor of Political
                           Economy, Trinity College Dublin.
                           1982-1987, Chancellor, International Academy
                           of Management.
                           1983 to date, Distinguished Professor of Public
                           Policy, International Management Centres,
                           UK.
                           1984-2004, Chancellor and President,
                           International Management Centres.
                           1984, Visiting Professor, Cranfield University,
                           UK.
                           1988, Executive-in-Residence, Indiana
                           University, US.

Degrees   1955, Master of Arts in Philosophy.
                           1984, Doctor of Business Administration.
                           1998, Doctor of Literature.

Awards   1981, Knight Commander of the Order of St.
                              Gregory the Great.
                              1981, Knight of St. George.
                              1982, LlD (*honoris causa*), National University
                              of Ireland.
                              1976, Companion of the Chartered
                              Management Institute.
                              1982, Life Fellow of the Irish Management
                              Institute.
                              1984, First Economics Award of the Economic
                              Development Foundation, San Antonio, Texas.
                              1985, CIOS Outstanding Contribution Award
                              for the Advancement of International Co-
                              Operation in Management, New York.
                              1998, Keris of Excellence for Outstanding
                              Doctor of the Year.

Private Sector   1986 to date, Independent News and Media
Boards   Plc.
                              1999 to date, IONA Technologies Plc.
                              1998 to 2001, Kerry Group Plc.
                              1991 to 1999, Odyssey PLC.
                              1991 to 1999, Typetec Limited.
                              1990 to 1992, Dublin Fine Meats Limited.
                              1983 to 1999, Smurfit Paribas Bank Limited.
                              1982 to 1987, Digital Telephone Co. Limited.
                              (UK).

Public Sector and Voluntary Boards	1966 to 1993, Gaeltarra Éireann. 1972, Government Commission on the Gaeltacht. 1968 to 1970, Commission on the Garda Síochána. 1971 to 1979, Royal City of Dublin Hospital Board of Governors. 1979, St. James's Hospital Board. 1981 to 1983, Government Commission on Adult Education. 1965 to 1983, Member of the Board of Trustees of the European Foundation for Management Development (Brussels) and of its Committee on the Educational and Training Needs of European Managers. 1980 to 1982, Co-Chairman of the European Societal Strategy Project of the EFMD and of the European Institute for Advanced Studies in Management (Brussels).
Pro Bono	Member, Development Committee, Christ Church Cathedral, Dublin. Member, Development Committee, Royal College of Surgeons in Ireland, now member, Court of Patrons. Member, Committee of the *Collège des Irlandais*, Paris. Member, Development Committees of Trinity College Dublin and of St. Patrick's College, Maynooth. Council member, Co-Operation Ireland.
Sport	Captain, UCG Boat Club. Member, London Rowing Club. Life Member and Coach, Garda Síochána Boat Club.

INDEX

Other books by Ivor Kenny from

FREEDOM AND ORDER
Studies in Strategic Leadership
€25 hb : ISBN 1-86076-120-8

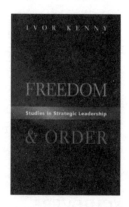

For the past 15 years, Ivor Kenny, Ireland's foremost management thinker, has worked closely with some of the top Irish companies to help them see clearly the issues they face. This work has produced a unique set of insights: how these organisations work, what makes them successful, what the stumbling blocks are, and where they are headed.

CAN YOU MANAGE?
€15 pb : ISBN 1-86076-266-2

Can You Manage? provides fresh ideas and inspiration for Irish businesspeople. This is a short book of short chapters, written for today's busy practising managers. In this book, Dr Kenny has distilled all the lessons learned from his experience of over 40 years dealing with Irish and international managers.

LEADERS
Conversations with Irish Chief Executives
€30 hb : ISBN 1-86076-221-2

Personal interviews with top Irish CEOs:
Richard Burrows, Irish Distillers; Bill Cullen,
Renault Distributors; Mark FitzGerald, Sherry
FitzGerald; Sean Fitzpatrick, Anglo Irish
Bank; Donal Geaney, Elan; Chris Horn, Iona
Technologies; Eddie Jordan, Jordan Grand
Prix; Stewart Kenny, Paddy Power; Kevin
Melia, MSL; Bernard McNamara, Michael
McNamara and Co – Builders; Michael
Murphy, Dairy Farmer; Martin Naughton,
Glen Dimplex; Denis O'Brien, ex-Esat; Fran
Rooney, ex-Baltimore Technologies; Peter Sutherland,
Goldman Sachs; David Went, Irish Life and Permanent.

ACHIEVERS
Visionary Irish Leaders Who Achieved Their Dream
€35 hb : ISBN 1-904887-03-1

Achievers is the fifth and concluding book
in the *Leadership* series. Those interviewed
in **Achievers** include: Lord Ballyedmond,
Denis Brosnan, Dermot Desmond, Moya
Doherty, Sean Fitzpatrick, Chris Horn,
Philip Lynch, Michael MacCormac, Hugh
Mackeown, Pádraig Ó Céidigh, Joyce
O'Connor, Sir Anthony O'Reilly, Tom
Roche, James Sheehan, Michael Smurfit,
Brody Sweeney, Ed Walsh and Ken
Whitaker. They are all different. The thing
they have in common was the ability to focus exclusively and
unremittingly on their ultimate objective.

OAK TREE PRESS
is Ireland's leading business book publisher.

It develops and delivers
information, advice and resources
to entrepreneurs and managers –
and those who educate and support them.

Its print, software and web materials
are in use in Ireland, the UK, Finland,
Greece, Norway and Slovenia.

OAK TREE PRESS
19 Rutland Street
Cork, Ireland
T: + 353 21 4313855
F: + 353 21 4313496
E: info@oaktreepress.com
W: www.oaktreepress.com